D1563423

IRELAND'S BIRDS

BIRDS

MYTHS, LEGENDS AND FOLKLORE

Do m'athair Dónal
le míle grá agus meas

IRELAND'S BIRDS

MYTHS, LEGENDS AND FOLKLORE

Niall Mac Coitir

Original Illustrations by Gordon D'Arcy

The Collins Press

First published in 2015 by
The Collins Press
West Link Park
Doughcloyne
Wilton
Cork

© Niall Mac Coitir 2015

Watercolours © Gordon D'Arcy

A CIP record for this book is available from the British Library.

Cased ISBN: 978-1-84889-247-7
PDF eBook ISBN: 978-1-84889-497-6
EPUB eBook ISBN: 978-1-84889-498-3
Kindle ISBN: 978-1-84889-499-0

Typesetting by Patricia Hope, Dublin
Typeset in Palatino
Printed in Malta by Gutenberg Press Limited

Contents

Introduction   1

Aspects of Bird Folklore   4

Robin	17	Eagle	113
Wren	25	Hawk	125
Kingfisher	45	Curlew	138
Seagull	48	Corncrake	143
Oystercatcher	53	Crane	147
Plover	56	Heron	158
Duck	59	Swan	165
Domestic Chicken	65	Goose	178
Skylark	75	Magpie	186
Swallow	80	Owl	194
Cuckoo	86	Hooded Crow	200
Dove	94	Raven	209
Blackbird	104		

Birds and the Ogham Alphabet   222
Postscript   231

References   235
Bibliography   253
Index   259

Introduction

Few things in nature are as beautiful as birds. Their colourful plumage, captivating song and, above all, their ability to fly enchant us. Even the person most indifferent to nature cannot but feel uplifted at the sound of birdsong in the morning, or at the sight of a bird soaring in flight against the evening sky. For these reasons, in human art and culture birds have always been important symbols of the power and significance of nature. In recent years there has been an upsurge in interest in wildlife and birdwatching, partly due to the high-quality wildlife photography and films now widely available, and partly due an increased desire of urban dwellers to reconnect with the natural world. This is reflected in the many excellent books on Irish wildlife and birds that have appeared in recent years. This book follows that trend, but it looks at a different aspect of our native birds from most other bird books. It is not concerned with the usual material, which focuses on natural history and providing identification guides to birdwatchers. Instead, it draws together the stories and customs in folklore and myths that have gathered around our native birds, stories from both Ireland and abroad.

The arrangement of this book also differs from the usual one. The birds are not arranged either by their ornithological classification or appearance, nor by the habitats in which they are found. Instead, it follows a seasonal cycle, based on what is most appropriate from the point of view of each bird's cultural associations in folklore and legend. Of course, this can often overlap with natural history, as this may have been what gave rise to the bird's cultural associations in the first place. For example, the cuckoo and swallow have become emblems of the arrival of summer in our culture, because that is when they arrive in northern Europe on migration. On the other hand, the first bird in the sequence, the robin, and the last bird, the raven, are placed more in accordance with cultural ideas. While it is true that the robin is one of the birds that continues singing in winter, its seasonal association with Christmas has more to do with its cheery red breast than anything else. In the same way, while the black raven as a carrion bird has obvious associations with death, giving it an affinity with Halloween, the season of the dead, there is nothing in particular from a natural-history point of view to link it to that time of year. The book also focuses on the most important Irish birds in terms of myths and legends, which means quite common birds that do not have much Irish folklore attached to them, such as the sparrow and chaffinch, are not included.

Birds feature strongly in early Irish myths and legends, and stories such as the *Children of Lir* and *St Kevin and the Blackbird* are probably familiar to most people. A wide variety of birds appear in the Irish legends recounted here, birds such as the swan, raven, eagle, hawk, dove, goose and crane. Early Ireland was also famous for its nature poetry, and again birds are frequently mentioned, often with an acute observation of their characteristics. A good selection of this poetry is provided here, translated into English by the author unless stated otherwise. The book also highlights the rich variety of Irish folklore that surrounds birds, covering everything from weather lore, to stories explaining how they acquired their song or plumage, to superstitions about how the various actions of birds are lucky or unlucky.

It is a sad fact that some of the most iconic Irish birds in myth and story became extinct in Ireland in recent centuries. Birds of prey like the eagle, osprey and red kite were exterminated by game-keepers, farmers and hunters, while birds like the crane were lost probably due to both hunting and loss of habitat. Other birds such as the peregrine falcon and sparrowhawk barely hung on against the double threat of shooting and poison, until legal protection and the banning of harmful agricultural chemicals revived their fortunes. The tide has also turned for the golden eagle, white-tailed eagle and red kite, which are being successfully reintroduced by the Golden Eagle Trust, despite setbacks. Perhaps in time the crane, too, will join the eagle on our island again. However, many other iconic bird species that have survived until now are under threat due to habitat loss, especially birds of open grassland and bog, like the curlew, lapwing, and corncrake. Efforts are under way by bodies like the National Parks and Wildlife Service and Birdwatch Ireland to preserve these birds, through protecting their habitat and raising awareness, but the struggle is ongoing. Many of Ireland's birds face continuing threats from urbanisation, intensification of agriculture and amenity uses, and the latest threat of climate change. It is hoped that this book, by showing how deeply birds have been intertwined with our culture, can play some small part in raising awareness of the need to save them.

Aspects of Bird Folklore

Birds have always been intimately associated with the lives of humans. Both wild and domestic birds have provided us with food from their flesh and eggs, and their feathers have provided us with warmth and ornament in objects as diverse as mattresses and hats. Birds have also always been powerful symbols of beauty with their colourful plumage, graceful flight and melodious song. The beauty of birds made them important symbols in Celtic art and they have been used to decorate objects as diverse as swords, shields and drinking vessels. In particular, the powers of flight and song have given birds an otherworldly beauty. This ability to soar into the sky and escape the earth also makes it entirely natural that in traditional beliefs the souls of the dead and of spirit beings were often thought to take the form of birds. In addition, the melodious songs of birds seem like music to us, and have the same power to enchant and transport us emotionally to another realm. Even birds with harsh and unmusical calls have traditionally been seen as significant. Birds whose cries seem to imitate the human voice, such as ravens, or which seem urgent and full of meaning, such as the wren, were widely regarded as birds with the power to foretell the future. All of these different aspects are recurring themes in the myths, legends and folklore of birds.

THEMES OF BIRD FOLKLORE

Birds are important symbols in Celtic art, and depictions of them have been found on a wide variety of objects.[1] While some of this no doubt is purely decorative, there are indications that some of it may have had a ritual value. For example, birds frequently appear on Celtic shields and scabbards, where they may have fulfilled some kind of talismanic purpose. A shield found in Wandsworth in London may be an illustration of this. It bears a design of long-tailed birds flying with outstretched wings, on which is engraved another bird. Images of birds' heads were also a favourite motif, often in association with foliage, where they play against each other as they emerge from abstract patterns. The evidence of archaeology is echoed in Irish legends.[2] For example, the beautiful maiden Étaín is described as washing herself from a silver vessel with four gold birds upon it. In another tale Queen Maeve presented to one champion a bronze cup with a bird raised in white gold upon it; and to another she presented a cup of white gold adorned with a golden bird. To Cúchulainn, however, she gave a cup of red gold with a bird made of precious stone. In the royal house of Conchubar, the king of Ulster, his room was said to be decorated with gold birds, their heads set with shining carbuncles.

Feathers used as personal adornments appear several times in Irish legends.[3] In one tale a warrior of Ulster is described as having a cover of birds' feathers over his head, while another warrior was said to adorn the frame of his chariot with bird feathers. In the ninth-century *Cormac's Glossary*, it is stated that the cloaks of Irish poets were made from the skins of birds, both white and many-coloured. Similarly, in the tale *The Wooing of Emer*, it states that the cloak of the chief poet of Ulster was adorned with beautiful bird feathers. The notion of houses thatched with wings or feathers also occurs several times in Irish legends. For example, one tale tells of the house of the fairy woman Crédhe of the Fair Hair, which was made of silver and gold, and thatched with the wings of birds in crimson, yellow and blue. Elsewhere, another otherworld woman, Eibhir, is described as living in a house thatched with the feathers of birds. The house of Manannán, the Irish sea god, was like a great king's house, with beams of bronze and walls of silver, and thatched with the wings of white birds.

Beautiful otherworldly birds often appear in Irish legends.[4] For example, the Irish god of love, Aongus Óg, was said to be surrounded by four little birds that had formed out of his kisses. In the tale *Tadhg son of Cian*, Tadhg and his men voyage to an island inhabited by great flocks of wonderful birds like blackbirds, but the size of eagles or cranes. The birds are red with green heads, and lay eggs of blue or pure crimson. Later, the men voyage to another island where they see a flock of multicoloured birds feeding on huge luscious grapes. The birds are white, with purple heads and beaks of gold, and sang 'music and minstrelsy' as they feed on the berries. The music is plaintive and matchless. The theme of birdsong having the power to lull to sleep and heal is a recurring theme in Celtic myth (see below). In another tale an otherworld fort is described as having beside it 'three trees of brilliant crystal, whence a gentle flock of birds call'.

However, birds can appear as demonic or destructive in Irish legends.[5] In one tale about the Fianna, the warrior band of early Ireland, it is related how three flocks of birds from the western seas arrived into west Munster wreaking havoc. The birds had beaks of bone and fiery breath, and the wind from their wings was as cold as a wind in spring. They devasted the crops of grain and fruit, and even took away small birds, animals and children. In the end, the birds were only defeated by a spell cast over them by Caoilte of the Fianna. In Keating's *History of Ireland,* an incident is recorded that malevolent jet-black birds appeared over the churchyard where the body of Donncha Mór of Ossory lay. However, the birds were unable to take the body or soul of the king on account of all the prayers and fasting that the clergy had made. According to a story about Cruachan, the royal centre of Connacht in County Roscommon, at one time a flock of white birds came out of the Cave of Cruachan, which withered everything they touched in all Ireland, until the men of Ulster killed them with their slings. The war goddess, the Morrigan, was also said to emerge from the cave at Samhain, or Halloween, accompanied by a flock of malevolent copper-red birds.

A common theme in the folklore of birds is the idea of various people or beings taking the form of birds.[6] For example, in the tale relating the birth of the warrior Cúchulainn, the god Lugh of the Long Hand appeared to Dechtire, sister of King Conchubar of Ulster, and turned her and fifty of her handmaidens into birds. Lugh took them with him to Brú na Bóinne in County Meath, and no one knew where they had gone. The birds reappeared a year later and led Conchubar and his men to where Dechtire and her maidens were hidden, and they were the most beautiful birds that the warriors had ever seen. They were in nine flocks, linked together two and two with a chain of silver, and at the head of each flock there were two birds of different colours, linked together with a chain of gold. In the tale *The Destruction of Da Derga's Hostel,* King Conaire of

Tara was conceived by an otherworld being with the power to take the form of a bird. He came to Conaire's mother by flying through a skylight in his bird form, before removing his 'bird hood'. Later, Conaire came upon a flock of huge white-speckled birds at Áth Cliath (Dublin). Thinking to hunt them, he pursued them in his chariot until they took off their bird hoods and informed him that they were the bird troop of his father, and he was forbidden to hunt them.

The souls of the dead could also take the form of birds in Irish legends and folklore.[7] For example, in the tale *The Voyage of the Hui Corra*, voyagers on a pilgrimage came to an island of red flowers, full of bright beautiful bird flocks which sang a plaintive, melodious music. A cleric on the island told them that the birds were the souls of holy human beings. During the same voyage, the pilgrims' jester died, and while they mourned, a little bird appeared on the side of the boat and spoke to them saying: 'I am your jester, and be not mournful any more, for I shall go to heaven.' Then the bird bade them farewell and flew off. In Irish folklore the souls of the departed were often said to appear in the form of various species of bird, for example, robins, doves and swans.

Angelic spirits also appear in the form of birds.[8] For example, during St Patrick's vigil on Croagh Patrick, he was visited by a flock of white angelic birds to comfort him. They beat the lake with their wings until it shone silver, and sang to him: 'O Patrick, rise and come! O Protector of the Gaels, bright in glory! O golden exalted star!' In the story *Voyage of St Brendan* the saint and his monks arrived at an island where there was a tree covered with snow-white birds beside a fountain. One of the birds flew to St Brendan and his wings made a sound like the tinkling of little bells. He informed Brendan that he and his companions were angels who took a small part in Lucifer's rebellion, and so were condemned to stay on the island. However, they suffered no pain and were able to see a part of the Divine Presence, and on feast days they took the form of birds to sing God's praises. In a lovely folktale, a monk heard a little bird singing in the rose bushes of the monastery, whose song the monk thought was sweeter than any he had ever heard before. After a while, the bird flew a short distance to a nearby grave and the monk followed it. The bird kept flying from place to place and the monk followed it, delighted with its enchanting song. At last it grew late, and the monk returned to the monastery. To his astonishment he recognised nobody, and learned that he had gone missing 200 years before. The monk then grew very old, died and was taken to heaven. The little bird was an angel that had carried out God's will to bring the monk to heaven in that way.

That birds sing is one of the most unique things about them, and a recurring theme in bird folklore is the idea of birds whose songs have a powerful effect on the listener, soothing them to sleep and healing them.[9] For example, in the tale *Tadhg son of Cian*, Tadhg voyages to an island where he encounters the otherworld maiden Cliodhna and her magical birds. There were three birds, a blue one with a crimson head, a crimson one with a green head, and a pied one with a golden head. They perched on an apple tree and ate an apple apiece, and warbled a melody so sweet and harmonious that the sick would sleep to it. Similarly, the birds guide Tadhg and his companions on their journey, lifting their spirits and reviving them with their song. In the tale *The Martial Career of Conghal Cláiringhneach* the three magical birds of the daughter of Cairthean Corr had the power to lull to sleep the wounded and sick people of the world with their music. In Welsh myth, the magical birds of Rhiannon entertained warriors, and had the power to 'wake the dead and lull the living'. The three birds entertained the company of Bran for seven years while they feasted, and forgot the grief they had previously suffered. It is interesting that in all three cases, the birds are connected to otherworldly women.

Sometimes the song of birds could have a negative effect. A tale from the *Metrical Dindshenchus* relates how King Cairpre was tormented by birds singing a sad, mournful song that took the strength from him. This continued until a druid managed to ensnare the birds in a spindle tree, which prevented the birds from singing by its perfume. Also in the *Metrical Dindshenchus* is a story of two brothers, Buide and Luan, who take the form of birds so that Buide can sleep with his married lover Estiu. The two brothers would arrive at the court of Nar, Estiu's husband, and sing a plaintive song until the court was lulled to sleep. Then while the court was asleep, Buide would sleep with Estiu. Eventually, growing suspicious, Nar asks his druid about the birds, who informs him of the truth. The next time Buide and Luan arrive in the form of birds, Nar is ready for them, and kills them with his slingshot.

Finally, another use of birds was to observe their flight or their song in order to foretell the future, a practice known as ornithomancy.[10] In ancient Rome ornithomancy was practised by the College of Augurs, who distinguished between '*oscines*' and '*alites*' – 'talkers' and 'flyers'. *Oscines* were birds that gave signs by their cries as well as by their flight, such as ravens, owls and crows. Birds which gave signs by their manner of flying alone were *alites*, such as eagles and vultures. The quarter of the heavens in which they appeared in flight, and their position relative to the observer, were significant factors. Also in ancient Rome were the auspices, or 'bird inspectors'. These ascertained the will of the gods by watching the behaviour of the sacred chickens, cared for by an official known as a 'pullarius'. This is the origin of the phrase used today that a particular thing is 'auspicious'.

Ornithomancy was practised by the ancient Celts as well. According to the Roman author Diodorus Siculus, the Gaulish druids foretold the future by watching the flight of birds. Similarly, in Keating's *History of Ireland* the Irish druids also used to listen to the chattering of birds in order to 'lay *geasa* on (command) the demons' and get information from them. Medieval Irish documents survive which outline how to determine the future from the calls of the wren and raven, giving detailed instructions as to the meaning of each kind of call (see Wren and Raven). At a folk level, a basic form of ornithomancy was also a popular belief until modern times in Ireland and elsewhere. For example, the calls of the cuckoo foretold various fates for the listener for the coming year, depending on when and where they first heard them (see Cuckoo). Indeed, the practice continues today, when people count the number of magpies they encounter to determine their future luck.

BIRDS IN EARLY IRISH LAW

Both wild and domestic birds feature in the early Irish Brehon Laws.[11] Hens and geese were kept for their meat and eggs in early Ireland, and were assigned various values under the law (see Domestic Chicken and Goose). Ducks were also kept, but more rarely, and do not appear to have been assigned a legal value. Most eggs consumed were hen-eggs, and it was considered that a hen was expected to lay about fifty eggs a year, far fewer than the modern hen, which can produce 300 a year. It was also stipulated that the egg of a full-grown hen should be 4 inches in circumference, and 5 inches long. Eggs were of particular value for clergy on penitential diets without meat, as they provided protein. A clerical penitent could eat only bread, gruel, milk, garden herbs and hard-boiled eggs. Finally, due to its fairly constant size, half of a hen-egg was used as a unit of measurement for liquids. Half an eggshell with a circumference of 4 inches (as mentioned above) can hold about half a fluid ounce, or 14.4 millilitres.

Regarding wild birds, the most important issues were hunting and trapping. Detailed regulations were laid down for the division of a bird's flesh and feathers between the trapper and landowner. The proportion depended on whether or not the trapper had secured permission, and on whether the landowner was a king, commoner or the Church. Unsurprisingly, the higher the rank of the landowner, the lower the proportion of the bird that went to the trapper. In the case of trapping on Church land without permission, the trapper had to do forty nights' penance, as well as surrendering two thirds of the bird's flesh, and all its feathers. If the trapper had been on Church land with permission, he only had to surrender one third of the flesh and two thirds of the feathers. However, the Brehon Laws also stated that three kinds of birds could be taken without any share going to the landowner: very small birds (*minnta*), herons (*corr*) or hawks (*séig*). Presumably small birds could be taken because they were not worth the landowner's trouble. The heron could be considered a pest because of its depredations on fish, while the hawk was allowed to be taken 'because it carries off young pigs and hens'. The word *séig* generally means 'hawk', but in this instance it must include bigger birds of prey, such as buzzards, kites, and harriers, as a sparrowhawk would not be able to carry off a young pig.

BIRDS IN IRISH PLACE NAMES
Many Irish places are named after birds, both wild and domestic.[12] Not surprisingly, many of our most common species of bird appear

most frequently. For example, a large number of names involve the crow. In County Limerick there is Ardnapreaghaun (*Ard na bPréachán*– Height of the Crow); while County Kerry has Carrignabreaghaun and Carrignapreaghane (*Carraig na bPréachán* – Rock of the Crow); and north County Dublin has Crowscastle (*Caisleán na bPréachán*). The hooded crow (*feannóg*) is specifically named many times. For example, there is Ballyfinoge (*Baile Feannóg* – Town of the Crow), County Wexford; Bawnnavinnoge (*Bán na bhFeannóg* – Green of the Crow), County Waterford; Cloonfinnoge (*Cluain Feannóg* – Meadow of the Crow) and Carrownafinnoge (*Ceathrú na Feannóige* – Quarter of the Crow), both in County Galway. County Cork has Gorteennafinnoge (*Goirtín na Feannóige* – Little Field of the Crow) and Knockanenafinnoge (*Cnocán na Feannóige* – Hill of the Crow); while County Mayo has Carricknafannoge (*Carraig na bhFeannóg* – Rock of the Crow).

There is also a large number of place names involving the pigeon or dove, many of them relating to rocks, caves or cliffs, indicating that the wild rock dove is involved. These include Pigeon Rock, County Mayo; Carrignagolur (*Carraig na gColúr* – Rock of the Dove), County Limerick; Coosnagolor (*Cuas na gColúr* – Hollow or Cave of the Dove), County Kerry; Pigeon Cove (*Úig na gColmán* – Sea cave of the Pigeon), County Donegal; and Pigeon Hole (*Poll na gColm*), County Galway. Some of the names suggest the domestic pigeon, including Pigeonpark (*Páirc na gColúr*) in Counties Offaly and Tipperary, and Pigeonhouse (*Teach na gColúr*) in County Offaly.

It is also not difficult to understand why there are many places named after the domestic chicken, both hen and cock. For example, County Sligo has Carrownagark (*Ceathrú na gCearc* – the Hen's Quarter); County Longford has Cloonnagark (*Cluain na gCearc* – Meadow of the Hen); and County Cork has Knockanenagark (*Cnocán na gCearc* – Hill of the Hen). County Galway has the townlands of Keeraunnagark South and North (*Caorán na gCearc Theas agus Thuaidh* – Heath of the Hens South and North), though this may refer to the grouse (*cearc fraoigh* or 'heather hen') rather than the domestic hen. Also in Galway are the townlands of Cockstown East and West, while in Monaghan is found Cavanaguillagh (*Cabhán na gCoileach* –

Field of the Cock). Finally, County Donegal has the intriguing Cullaghcro (*Coileach an Chró* – Cock of the Bothy). The duck also appears in some names. Duck Rock is in County Galway, while Duckspool (*Clais na Lachan* – Ditch of the Duck) is in County Waterford. Duck Island appears in Counties Longford, Donegal and Galway. Similarly, Goose Island (*Oileán na nGé*) appears in Counties Galway, Clare, and (*Inis na nGé*) in Mayo, and the islands Inishkea North and South (*Inis Gé Thuaidh agus Theas* – Goose Island North and South) are also in Mayo. Interestingly, Coolock in north Dublin city has two townlands – Gooseacre and Goosegreen – which may refer to the domestic goose rather than the wild variety.

Some other birds appear frequently, often in areas which reflect their natural habitat. For example, the eagle usually appears in place names of mountainous or remote areas where eagles might be expected to be found. These include, among others, Loch Ouler (*Loch Iolar* – Eagle Lake) in the mountains of County Wicklow; Eagle's Crag, County Wicklow; Eagle's Nest (*Nead an Iolair*), County Donegal; and Eagle's Hill (*Cnoc an Iolair*), County Kerry. Similarly, the raven occurs in quite a few names, such as Aillenaveagh (*Aill na bhFiach* – Cliff of the Raven), County Galway; Ardnaveagh (*Ard na bhFiach* – Height of the Raven), County Limerick; Ballybofey (*Bealach Féich* – Pass of the Raven) County Donegal; Raven Island, County Galway and Ravenhill, County Down. The hawk appears in such names as Shouks (*Cnocán Seabhac* – Hill of the Hawk), County Wexford; Srashouke (*Sraith Seabhac* – Moor of the Hawk), County Galway; Hawkswood (*Coill na Seabhac*), County Offaly; and Hawkfield, County Kildare. As might be expected, place names involving the seagull usually indicate a location near the sea or water. These include Gull Island (*Carraigín na bhFaoileáin* – Rock of the Seagull) and Carrickaweelion (*Carraig na bhFaoileáin* – Rock of the Seagull) in County Mayo; Seagull Rock in County Galway; and Reennaweelaun (*Rinn na bhFaoileann* – Headland of the Seagull) in Counties Kerry and Donegal. The curlew is found in place names reflecting its preference for hills and moorland, such as Curlew Hill (*Cnoc an Chrotaigh*), County Mayo; Curlew Rock (*An Chreag Chrotach*), County Donegal; and Curlew Island (*Oileán an Chrotaigh*) County Galway. However, the Curlew Mountains in Counties Sligo and

Roscommon probably have nothing to do with the bird, but derive their name instead from the Irish *Corrshliabh* meaning 'steep-sided, pointed mountains'. Finally, the plover makes an appearance in some place names. These include Barrnaveddogue, County Louth and Barranafaddock, County Waterford (*Barr na bhFeadóg* – Height of the Plover); Cloonnavaddogue (*Cluain na bhFeadóg* – Meadow of the Plover), County Galway; Drummeennavaddoge (*Droimín na bhFeadóg* – Ridge of the Plover), County Mayo; Crocnavaddoge (*Croc na bhFeadóg* – Hill of the Plover), County Donegal and Ploverhill, County Tipperary.

Birds In Early Irish Poetry

Early Irish poetry is famous for its vivid portrayal of nature, and birds feature in many verses, often with a clear appreciation of their habits and characteristics.[13] For example, in the story of the doomed lovers Deirdre and Naoise, Deirdre declares in one poem: 'sweet the cuckoo's note on bending bough, / on the peak above Glen Daruadh'; while an early Irish poem about the mountain Beann Ghualann praises 'the turtle doves (*fearáin*) of your sheltering trees'. The blackbird was also a favourite, with a famous poem about the blackbird of Belfast Lough (see Blackbird) and numerous mentions of its sweet song. For example, Fionn of the warrior band the Fianna says: 'Blackbird of Doire an Chairn, your voice is sweet; I never heard on any height of the world, music was sweeter than your voice.' However, more warlike birds that were less sweet of voice were also praised. A poem about the Fianna states that dear to them was 'the scream of the eagle on the edge of the wood'. A story about the poet Athairne states 'raw and cold is icy spring – passionately wailful is the harsh shrieking crane [heron]'. In addition, some poems have several verses praising many different kinds of birds.

An example of this appears in a poem in the well-known tale of Diarmuid and Gráinne. The two lovers were fleeing across Ireland from Fionn Mac Cumhaill and the Fianna, who were furious that they had eloped together, betraying Fionn, who had been Gráinne's lover. The pair were exhausted from their wanderings and often Gráinne would watch over Diarmuid and sing a song to help him sleep. Later she would sing a song to rouse him, in which she would tell him that even the animals and birds of the forest were awake:

Ní chodail in dam so soir	The stag in the east is awake
Ní sguirionn do bhúirfedhaig	Loudly he roars without cease
Cía bheith um dhoiribh na lon	Though with blackbirds in the oaks
Ní fuil na meanmhuin codladh	He has no mind to sleep.
Ní chodail in eilit mhaol	The hornless doe is awake
Ag buirfedhaig fo breclaoch	Calling for her speckled fawn
Do ghní rith tar barraibh tor	Running over the bushy brakes
Ní dhén na hadbhaidh codal	In her den she waits for dawn.
Ní chodail in caoinche bhras	Many birds are still awake
Os barraibh na crand caomh cas	In the tops of tangled trees
Is glórach atathar ann	All night a noisy din they make
Gidhbe an smólach ní chodlann	Even the song thrush does not sleep.
Ní chodail in lach lán	The broody duck is wide awake,
Maith a lathor re degh-snámh	And though her swimming is the best
Ní dhein súan no sáimhe ann	She has no peace, nor rest she takes,
Ina hadbhaidh ní chodlann.	And does not sleep within her nest.
Anocht ní chodail in gerg	The grouse is still awake tonight
Os fraochaibh anfaidh imaird	On the storm-tossed mountain heath.
Bin fogher a gotha gloin	Sweet the sound of her clear cries
Eidir srothaibh ní chodail	Amongst the streams she does not sleep.

Birds feature often in the well-known story of *Suibhne Geilt* or Mad Sweeney. Mad Sweeney was a king in early Ireland who later lived as an outcast in the woods, fleeing under a curse after insulting St Ronan. In the following verses he describes his life in the wild as an outcast, living in fear even of the harmless wild birds around him:

Teichim riasna huiseóga	At the sight of larks I flee
As é an trenrioth tenn	Running hard, afraid to stop
Lingim tar na guiseoga	Leaping over little streams
A mullaighibh benn.	That flow on the mountaintop.
Feran eidhinn iomuallach	The turtle dove makes quite a stir
An tan éirghuis duinn	When she flies as I draw nigh
Gairid bhím ag tharrachtain	But soon I am surpassing her
Ó rofas mo chlúimh.	Such a feathery state have I.
Creabhair oscar antuicseach	The silly woodcock does not know
An tan éirghuis damh	Why before my step it flies
Indar liom as dergnámha	But I face a mortal foe
An lon do gní an sgal.	In the blackbird's scolding cries.

In time however, Sweeney comes to feel at one with the nature around him, and begins to love the animals and birds of the wild woods. As he approaches death, though still an outcast, he has reached some kind of inner peace and so he praises his life in the woods that is about to end forever.

Ba binne lium robhaoi tan	Once a sweeter sound to me
Ná comhradh ciúin na muintear	Than local people's quiet speech
Bheith icc lúthmhaireacht im linn	Was the rustling by the pool
Cúchaireacht fhéráinn feraiñ eidhinn.	Of turtle doves that call and croon.
Ba binne lium robhaoi tan	Once a sweeter sound to me
Ná guth cluigín im fharradh	Than little bells tolling near,
Ceileabhradh an luin don bheinn	The blackbird's song upon a crag
Is dordán doimh ar doininn.	And in a storm the roaring stag.
Ba binn lium robhaoi tan	Once a sweeter sound to me
Ná guth mná áille im fharradh	Than women's voices softly near,
Guth circe fraoich an tsléibhe	the grouse on the steep hillside
Do cluisin in iarmh-éirghe.	Raising her voice to greet sunrise.

Finally, a beautiful nature poem from the seventh century concerns the hermit Marbán and his life in a hut in the woods, close to the trees, wild plants, animals and birds that live there. In these verses Marbán describes how the birds around him provide him with some company, describing them affectionately as if they were old friends.

> Turtle Doves,
> Neat, red-breasted
> Are dearly known.
> Thrushes' sweet refrain
> Calling once again
> Around my home.

> Bumblebees, chafers
> Plump music makers
> Gently drone.
> Barnacles, brent geese
> Close to Halloween
> A dark, rough tone.

> Singing lively
> Wren so sprightly
> On the hazel staff.
> Bright headcover,
> Bold woodpecker
> In a flock so vast.

> White birds come
> Herons, seagulls,
> The shy cuckoo hides.
> No call morose
> The red grouse
> On the heathered hillside.

Robin — Spideog — *Erithacus rubecula*

The robin's red breast and cheerful, friendly manner and song gave it a role in European tradition of bringing comfort to the wounded and suffering, especially to Jesus Christ; and have made it one of the most popular images of Christmas today. The robin was also traditionally said to show respect to the dead by covering them with leaves and moss. In Irish folk tales the robin often helped heroes in their adventures, with encouragement and advice.

FOLK BELIEFS AND CUSTOMS

The most common folk tales in Ireland about the robin explain how it got its red breast. A widespread story is that when Jesus was hanging on the cross, the robin came and plucked a thorn from the crown of thorns on Jesus' head.[1] A drop of Christ's blood fell on the robin's breast, and it has remained that colour ever since, in remembrance of the deed. Alternatively, the robin's breast became stained with blood as it was trying to staunch or cover Christ's wounds with moss or leaves, or from covering up with leaves the drops of blood that fell to the ground. Another version from County Mayo held that the robin was trying to pull the nails out of Christ's hands and feet, when a drop of blood fell onto its breast. Yet another variation on the theme held that the robin got its red breast from trying to save Jesus from his persecutors. According to this story, Jesus was being pursued by soldiers and passed through a wheat field, leaving a trail of drops of blood behind him. The robin lay upon every drop of blood to cover the trail, and did not leave a trace of it for the soldiers to find. Unfortunately the robin's good works were then undone by the wren, which alerted the soldiers to Jesus' whereabouts (see Wren). Similarly, another tale relates that the robin helped the Virgin Mary on the flight into Egypt.[2] According to this story, Mary was cut by brambles, but the robin followed her trail, covering the blood with leaves so that the pursuers could not find it. In Brittany it was said that Christ thanked the robin for plucking out the thorns by making it a lucky bird, and giving it sky-blue eggs.[3] In Greece it was said that as a child Jesus would feed the robins outside his home. A close bond thus formed, and many years later, the robin refused to leave Jesus' tomb until he had risen from the dead. It then sang with the angels as Jesus ascended into heaven.[4]

An alternative Irish version of how the robin got its red breast contends that it was fire, and not blood, that was responsible.[5] According to the tale, a boy was minding a fire when he fell asleep, and a wolf came and quenched the fire. A nearby robin saw what had happened, and noticed that one spark of the fire was still alight. The helpful robin started clapping his wings until the spark grew into a flame again and burned his breast, giving him its red colour from then on. In the north of England it was said that the fire that burned the robin's breast emanated from hell, where the robin would travel carrying a drop of water in its beak, to alleviate the suffering of those incarcerated there.

A variation on the theme of the robin helping or comforting those suffering or dying is the widespread European tradition that the robin covers up the face of a dead person, or the whole body, with leaves or moss out of respect.[6] The tradition was found in seventeenth-century England, Germany and France. For example, an English poem entitled 'The Owl' by Michael Drayton, dating from 1604, includes the lines: 'Covering with moss the dead's unclosed eye, / the little redbreast teacheth charitie.' The most famous story involving the tradition however, was that of the 'Babes in the Wood' which tells of how two children, abandoned by their wicked uncle in Wayland Wood in Norfolk, starved to death and were covered with leaves by a merciful robin. This tradition was held in Ireland also, and for this reason it was believed that the robin should never be killed or put into a cage, despite its sweet voice. In Brittany it was believed that robins sang songs of pity around dead bodies, and would not give up singing until the bodies were found and interred.[7] Similarly, it was said that robins would attend funerals, and at the funeral of Queen Mary II in 1695 in Westminster Abbey, a robin was supposed to have perched on the queen's catafalque.[8] Because of the assistance the robin gave to Jesus, it was also regarded in Ireland as a bird anxious to console the sick and dying, and it was claimed by some that the robin was given to landing on the windowsill of a house where someone was dying, in order to sing and bring comfort to the dying person within.[9]

Naturally, given the belief in the robin's good deeds, it was considered to be a blessed bird in many parts of Europe.[10] In Ireland generally it was considered to be very bad luck to kill or interfere with a robin, and boys were told that if they robbed a robin's nest they would get sore hands. In County Donegal it was said that when a robin discovered its nest had been robbed, it would utter the following curse: *Má's duine beag a thóg mo nead, / go dtabhairidh Dia ciall dó / Má's duine mór a thóg mo nead / Go gcuireadh Sé faoi chlár é* – 'If it's a little person (a child) who took my nest / May God give him good sense / If it's a big person (an adult) who took my nest / May God send him to death'.

In Counties Kerry, Tipperary and Limerick, boys who trapped birds would always release a robin if they caught one, but only after taking a feather from its tail and telling it to swear an oath to send a blackbird or a thrush next time. In Suffolk in England, it was said that a broken leg would follow from taking a robin's eggs. In Tyrol in Austria, harrying a robin's nest would bring epilepsy, while in Bohemia it would bring permanent trembling of the hands. In Britain it was believed that to kill or harm a robin or its nest would bring bad luck, and an old saying in England made this clear: 'The Robin and the Jenny Wren, are God Almighty's cock and hen.'

The behaviour of the robin also gave rise to some superstitions.[11] In Ireland it was said that if a robin perched directly in front of someone, that person might expect some important news, or an important letter. In many parts of Ireland it was thought that a robin coming into the house was lucky. However, it was said simultaneously in many places in Ireland that the robin coming into the house was in fact unlucky, or that it was a sign of death. For example, in County Cork it was said that if a small bird like a robin or a wren came into the house, it was a sign that someone in the house would die. In Ireland a robin pecking at the window of a house was also a particularly bad omen. Similar beliefs about the robin existed in Britain. In Wales it was believed that a robin pecking at the window of a house signalled death. In many parts of England, a robin appearing at the door or around the house was considered an omen of death.

Some weather lore surrounded the robin.[12] In Ireland generally it was said that a robin singing from the top of a tree was a sign of good weather. On the other hand, a robin entering the house in the autumn was said in Ireland to foretell hard weather, frost and snow. In County Donegal it was said that the robin flew near the house and barn when snow was forthcoming, and flew right into the kitchen if a heavy snowfall was fast approaching. In County Waterford it was said that the robin would come into the house if it was going to snow, but hide in a bush if a storm was approaching. In County Donegal, if the robin sang in the evening in spring or summer then rain was sure to come the next day.

The robin was also involved in some Irish folk cures.[13] For example, the robin was said to be able to cure the skin disease scrofula by being rubbed three times against the affected area. Given its associations of helpfulness and bravery, it is not surprising that the robin was also thought to provide an Irish folk cure for combating depression. The rather cruel cure involved killing a robin, removing its heart and stitching it into a sachet. The sachet was then put on a cord, and worn around the neck of the sufferer.

The robin was traditionally known in Ireland, especially in Munster, as *Spideog Mhuintir Shúileabhain* or 'Robin of the O'Sullivans', and was said to be the champion and supporter of their heroes in battle.[14] It was said that one ancestor of the O'Sullivans', Maolughra, gave away an eye as an act of generosity, thus mirroring the generosity of the robin when it plucked the thorns out at the crucifixion. The robin appears on the coat of arms of the O'Sullivans, apparently to exhort the clan that in victory it is better to be kind to the vanquished, the wretched and those who suffer calamity, as the robin covers the limbs of the fallen.

In Donegal children up to seven years old were called by the names of birds to confuse the fairies and so prevent them from taking the children.[15] Girls were called *Spideog, Eiseog* and *Cuach* (Robin, Lark, and Cuckoo) and boys were called *Colmán* (Dove). The name *Spideog*, anglicised as 'spidogue', was also used in many parts of the country to mean a delicate, weak or slender child. The robin was also known by some other names.[16] A widespread name for the robin in Britain and Ireland is 'redbreast' or 'robin redbreast', and the same name is found in Ulster Irish as *broinndearg*. The robin was also widely known in Irish as *spideog Mhuire*, 'the Virgin Mary's Robin', reflecting the belief that it was a blessed bird. The robin also appears in some Irish place names such as Graiguenaspiddoge (*Gráig na Spideog* – Hamlet of the Robin), County Carlow; Kylespiddoge (*Coill Spideog* – Robin's Wood), County Laois; and Turnaspidogy (*Tír na Spideoige* – Land of the Robin), County Cork.[17]

The robin has been associated with Christmas in Britain and Ireland since at least the eighteenth century, which is not surprising as its red breast and cheerful manner make it a natural fit for the season.[18] The robin is also one of the few birds to carry on singing in wintertime, giving it a high profile at that time of year. The image of the robin as a Christmas bird was cemented in Victorian times when it began to appear as a popular motif on Christmas cards from about 1860. Part of the appeal of the robin on Christmas cards was that its bright red breast echoed the red of postboxes and postmens' uniforms, making it a bird associated with the glad tidings of the season. These newer associations made a very good fit with the older blessed images of the robin, which is perhaps why the link between the robin and Christmas is as powerful as ever today.

MYTHS AND LEGENDS

The robin plays a helpful role in many Irish folktales.[19] For example, in one tale the hero Mionn had to complete a series of tasks, one of which involved getting some bread from a baker. However, the baker would not give any bread unless Mionn filled a sieve full of water from a nearby river. Naturally, every time Mionn tried to fill the sieve, the water would simply run out the bottom. A robin appeared and advised Mionn to get some cow dung and daub it on the bottom of the sieve. Once Mionn did this the water stayed in the sieve, and he was able to bring some back to the baker. In another tale, a priest hurt and left deaf and dumb by witches is helped by a robin, who gives him a herb which restores him to full health. The priest asked why the robin had helped him, and she replied that she was the same robin that the priest had helped two years ago when she had a broken foot. The robin could also punish those who were not helpful to it in turn. In one story, a girl who had been banished by her stepmother sat down beside a well to eat the little bit of food she had. A robin appeared and asked her for a few scraps for her chicks. The girl told her to help herself, and welcome. In return, the robin stuck its tail into the well, and divided the contents into honey above and blood below. The girl was able then to enjoy her fill of the honey. Later, the stepmother's daughter came the same way and also sat down by the well to eat her lunch. The robin appeared again and asked for some crumbs, but the daughter shooed the robin away with disdain. Before it left, the robin stuck its tail into the well and divided the contents of the well into blood above and honey below. Then when the selfish daughter tried to drink from the well she nearly choked.

The most common appearance of the robin, however, is as a help to various heroes on their quests.[20] For example, a widespread story concerns the adventures of three sons of a widow who each set out on a quest. The first son sat near a well to eat some cake, and was asked by a robin for some crumbs. The son refused to spare anything, telling the robin to be off and not bother him. He later encountered a witch in the forest and was killed by her. The second son also stopped at the well to eat some cake and similarly refused to share any cake with the robin. He also ended up killed by the witch in the same way. Finally, the third and youngest son stopped at the same well, but unlike his brothers was happy to share his cake with the robin. In return, the robin told him about the witch that he would soon encounter, and advised him of the way to defeat her. The youngest son followed the robin's advice, killed the witch, met the inevitable princess and married her, and restored his brothers to life into the bargain (not a bad return for sharing a few crumbs!). In another tale, a robin helps a hero fighting a giant by advising him to stand between the giant and the sun, and 'to remember where men draw blood from sheep in Erin'. Taking the robin's advice, the hero stood so that the sun was always behind him as he fought, thus half blinding the giant. This forced the giant to stick its neck out to squint, and the hero, remembering the second part of the robin's advice, struck the giant a blow to the neck that killed it. In other stories the robin helps the hero by egging him on to fight, normally by making him angry. For example, in one tale the robin said to the hero fighting a giant: 'Isn't it a shame for you, and you haven't a friend nor a relation here but me, if that dirty beast should kill you, [you would have no-one] to cover you, but me with the little leaves that I'd gather with my bill.' The hero was so enraged by this thought that he killed the giant by beheading it.

The robin is also associated with some saints.[21] A folk tale links the robin with St Columba (or Colmcille). According to the tale, the saint was alone in his room when a robin hopped onto the window beside him. 'Will you sing me a song, birdie?', asked Columba. The robin began to sing the following words: 'Holy, holy, holy, a wee brown bird am I. / But my breast is ruddy, because I saw Christ die.' In Scotland the robin is associated with St Kentigern, who according to legend brought a robin back to life. The robin had been the companion of St Serf, Kentigern's teacher, and would feed off Serf's hand and sit on his shoulder twittering while the psalms were being sung. Some of the other young men grew jealous of the fact that Kentigern was Serf's favourite, and killed the robin with the aim of placing the blame on him. However, Kentigern blessed the robin's corpse and returned it to life, by crying and praying, and making the sign of the cross over it. A robin appears on the coat of arms of the city of Glasgow in remembrance of the tale.

NOTABLE FACTS

The robin is famous for building its nest anywhere it can find a suitable spot, without any fear of being close to humans. Robins' nests have been found in an extraordinary variety of objects, including abandoned kettles, tins, saucepans, rolls of wire and the pocket of a gardener's jacket.[22] The robin has also been known to build its nest quite happily in places such as a row of books, a pigeonhole in a writing desk, the lectern of a church, and even under the bonnets of cars. Despite its friendly reputation, robins are actually fiercely territorial, with male birds defending their patches aggressively against other males all through the year, winter included.[23] The robin is also famous for following the gardener as he or she digs, in the hope of getting some juicy worms or other invertebrates, and they would once have followed foraging animals in woodland, such as wild boar, in the same way. The robin is noted in Britain and Ireland for being a bolder, friendlier bird than its counterpart on the European continent, which may perhaps be because it is a subspecies: *melophilus*.[24] Whatever the reason, few people would dispute that our lives would be poorer without the cheeky robin to keep us company when we venture outdoors.

Wren — Dreoilín — *Troglodytes troglodytes*

*A*lthough it is one of our smallest native birds, the wren's lively, bold manner and loud song ensured that the story of how it became 'the king of the birds' was well known throughout Europe since ancient times. This story in turn led to the custom of the wrenboys parading the wren on St Stephen's Day in Ireland and Britain, and on various dates around Christmas and New Year in France. In early Ireland the loud song of the wren made it a sacred bird to the druids, as it was believed to have the gift of prophecy.

FOLK BELIEFS AND CUSTOMS

The most common theme in Irish folklore about the wren is the justification for why it is hunted on St Stephen's Day.[1] A popular story was that St Stephen was hiding from his enemies, but the wren flitted all about the bush or the cave where he was hidden until he was revealed to his pursuers. The wren was also said to have been hunted because it betrayed Christ to soldiers pursuing him. It did this by informing them that he had escaped through a field of wheat, which had miraculously sprung up to hide his tracks when drops of his blood had fallen on a newly sown field. The wren was also believed to have betrayed Fionn Mac Cumhaill, the hero of the Irish warrior band, the Fianna, who was hiding in a clump of bushes from his pursuers. As they drew near, the wren pinched him on the ear with its beak and thus betrayed him (presumably because he cried out in pain). It was said that the little nip was visible in the hero's ear until his death.

Some versions lay the blame for the wren's unpopularity on more modern events.[2] For example, it was said that the wren was supposed to have pecked on the drum of a Williamite soldier, alerting him to a surprise attack by Jacobite forces. Similarly, a flock of wrens was supposed to have alerted Cromwell's army to a surprise attack by the Irish army, by flapping their wings on the drums of the Irish. Writing in 1625, O'Sullivan Beare in his *Natural*

History of Ireland gives yet another reason for why the wren was hunted, accusing the wren of being a miserable bird that 'pecks the dead with its beak with such cursed savagery'.

It is more likely, however, that the custom of hunting the wren is related to the most famous story about it, namely how the wren became king of the birds.[3] This story is very old, being known to the ancient Romans (see below). According to the story, all the birds held a parliament to decide which among them should be king, and it was agreed that the bird that could fly the highest would claim the honour. The eagle soared far above every other bird on its great wings, and looked set to be the outright winner. However, the wren hid in the eagle's tail, and when the great bird grew tired and could fly no higher, the clever wren jumped out and flew up a little further, thus taking the title of king. Some Irish versions add that as they were returning the eagle hit the wren on its back with his beak. This injured the wren and meant that from then on it could not fly properly, but only flit from hedge to hedge. Some European folk tales concern the aftermath of this, relating how the other birds were

displeased that the wren had achieved the title through trickery, and how they tried to reverse the result. However, the folktales go on to say that their efforts were thwarted by the clumsy interventions of the owl (see Owl).

The custom of hunting the wren was found all over Ireland, except for most parts of Ulster.[4] Generally, in the days and weeks leading up to Christmas, young boys and youths would search the hedgerows for the wren. When one was discovered, it was chased with great excitement and assaulted with a variety of missiles, sticks and stones, until it was successfully killed. Then on St Stephen's Day, 26 December, the dead wren or wrens were triumphantly paraded through the district, usually attached to a holly bush elevated on a pole. The boys would stop at various houses of the district, where they would recite the wren song, looking for a contribution to the 'wren party'. This usually consisted of a carousing drinking session based on the proceeds of the day's collection, which would be held that night or later during Christmas week. The wren song varied from place to place, but a common version went something like this:

> The wren, the wren, the king of all birds,
> On St Stephen's Day, was caught in the furze;
> Though he is small, his family is great,
> So, if you please, your honour, give us a treat.
> On Christmas Day I turned a spit;
> I burned my finger: I feel it yet,
> Up with the kettle, and down with the pan:
> Give us some money to bury the wren.

Often there would be further verses referring to the holly and ivy tree, and describing the chase for the wren. For example, another version of the wrenboys' song from Cork city includes the lines:[5]

> *Dreóilín, dreóilín,* where is your nest?
> 'Tis in the tree that I love best.
> 'Tis in the holly and ivy tree,
> Where all the birds come singing to me.

Another version from Cork city has a well-known chorus:[6]

> Knock at the knocker, ring at the bell,
> Please give us a copper for singing so well,
> Singing so well, singing so well,
> Please give a copper for singing so well.

The wrenboys would generally be in fancy dress and wearing comic masks, often in women's clothing, with ribbons and coloured pieces of cloth pinned to their clothes. Usually among the wrenboys would also be some who played music to accompany the song, with pipes, melodeons or mouth organs. The holly bush would generally be decorated with coloured ribbons, and sometimes the wren would be displayed in a little box. On occasion the wren was captured alive and fastened by a string to the holly bush, but this was less usual. Despite the words of the rhyme, holly was almost always the preferred choice of bush, and the use of furze was only exceptional. At the end of the day the dead wren was buried, either in front of a household that had refused to give money (something that was supposed to bring bad luck for the coming year), or simply at the place where the wrenboys had finished their collecting.

The custom of hunting the wren was always strongest in Munster, and here the wrenboy customs were more elaborate. The boys were generally headed by a 'captain', dressed in quasi-military style and carrying a sword, and were accompanied by two other characters, an *amadán* (a male jester) and an *óinseach* (a female jester). This pair would keep onlookers amused by merry jokes and pranks while the wrenboys sang. Around Tralee and the Dingle Peninsula in County Kerry, the wrenboys would also be accompanied by the *lair bhán*, the 'white mare' or hobby horse, which consisted of a wooden horse's head with a moveable jaw which could snap at the unwary, or those slow to contribute. This was worn over the head of one of the boys, who was dressed in a white sheet.

The wren was also one of the characters that appeared in the plays of the Christmas mummers in Ireland.[7] The mummers usually performed at any time during the twelve days of Christmas (25 December – 5 January), generally going from house to house and giving the play in the kitchens or living rooms of the houses they visited. Among the characters was the wren who would appear with a version of the wren song, such as the following: 'The Wren, the Wren, the King of All Birds / St Stephenses Day he was caught in the furze. / She dipped her wing in a barrel of beer / And wishes you all a Happy New Year'. The fact that the wren appears to change gender between the second and third lines did not seem to matter to the mummers or their audience.

A wrenboy rhyme in Irish from County Kerry goes as follows:[8] *'Dreóilín, dreóilín, cois chluí an chloch / Cathas mo mhaide leis; bhriseas a chos, / Éirig' id'shuí, a bhean a' tí, agus tuir dúinn deoch / Nú sáthad an dreoilín siar i'd chorp'* ('O Wren, O wren, on the stone ditch, / I threw my stick at him, I broke his foot, / Get up now, lady of the house and give us a drink, / Or the wren will be shoved into you right quick'). A rather nicer rhyme was recited in Connemara: *'Dreóilín, dreóilín, rí na n-ean / Lá Fhéile Stiofáin rugadh é / Is mór a mhuintir gidh beag é féin / Tabhair dhom pingin as ucht Dé.'* (The wren, the wren, king of the birds, / On Stephen's Day is carried about / Its family is great, though it is small / Give us a penny for the love of God').[9] In Connemara the wren was always alive as it was considered bad luck for it to be killed, and it was carried around on a bush of furze rather than holly.

It is probably a surprise to many Irish people to learn that the custom of hunting the wren was also a widespread tradition in England, Wales, the Isle of Man and France. In England the wren hunt was practised across a wide area of England, from Devon in the west to Suffolk in the east, and through the midlands as far north as Derbyshire.[10] The wren hunt had largely died out in England by the end of the nineteenth century, so details are sketchier, but what details do exist suggest customs similar to those in Ireland. In Essex at Christmas time, the wrenboys sang a similar rhyme to those found in Ireland, beginning with the words 'The wren, the wren, the king of all birds / St Stephen's Day was caught in the furze / Although he is little his honour is great / And so good people give us a treat.' In many parts of England such as Devonshire, Oxfordshire and Gloucestershire, another song was sung that suggested humorously that the 'Cutty Wren', as it was usually called, was of enormous size and needed to be lifted into a cart and dismembered after being shot. Various versions existed, but a popular one called 'The Wren Shooting' went as follows:

> 'We'll go a shooting', says Robin to Bobbin;
> 'We'll go a shooting' says Richard to Robin,
> 'We'll go a shooting' says John all alone
> 'We'll go a shooting' says everyone.
>
> 'What shall we kill', says Robbin to Bobbin, etc.
> 'We'll shoot the wren' says Robin to Bobbin, etc.

And so on for many verses, until the song ends: 'So they brought her away, after each plucked a feather, and when they got home, shar'd the booty together.'

In Wales the wren hunt took place on Twelfth Night (5 January) rather than St Stephen's Day, and appears to have been largely confined to Pembrokeshire, although the wren song has been found in most counties of north Wales, suggesting it may have been there too.[11] The wren was paraded about from door to door in a decorated 'wren house' with glass windows, hoisted on four poles and borne by four men. The procession was accompanied by a song similar to some of those found in England:

> 'O! Where are you going?' says Milder to Melder;
> 'O! Where are you going?' says younger to elder;
> 'O! I cannot tell,' says Festel to Fose;
> 'To catch Cutty Wren,' says John-the-red-nose.

In the Isle of Man, the customs were again similar, with the wren being hunted in the small hours of Christmas Day, and paraded the following day on a long pole decorated with ribbons.[12] The wren song was similar to that in England, involving 'Robin the Bobbin' hunting the wren.

In France the wren hunt was found in the south around the Marseilles region and Carcassonne, and was rather more elaborate.[13] In Carcassonne the hunt took place on the first Sunday in December, when the boys of the Rue Saint-Jean went out of the town armed with sticks to hunt the wren. The first boy to kill a wren was proclaimed the King, and led the procession back into town, carrying the wren on a pole. In La Ciotat near Marseilles the wren hunt took place at the beginning of Nivôse (the end of December). After being hunted, the wren was carried on the middle of a pole, which two men carried as if it were a great burden, and paraded around the town, after which there was a feast.

The wren was traditionally known for the large size of its broods, often with eleven or twelve eggs in a nest, leading to the traditional Irish saying about the wren: 'though he is little, his family is large.' An identical saying was found in Scotland: 'Little as the wren is, its family is large.'[14] This is reflected in some Irish folktales where the wren appears along with a large family.[15] For example, in a well-known tale, the wren was once a farmer who had twelve sons who looked exactly like himself. During a harsh winter, he ran out of food and had to borrow some grain. The following year the wren had a fine crop, but made no effort to repay the debt. When the creditor went to collect what he was owed, he was confronted by thirteen identical birds, and did not know to which of them he should address his demand, much to the delight of the old wren. However, the creditor came up with a plan to get the better of him. He shouted enthusiastically that the old wren was a much harder worker than any of his sons. Hearing this, the old wren jumped up and beat his breast with pride, pleased that his own opinion had been justified at last. However, this was a mistake, as now the creditor knew to whom he should look for repayment.

Another tale with a similar theme from the Aran Islands concerns how the wren outwitted a fox. One day a fox set out to kill a wren and so went to the wren's house, where he asked the bird to come out. However, the clever wren said: 'You can come in and get me, if you promise not to hurt my family.' The fox promised to do that, and went into the house. Then the wren said to his family, 'All together now, my family' and the wrens all mixed themselves up together. As a result, the fox could not recognise the original wren to which he had made the promise. There was nothing he could do, and so the fox went away disappointed. Thus the clever wren lived for another day.

The wren was often seen as a mouse-like bird, as it is small and brown and bobs about in the undergrowth. The wren is also happy to go into holes and crevices that other birds would avoid, from which habit derives its Latin name *Troglodytes*, which means 'cave dweller'. Perhaps because of this some folktales portray the wren and the mouse as rivals, rather than the wren and eagle.[16] Usually this involves the wren and the mouse having a dispute with each other, which escalates into a great battle between the animal and bird kingdoms. In one version, the wren and mouse began to quarrel, because the wren called the mouse dirty for licking its paw and dipping it into the porridge. The winged creatures sided with the wren, and the four-legged creatures sided with the mouse. The fox agreed to be umpire for the two sides, by standing on a hill and indicating who was winning with his tail. If the four-legged creatures were winning, he would raise his tail, and if the birds were winning he would lower it. The battle commenced and the animals were soon winning, and accordingly the fox raised his tail. However, the bee, which had hitherto been neutral, decided to join the side of the birds and so stung the fox on the behind. Howling in pain, the fox lowered his tail to protect himself, and seeing this, the birds rallied and routed the animals from the field. Ever since, the birds have had jurisdiction over both the air and the ground, while the animals are confined to the ground only.

In another version of the tale, the mouse undertook to feed the wren all winter, and would gather scraps from a carpenter's meals for him. One day the carpenter caught the mouse taking scraps, and cut off its tail with an adze. When the mouse told the wren what had happened, the wren said that it did not care, and that it was leaving. The mouse was furious and was determined to call the wren to account. He therefore called all the wild beasts together, while the wren called on all the birds to defend him. The two sides began to fight and soon all the birds were being killed one by one, until there was only the eagle left. He fled the scene of the battle and landed on top of the king's mansion, where he was rescued by a king's son.

The wren was frequently seen as a bold and boastful bird.[17] An Irish nursery rhyme tells of how the robin nursed the wren when she was sick by bringing her food and wine, but when the wren got better she was less than grateful. The rhyme ends as follows: 'Robin being angry hopped upon a twig / Saying "out with you! Fie upon you! Bold-faced jig!"' A humorous story about the wren from the Aran Islands says that one day the wren wanted a new jacket and so went to a tailor's house. The vain wren kicked in the door of the tailor's house, breaking a panel of it, and declared: '*Mar a ndéanfaidh tú mo jaicéad, agus veilbhit lena chába, / beidh mise ag gabháil de mhaide ort, nó go mille mé do chnámha*' (If you don't make me a jacket, with a velvet collar bold, / I'll take a stick to you, and break all your bones'). Interestingly, a version of the wrenboy song in Irish mentions the wren wearing a silk cravat. In Brittany the wren is seen as a vain and presumptuous bird, which chooses the biggest branch it can find to sing from in order to make itself look important.

Despite the custom of hunting the wren, it was perceived in Ireland and Britain as a blessed bird, that should not be interfered with at any other time than St Stephen's Day.[18] From the eighteenth century onwards in Britain, the robin and the wren were often seen as a male and female respectively, and depicted as a married couple, particularly at Christmas time, and in festive imagery such as Christmas cards. However, the wren could also be seen as an unlucky bird.[19] For example, in County Cork it was said that if a small bird like a wren or a robin came into the house, it was a sign that someone in the house would die. In County Donegal it was said that if a wren tapped on the window, it was a sure sign that there would be a death in the house.

The wren was associated with some weather lore.[20] In Donegal it was said that if the wren built its nest on a branch overhanging a stream or river, then a good summer was on the way. However, if it built its nest in a dry ditch or in the eaves of a house, there would be heavy rain and floods during the summer. In Mayo it was said that when the wren hid in a hole in a wall, snow was expected. The wren appears in the Irish place names Knockadroleen (*Cnoc an Dreoilín* – Wren Hill), County Cork, and Wren Island (*Oileán an Dreoilín*), County Donegal.[21]

MYTHS AND LEGENDS

The wren was associated with prophecy in early Ireland, doubtless because of its loud call.[22] Famously, the ninth-century text *Cormac's Glossary* defined the old Irish word for wren – *dreann* – as being derived from 'druid bird'. What is less often stated is that this name derives from its supposed powers of prophecy, with no mention of any ritual killing: '*Dreunn* wren – from *der* "small" *én* "bird" or *drui-én* "druid-bird" i.e. a bird that makes prophecy.' The power of the wren to provide prophecies or auguries is confirmed in a medieval Irish text *Dreanacht* or 'Wren Lore', which sets out in great detail the meaning of each call of the wren in terms of foretelling future events. The direction from which the call of the wren was heard usually signified what was about to happen. For example, if the wren was heard calling from the south-east it meant that proud jesters were coming to visit; from the north, the visit of someone precious to the hearer; and from the north-west, pious folk. If the wren was heard calling from the south it meant a 'fond visitation', but only if the wren was not between the hearer and the sun. Things were better if the wren called from the east, as it signified the arrival of poets, or at least tidings of them. However, hearing the wren calling from the west was bad, as it heralded the arrival of wicked kinsmen!

The power of the wren to foretell events is mentioned in a few early Irish texts.[23] The *Life of Saint Cellach of Killala* recounts how he was ordered to be killed by King Guaire. As he was led out to be killed, scaldcrows, ravens, kites and wrens gathered around, anticipating his death. St Cellach addresses each of them in turn, saying to the wren: 'O tiny wren most scant of tail! Dolefully thou hast piped prophecy lay, surely thou art come to betray me, and curtail my gift of life.' After the saint is killed, the birds of prey (not including the wren) have their fill. Similarly, an incident in the *Life of Saint Moling* concerns the saint cursing the wren. The saint lived as a hermit, with a madman, a fox, a wren and a fly to keep him company. One day the wren hopped on the fly and killed it, so Moling cursed it, saying: 'let his dwelling be forever in empty houses, with a wet drip therein continually, and may children and small people be destroying him!' Then the fox killed the wren, a dog killed the fox, and a cowherd killed the madman, so that St Moling was left on his own. The incident is also interesting because it suggests that the wren was hunted in Ireland at the time when the *Life* was written, at the end of the fourteenth or early fifteenth century. A poem in Irish by Donnchadh Mór Ó Dálaigh of the Early Modern period describes the wren as a prophet, seer and poet.

The wren is mentioned sometimes in other early Irish texts.[24] An eleventh-century poem about a cold winter's night in Moylurg states: 'the little wren does not find shelter for her nest on the slope of Lon', while a tenth-century poem mentions a wren on a branch of hazel. The wren is also mentioned in the well-known story of *Suibhne Geilt* or Mad Sweeney. In the story, the hermit Sweeney remarked that so frightened of people was he that: 'I would flee from them as fast / as at the flight of a wren.' The wren also appears in some Welsh legends.[25] In the tale *Math Son of Mathonwy*, the boy Lleu Skilful Hand gets his name from aiming a shot at a wren from a great distance, and hitting it between the sinew and the leg. In another tale, one of Arthur's men, Medyr son of Medyredydd (Aim son of Aimer) was such a good shot that he could hit a wren in Ireland while aiming from Cornwall.

The story of the rivalry between the wren and the eagle can be traced back as far as ancient Rome.[26] The Roman writer Pliny remarked that there is antipathy between the eagle and the wren because the latter received the title of 'King of the Birds'. Similarly, Aristotle in his *History of Animals* stated that the wren goes by the nickname 'old man' or 'king', and for this reason the eagle is at war with him. It is possible that the bird *trochilus* mentioned by both Classical writers was originally the goldcrest *Regulus regulus*, on account of the fact that the goldcrest has a yellow bar or crest on its head, reminiscent of a king's crown. As the goldcrest is smaller even than the wren, this probably gave rise to the legend of the 'little king', which was later transferred to the wren. The goldcrest's present-day Latin name *Regulus* in fact means 'little king'.

ORIGINS OF THE WREN HUNT

The custom of hunting and killing the wren, before parading it around for alms and then burying it, is so striking and unusual that it has given rise to much speculation as to its origins. A popular theory, maintained by many writers, is that it is a relic of pagan rites of sacrifice and renewal, whereby the wren is ritually killed at the winter solstice to ensure the fertility of the land for the coming year. This argument has been put forward in various forms by writers such as James Frazer, Edward Armstrong, Sylvie Muller and Elizabeth Atwood Laurence. It is generally argued that the rite is ancient in origin, even going as far back as the Stone Age, with the implication that it has survived in Western Europe longest, perhaps due to Celtic influence. There is not sufficient space here to go into these theories in detail. It is enough to say that each writer argues that the custom of hunting the wren is at the centre of an elaborate and ancient cult of immense significance, in which each detail of the wren hunt has an important symbolic function.

However, there are several problems with the 'wren cult' theory. The first of these is that the burial of the wren is marginal to the custom of the wren hunt. Given that the ritual killing of the wren is supposed to be central to the wren cult, the expectation would be that the wren would be buried with ceremony in a place of significance. For example, a symbolic location in the fields to ensure the success of the crops for the coming year, or next to the barn or farm buildings to ensure the good health of the livestock. Failing that, there are other important locations where the wren could be buried, such as at a holy well, parish boundary, fairy fort or crossroads. In fact, far from any of these, the most common custom was to bury the wren outside a household that did not contribute to the wrenboy collection, where it was supposed to bring bad luck, not any benefit. Other than that, the custom was to simply bury the wren without ceremony at the spot where the wrenboy rounds ended, or even just to throw it away. The only example of the wren being treated with any respect seems to be in the Isle of Man where the custom was to bury the wren in a local churchyard. Given that ritual burial is normally of such importance to pagan sacrifice, the casual, almost dismissive disposal of the wren is remarkable and difficult to explain. It also cannot be argued that this lack of regard is due to the deterioration of the custom in a Christian context, as there have never been any archaeological discoveries of the ritual burial of wrens by Pre-Christian Celtic or Pre-Celtic peoples.

The second problem is that there is almost no evidence that the wren was a bird of any symbolic importance prior to the Middle Ages. Apart from a tenuous link to Lleu Skilful Hand, in which hitting the wren demonstrates his prowess as a good shot (see above), the wren does not appear in any legends or mythology in association with gods or goddesses. Unlike, for example, the eagle, raven or swan, there is no suggestion of the wren embodying any deity, or being companion to one; or of playing any important role in any central myths. Considering that the themes of death and resurrection, and of kingship and the fertility of the land, are central to so many Celtic legends, the absence of the wren in any of these stories is difficult to explain in terms of the theory of the wren cult. The only evidence of a major role for the wren in early Celtic society is that of being a bird of augury or prophecy in Ireland, on account of its loud song (see above). The wren also does not have any significant presence in Celtic art or imagery. Apart from a sixth- or seventh-century gold filigreed ornamental brooch in the shape of a wren found at Garryduff, County Cork, it is not depicted in any Celtic decoration or sculpture. It is also not depicted at any Romano-British or Gallo-Roman sites such as temples or holy wells, where images of other animals and birds regularly appear. Indeed, such a wide variety of animals and birds appear in Celtic art that it has been described as a 'Celtic Zoo'.[27] If the wren was of such symbolic importance to the Celts, its absence from Celtic imagery is highly unusual.

Another weakness of the wren cult theory is the argument that the use of the name 'little king' for the wren in many of the languages of Europe is proof that the custom of hunting the wren was once in existence across Europe in Pre-Christian times. For example, in France it is *roitelet*, in Italian *regolo*, in Greek *basiliskos*, in Russian *korólyk* and in German *zaunkönig* ('hedge king').[28] However, these names reflect the fact that the Classical story of the wren becoming king of the birds had entered those cultures, and nothing more. By itself it is not evidence of the custom of hunting the wren in regions where that language was spoken. Indeed, in the very places where the custom of the wren hunt existed, the names for the wren have little to do with the 'little king' story. For example, the Irish word for wren is *dreoilín*, which either derives from *drui-én* 'druid-bird', or from the word *der* or *dher* meaning to jump. [29] Some names in Irish connect the wren to kingship: *breas-én* 'prince bird', *righ-beag* 'little king', *ri-eitile* 'flying king', but they do not appear in the folk tradition, and appear to be scholarly borrowings from English or Latin. [30] It also seems that none of the other languages of Britain or Ireland have a name for the wren based on 'king' or 'little king' either. The English word 'wren', and similarly Scots Gaelic *Dreòlan* or *dreathan*, Manx *drean*, Welsh *dryw*, or Cornish *gwradn* appear to be unconnected with the idea of a king.

Yet another problem for the wren-cult theory is the assertion that the custom of hunting the wren survived into modern times in the more remote locations of Western Europe, where a Celtic or Pre-Celtic cultural influence lasted longest. The evidence for the distribution of the wren hunt does not tally with this. For a start, the south of France appears to be the place where the wren hunt survived longest in its oldest and most elaborate form, and this region bordering the Mediterranean could hardly be called remote in European terms. Regarding Britain and Ireland, far from the remote regions of these islands being centres of the wren hunt, in fact, almost the opposite is true. There is little or no sign of the wren hunt in Scotland, apart from one location in the lowland region of Galloway. [31] It played no part in the Gaelic Celtic culture of the Highlands, and it was not found in the historic heartlands of the Picts. Given that the Picts are widely believed to have retained Pre-Celtic elements in their culture, its absence from Pictish areas is particularly striking. The evidence points instead to the wren hunt in Britain and Ireland corresponding to areas of Anglo-Norman control. In England the wren hunt is widespread throughout the country, but is strongest in the south, and declines in importance further north, which corresponds well with probable Norman influence. Again, in Celtic Cornwall there appears to be no direct evidence of the wren hunt. Regarding Ireland, the absence of the custom of hunting the wren across Ulster has been noted by scholars. [32] What is striking is that the line of demarcation between areas where the wren hunt is practised and those where it is not is quite sharp. It cannot be blamed on the seventeenth-century plantations, as it is also missing from areas that were untouched by them. It cannot be a coincidence that this area largely corresponds to the heartlands of the Gaelic chieftains of Ulster, the only area of Ireland that never came under any kind of Norman control or influence, and which only became subject to English control in modern times after the Flight of the Earls in 1607. In Wales the evidence of the wren hunt is particularly telling. It was strongest in Pembrokeshire around Tenby, in an outpost of Anglo-Norman control known as 'the little England beyond Wales'. The other main area where there is Welsh evidence of the wren hunt is in north Wales. This is also an area of early Anglo-Norman settlement, around the ring of castles and fortified 'bastide' towns built by Edward I of England in the thirteenth century, which functioned as outposts of Anglo-Norman culture in an otherwise native Welsh area. In the rest of Wales, where the native Celtic culture remained strong, there is much less evidence of the wren hunt.

The other region where the custom of the wren hunt was strong was in the Isle of Man. Although the Normans did not invade the island as such, it alternated between the English and Scottish Crowns from the thirteenth century. More relevant is the fact that the island was under the control of the Earls of Derby, the Stanley family, on behalf of the English Crown from 1405 to 1627. There is evidence for the wren hunt existing in Derbyshire, and the most likely explanation is that the Stanley family took the custom of the wren hunt over with them when they took control of the island. Interestingly, the crest of the Stanley family famously features an eagle and child (see Eagle), so it may be that the wren hunt was a particular custom among their retainers and servants. Finally, with regard to the absence of the wren hunt in Scotland, the different pattern of Norman settlement is probably relevant. Unlike the rest of Britain and Ireland, the Normans did not invade Scotland, but were invited to settle there by David I of Scotland in the twelfth century. The likelihood is that some difference in those who settled and their role in Scottish society accounts for the fact that the custom of the wren hunt did not follow them there.

The evidence therefore points to the custom of hunting the wren as being of Medieval origin. As a result, there is no need to seek an explanation for the custom of hunting the wren other than the obvious, which is that it provided sport and entertainment.

Coupling the entertainment of the hunt with the parading of the wren and seeking of alms also do not need any ritual explanation, as they are clearly part of the Medieval traditions of hunting, pageantry and general revelry. In particular, there can be no doubt that the custom of the wrenboys should be seen in the context of Medieval Christmas and New Year customs such as the Feast of Fools and the Lord of Misrule, as the parallels with the wren hunt are obvious. This, in fact, has regularly been remarked upon by wren-cult theorists, only to be dismissed, or else glibly asserted by them to be further evidence of the wren hunt's supposed pagan nature.

While the Feast of Fools and similar customs ultimately grew out of the pagan Roman festivals of Saturnalia on 17 December and of the New Year Kalends on 1 January, by the Middle Ages they had lost any religious connotations and become simply occasions of revelry when the normal moral and social constraints were abandoned.[33] This notion of the normal order of things being reversed was practised at Saturnalia, when masters made merry with their servants and slaves, and a '*Rex Saturnalitius*' was chosen by lots to lead the revels and enliven them by issuing outrageous commands which had to be obeyed. Again, at the Kalends festival of New Year, masters drank and played dice with their servants, and bands of revellers paraded through the streets dressed in women's clothes or the skins of animals. These traditions continued in some fashion up to the Middle Ages, although there were frequent efforts to suppress them by the Church authorities.

Usually the Feast of Fools took place on 1 January and was carried out by the lower clergy in medieval cathedrals and collegiate churches.[34] A Bishop, Lord or even Pope of Fools was appointed for the duration, whose job it was to lead the festivities. The priests and clerks wore masks and danced in the choir dressed as women or minstrels, and sang bawdy songs. The custom mostly took place in France from the end of the twelfth century onwards. Allied to it was the Feast of the Ass, when an ass (a donkey) was led in procession, often decorated and accompanied with music, and sometimes even into the church itself.[35] After the Feast of Fools was suppressed, it was continued in many places by the townsfolk with a *roi des sots*, who wore a hood with ass's ears.

Another similar custom was that of the Boy Bishop, which was celebrated in France and England on the Feast of the Innocents, 28 December , or else on St Nicholas' Day, 6 December.[36] One of the boys of the church choir would be appointed 'bishop' for the day and would lead the Mass, after which there would be a supper for all the choirboys. In England the Feast of Fools was never very widespread, but instead there would be a 'Lord of Misrule' or 'Abbot of Misrule' appointed for the Christmas season in the houses of the nobility and the legal profession. The common theme of all these customs is the inversion of the normal order of things, whereby the appointment of a lowly figure such as a fool, ass or boy is made a mock 'king' (or lord, bishop, abbot and so on) for the period of the festival. The mock king is paraded around surrounded by pageantry, and afterward there is a celebration or a feast. The parallel with the wren hunt is obvious, whereby the lowly wren is made a mock king and paraded around, followed by a celebration. In the case of the wren, the mockery is clearly of the royal eagle, which leaves an obvious question: what eagle is being mocked, or rather *whose* eagle?

It is time now to propose a new theory for the origin of the custom of hunting the wren. It is hereby proposed that the custom of the wren hunt arose in Medieval France in the wider context of the Feast of Fools, and involves a search for alms through a humorous parody of St John the Evangelist. There are several reasons why the evidence points to St John the Evangelist.

His symbol is the eagle. Each of the four Evangelists has had his own symbol since the early days of Christianity: Matthew the winged man or angel, Mark the winged lion, Luke the winged calf or ox, and John the eagle. The reason why the eagle is the symbol of St John is because it was traditionally said that his gospel soars to lofty heights like the eagle in discussing theological issues and the divinity of Jesus.

The festival of St John the Evangelist is 27 December. This is during the time of the Feast of Fools. The custom of the parading the wren could originally have been held on this date, and then migrated over time to other dates during the Christmas and New Year period. In Britain and Ireland, this involved merely switching to the previous day, St Stephen's Day on 26 December. The shift may have occurred because it was considered that other times closer to the main celebrations afforded better opportunities for collecting alms, or it may have been due to Church hostility. Parading with a wren in mockery of the eagle of St John could have been seen as quite scurrilous and sacrilegious, and the Church authorities may have initially tried to suppress it. Switching to another date and dropping any explicit religious connotations of the wren may have been a strategy employed to enable the custom to survive.

St John the Evangelist is associated with wine. According to legend, an enemy of St John tried to kill him with a poisoned cup of wine, but the saint overcame the attempt by taking the cup and blessing it, thereby drawing out the poison. Also, the miracle of Jesus turning water into wine at the wedding feast at Cana occurs only in the gospel of St John. These associations led to the European custom on the Feast of St John the Evangelist of taking wine or cider to the church to be blessed. The blessed wine was then taken with a meal afterwards, where it was supposed to bring blessings to the household for the coming year. Some of the wine would also be kept for special occasions throughout the year, for example for weddings, and for those setting out on a journey. This custom of blessing and drinking wine was known as the 'Love of St John'.[37] These associations are probably the reason why the custom first began. The original wrenboys would have paraded with the purpose of looking for alms to buy wine, ostensibly for the purpose of having it blessed on the feast day.

The wren is traditionally called 'Jenny'. This has been assumed to be the female name, but it may originally have been French *Jean* or *Jeannot*, 'Little John'. It is interesting to note in the English stories of the outlaw Robin Hood that his companion is Little John, and their activity is 'robbing the rich to help the poor'. Could the Robin Hood and Little John stories have been influenced by the tradition of the robin and wren being a pair, and by the custom of hunting the wren?

There are other hints that point to St John the Evangelist. Firstly, in Carcassonne, the wren hunt was led by the boys of Rue Saint-Jean. This is significant because the wren hunt in Carcassonne appears to have survived in a form very close to the original custom. Secondly, another French custom of the 'Bachelleries' can be connected to the saint.[38] This custom generally took place in May and involved young unmarried men and women presenting the local abbot or lord with a wren, in return for which they would receive wine and be allowed to hold a celebration together. Sometimes this custom involved young married couples. In Villiers in central France, newly-wed couples had to visit the steward of their local estate on the next Trinity Sunday after their wedding, holding a wine barrel on their shoulders with a wren inside. These customs involving wine and wrens can be linked to St John, as a second feast day is associated with him: St John before the Latin Gate, on 6 May. The association with newly-weds also points to a reference to the wedding feast at Cana. Thus the wren hunt is not a vestige of pagan ritual, but is instead steeped in Medieval Christianity.

While this theory provides an explanation for the origin of the custom of hunting the wren, it does not quite explain its enduring popularity. It would not be right to be too cynical about the custom. For all that it was a humorous parody with the aim of seeking alms, it can be argued that there was something about the wren with which the wrenboys identified at a deeper level. It is not too difficult to see how they might have felt an empathy with a lively, restless little bird known for its loud voice and bold manner. There is something subversive about the image of the wren as the 'little king', getting the better of his supposed noble superior through wit and bravery. Perhaps the wren represented to them the plucky outcast, the underling who cocks a snook at the powerful of Church and state. Indeed, it is not too far-fetched to see a whiff of rebellion in the custom of hunting the wren, to see in it low-status and usually ignored youths demanding their moment of attention and respect.

NOTABLE FACTS
The wren is noted for several striking features in its nature and habits.[39] The first, as has been remarked upon already, is its extraordinarily loud call for a bird of its small size. The loudest part of the song is an intense trilling, lasting just five seconds and repeated four or five times a minute, and such is its intensity that it

has been known to carry up to a kilometre. The wren is also noted for its large broods, often with eleven or twelve eggs in a nest, and as many as eighteen.

Another unique feature of the wren is its habit of roosting together in large numbers in cold weather: up to seventeen have been counted huddled close to each other in the old bird nests of other species. The wren is found all over Ireland, in every kind of habitat, including remote uninhabited islands, and there are up to 3 million pairs of this endlessly adaptable bird in the country. Finally, a remarkable feature of the wren is that it is American in origin, one of the very few bird species which have successfully invaded the Old World from the New, crossing the Bering Strait to Russia and spreading all the away across Eurasia to our shores.[40] Somehow, that is not at all a surprising fact to learn about this indomitable little bird.

Kingfisher — Cruidín — *Alcedo atthis*

The kingfisher, with its beautiful, bright colours, was a symbol of peace and good fortune in ancient times. In Classical myth the kingfisher or halcyon was associated with the Halcyon Days, a period of calm in otherwise stormy times.

FOLK BELIEFS AND CUSTOMS

In England it was traditionally believed that a kingfisher hung up by its beak would act like a weathervane, and point in the direction where the wind would blow.[1] This belief was mentioned by Shakespeare in *King Lear*: 'Renege, affirm, and turn their halcyon beaks, with every gale and vary of their masters.' It was further believed that it had the power of enriching its possessor, preserving peace and harmony in families and imparting grace and loveliness to those who wore its feathers. In Ireland similar beliefs were held in Kerry, where as well as acting as a weathervane, the kingfisher in full plumage was considered to be an antidote to certain diseases. It is likely that these beliefs developed out of the Classical myth of Halcyone and Ceyx (discussed in the next section), when the winds were calmed for the kingfisher's benefit and a period of peace prevailed.

In Western Europe it was believed that the kingfisher laid its eggs around the time of St Martin's Day (11 November), and that for a fortnight around this period the seas would remain calm, a period known as the Halcyon Days.[2] In France one of the local names for the kingfisher, *martin-pêcheur*, reflects this belief. This belief goes back to Classical writers, although the period concerned was said by them to take place around the winter solstice. In Brittany it was said that a kingfisher's head shines by night like a will-o'-the-wisp, and it is much given to swearing.[3] The first belief is probably due to the kingfisher's brightly coloured feathers, while the second might be due to the kingfisher's call, which is loud and shrill.

MYTHS AND LEGENDS

Gerald of Wales, in his twelfth-century work *The History and Topography of Ireland*, describes the kingfisher and relates some curious lore about it.[4] According to Gerald, if a dead kingfisher was kept in a dry place it would never putrefy. On the contrary, if placed between clothes it would keep them free from moths and impart a pleasant perfume to them. Also, if a dead kingfisher was hung in a dry place by its beak, its feathers would miraculously renew themselves every year.

Classical writers also had some curious beliefs about the kingfisher.[5] It was thought the kingfisher built its nest hanging over the sea for the seven days leading up to the winter solstice, and hatched its eggs in the seven days after. During this period the seas would be calm and safe. According to Aristotle, the kingfisher's nest was a gourd shape that hung over the sea, with a tiny entrance so that the sea could not enter. This has no basis in fact, as the kingfisher actually lays its eggs in tunnels in riverbanks between April and August. However, kingfishers are seen beside the sea in wintertime, as they often migrate to the coast in winter to feed along the seashore.

The Classical beliefs have their origin in the most significant myth about the kingfisher, namely the Greek story of Halcyone and Ceyx.[6] According to the myth, Halycone was the daughter of Aeolus, the god of the winds, and was married to Ceyx, king of Thessaly. Despite Halcyone's feelings of foreboding, Ceyx embarked on a long sea voyage to visit the oracle of Apollo. Halcyone's misgivings were proved right when Ceyx was drowned, after his ship sank in a terrible storm. As the days passed with no word of her husband, Halcyone became increasingly distressed and prayed incessantly to the gods for his safe return. Eventually the gods took pity on her and revealed to her in a dream that her husband was dead. When she awoke, Halcyone immediately rushed down to the seashore to the spot where she last saw Ceyx, only to find his body washed up on the shore. Taking pity once again on Halcyone in her grief, the gods then turned her and her husband Ceyx into a pair of kingfisher birds to live forever on the seashore. From then on, every year for a period in midwinter Halcyone built her nest on the sea and guarded it until the eggs hatched. Her father, Aeolus, ensured the seas

remained calm and undisturbed by wind during this time, and so the Halcyon Days were a period of placid weather around the winter solstice when it was safe for sailors to travel between the storms of winter. Since then the term Halcyon Days has come to mean any period of calm or happiness during troubled times.

NOTABLE FACTS

The kingfisher is noted for its beautiful iridescent blue and orange feathers, which seem to shimmer and dazzle as the bird streaks past. This led to kingfisher feathers being popular with Victorian milliners who used them in ladies' hats and other items of feminine costume.[7] The kingfisher is also excellent at catching fish, and a pair can provide up to 115 fish a day for their young.[8] The Irish name *cruidín* or *cruitín* means 'little hunchback', which refers to the kingfisher's rather hunched posture.

Seagull — Faoileán — *Larus* spp.

The seagull is seen by many people as a mischievous and opportunistic bird as it scavenges and squabbles for fish. But for many others, there is also something romantic and mysterious about it as it soars over the sea. In traditional lore, the souls of those lost at sea would often take the form of a seagull.

Herring gull – Faoileán scadán – *Larus argentatus*

Lesser Black-backed Gull – Droimneach beag – *Larus fuscus*

Greater Black-backed Gull – Droimneach mór – *Larus marinus*

Black-headed Gull – Sléibhín – *Larus ridibundus*

Common Gull – Faoileán bán – *Larus canus*

FOLK BELIEFS AND CUSTOMS

Some weather lore surrounded the seagull.[1] In Donegal it was believed that in late winter or early spring to see seagulls flying inland was a sign of a bad season ahead. Similarly, in Mayo it was believed that when seagulls moved inland it was a sign that a storm was expected. In Ulster and Scotland this belief was expressed in the following rhyme: 'Seagull, seagull, sit on the sand / It's never good weather while you're on the land.' Seagulls were traditionally held in high regard by fishermen.[2] In Donegal fishermen do not like any harm to be done to the seagull, even if it angers them by stealing their bait. The reason given is that they can learn a lot about where the fish are by watching them. In Scotland it was said to be unlucky to catch a seagull and keep it on board a boat. Irish and Cornish fisherman traditionally believed that seagulls embodied the souls of drowned people. Similarly, in Liverpool seagulls were said to be the souls of drowned seamen.

In Clare it was thought that when the seagulls called out to each other, they were saying the following:[3]

First seagull: *Iasc! Iasc! Iasc!*
(Fish! Fish! Fish!)

Second seagull: *Coinnig! Coinnig! Coinnig!*
(Keep it! Keep it! Keep it!)

First seagull: *D'imig! D'imig! D'imig!*
(It's gone! It's gone! It's gone!)

Second Seagull: *Lá léin ort! Lá léin ort!*
(Woe to you! Woe to you!)

If the Irish words are said out loud, an echo of the seagull's cry can clearly be heard. In Aberdeen in Scotland it was believed that seagulls cry before any disaster.

Some Irish folktales involve the seagull.[4] A widespread tradition tells of how the seagull stole the ability to swim from the oystercatcher. In west Cork the story goes that the seagull could not swim until he asked the oystercatcher for a loan of its webbed feet. The oystercatcher agreed to lend them for one day only, but when he went looking for them, the selfish seagull would not give them back. So the poor oystercatcher is now forever wading along the tide's edge, unable to swim and mournfully crying for its loss. The story gave rise to an old saying: *'Iasacht na roillí don fhaoilin'* (the oystercatcher's loan to the seagull), to describe a loan that is never got back. A Donegal version goes further and says that the deceitful seagull is constantly laughing at the poor oystercatcher, who is unable to go out to sea and reduced to picking seashells off the rocks. However, the story adds that the seagull gave his power to whistle to the oystercatcher while his ability to swim was borrowed, with the result that the oystercatcher kept that power, even if it is the loneliest whistle in the world. However, in another Donegal story the seagull comes out second best. The story related that a duck and a seagull had a bet to see which of them would be first to see the day. The duck was the first to wake and cried out *'Wác! Wác! Wác.'* *'Hó'* said the seagull knowing he was beaten, 'that's the day – I'm too late!'

Some Scottish folktales involve witches taking the form of seagulls.[5] In one tale a witch was engaged to destroy a boat coming to the Isle of Tiree in the Hebrides. She hovered about the boat in the form of a gull, keeping it back. However, another witch wished to ensure its survival and followed the wake of the boat in the form of a cormorant, keeping it safe. In another tale, a witch in the form of a gull is the protector of the boat. In this story, a boat on its way to the islands of Uist was fought over by two witches: Yellow Claw who wished to sink the boat and took the form of a skua, and Blue Eye who took the form of a gull and sought to protect it. The two witches fought each other in their bird forms, and Blue Eye won, thus ensuring the boat's safety. A witch in the form of a gull also plays a helpful role in another tale about a boat from Tiree. The boat concerned was caught in a violent gale but managed to take shelter in a creek. However, the crew had to remain there for four days until the seas calmed down. Their relatives were worried about them and asked a local witch if she could tell them their fate. The witch said she could, and told the relatives to come back to her the next day. When the relatives returned, the witch confirmed that their menfolk were safe and well and would soon be home. When the men returned home they were asked if they saw anything unusual, and they confirmed that a grey gull had come and sat on rocks near to them, peering at them closely.

MYTHS AND LEGENDS

According to legend, the Welsh saint Kenneth or Cenydd was raised by seagulls.[6] The legend goes that some black-headed gulls at Worm's Head Island on the Gower peninsula in south Wales came upon a newborn human baby floating in a coracle upon a cloth. Instead of attacking the child, several of the gulls seized the cloth and carried it to a cliff ledge where they made a soft nest for the baby with their feathers. They persuaded a doe to give him milk and he stayed there until adulthood, becoming a man full of laughter, singing and kind words. Angels ensured he was educated as a Christian, and he became a hermit known for his piety.

Seagulls are mentioned several times in early Irish works.[7] According to *Lebor na Cert* or 'The Rights of Kings', the King of Ulster was traditionally entitled to twenty gulls' eggs as part of the tribute received every three years from the King of Ireland. Interestingly, in the tale *The Martial Career of Conghal Cláiringhneach*, seagulls appear along with crows in the role of scavengers. When Conghal and his rival Lughaidh muster to do battle at Tara: 'Royston [hooded] crows and ravens and seagulls came around Tara at the noise, mindful of the enmity of one to the other.' Finally, an early Irish poem in praise of a beauty spot called Beann Ghualann mentions 'the music of your seagulls and swans'.

NOTABLE FACTS

Gulls have become rather unpopular birds because of their success in moving from the coast to our towns and cities where they feast on scraps and all the rubbish left behind by people. They have long been a staple of rubbish tips and now can be seen in many urban streets, where they are considered a nuisance by many. In Britain gulls first began to nest on urban rooftops in Devon and Cornwall in the 1920s, but by the Second World War the habit had begun to spread more widely.[8] By the twenty-first century, they were firmly established in urban areas all across these islands. The habit of raiding rubbish dumps has had negative consequences for the herring gull, however, as botulism from eating rotten meat has led to a decline in their numbers. Numbers in Ireland have declined from about 60,000 pairs in 1969 to only about 6,235 pairs in 2006.[9] Despite their modern reputation as an unclean scavenger, gulls' meat and eggs were regularly eaten for centuries.[10] Black-headed gulls in particular were favoured, and in the mid-nineteenth century the eggs were regularly sold in Dublin markets alongside those of lapwings, where they were highly regarded. In Britain, a famous 'gullery' in Norfolk collected up to a thousand black-headed gull eggs a day, until the early 1900s.

Oystercatcher — Roilleach — *Haematopus ostralegus*

The oystercatcher's mournful cry and habit of running along the seashore led to the story that it had been tricked out of its ability to swim by the seagull. Nevertheless, it was said to be under the protection of St Brigid.

FOLK BELIEFS AND CUSTOMS
Despite its name, the oystercatcher rarely eats oysters, though it is very partial to other shellfish as it feeds along the shore.[1] The oystercatcher is associated in Gaelic tradtion with St Brigid.[2] The oystercatcher is known in Connacht by another name – *Giolla Bríde* (St Brigid's page) – and is said to be conspicuous on the shore around the saint's day. The oystercatcher is also called the Page of Bride in the Scottish Highlands, and its call is said to be the words *'Bi glic, bi glic'* (be wise, be wise). The oystercatcher has a faint cross on its chest which it is said to have got from St Brigid. The story goes that the saint was fleeing from her persecutors and collapsed at the seashore. Seeing her distress, oystercatchers covered her with seaweed and hid her. In gratitude St Brigid blessed the birds and gave them the sign of the cross. Alternatively, it was said in Ulster that when Christ was hiding from his enemies by the Sea of Galilee an oystercatcher covered him in seaweed so that he could not be found, and so was rewarded with the cross in thanks.[3]

Various stories exist to explain the oystercatcher's mournful cry.[4] In west Cork the explanation is that the seagull could not swim until he asked the oystercatcher for a loan of its webbed feet. The oystercatcher agreed to lend them for one day only, but when he went looking for them, the seagull would not return them. So the oystercatcher is now forever wading along the tide's edge unable to swim and crying out: *'Tó-ó-óg mé! Tó-ó-óg mé! Ní fhéatainn é! Ní fhéatainn é! Tá an tráig líonta. Tá an tráig líonta'*. ('Ta-a-ake me! Ta-a-ake me! I can't! I can't! The tide is full. The tide is full.')

A longer version coming from Donegal has it that the story began at a wedding in Inishdooey (a small island near Tory Island)

and all the birds that could swim were invited. Although the oystercatcher could swim, he was nervous and did not really want to go. The seagull, on the other hand, wanted to go but could not swim. Realising the oystercatcher was not keen, the seagull asked him if he could borrow the ability to swim so that he could go to the wedding. 'I will, surely,' replied the oystercatcher, 'if you give it back to me when the wedding is over.' 'Agreed,' the seagull readily replied, but when the wedding was over, he never returned to the oystercatcher, and that is why you will see the oystercatcher running up and down the seashore, crying mournfully. In another version of this tale, the seagull's raucous cries are explained by saying it is for ever after laughing at the poor oystercatcher (see Seagull).

In the Scottish Highlands a different explanation is that the oystercatcher laid three lovely eggs, but went off exploring along the seashore. A grey crow came along and took the eggs one by one. When the crow had the last egg sucked, the oystercatcher returned. Seeing the eggs destroyed she flew hither and thither in great distress, crying out, '*Co dh'ol na huibhean? Co dh'ol na huibhean? Cha chuala mi riamh a leithid! Cha chuala mi riamh a leithid!* (Who drank the eggs? Who drank the eggs? I never heard the like! I never heard the like!). The grey crow answered her in mock sympathy: '*Cha chuala na sinne sinn fhéin sin, ged is sine is sine's an aite*' (No, nor heard we ourselves that, though we are longer in this place).

The osyercatcher appears in the Irish place names Cregnarullah (*Sceir na Roilleach* – Oystercatcher Rock), County Mayo and Stackanrelagh (*Stacán Roilleach* – Stack of the Oystercatcher), County Donegal.[5]

NOTABLE FACTS

The oystercatcher's shrill cries reach a crescendo in spring, when they have a remarkable 'piping display' during courtship.[6] This involves several birds running around in a frenzied fashion, with their heads and bills pointed down, and their shoulders lifted, making a piping sound with their bills open. This can involve up to twelve birds and go on for several minutes. The oystercatcher is also noted for the great physical strength of its bill, which enables it to prise open a mussel shell or hammer limpets off a rock.[7] Another interesting trait of the oystercatcher is that it feigns lameness to decoy away those who approach its nest, in a similar manner to the lapwing.[8]

Plover — Feadóg — *Charadriidae*

The plover is noted for its piercing, mournful cry, which was thought to be a warning of bad weather or of trouble ahead. The lapwing or green plover is noted for its habit of feigning injury to draw potential predators away from its nest before flying away. This gave it a reputation for deceitfulness in European folklore.

Golden Plover – Feadóg bhuí – *Pluvialis apricaria*

Grey Plover – Feadóg ghlas – *Pluvialis squatarola*

Ringed Plover – Feadóg chladaigh – *Charadrius hiaticula*

Lapwing – Pilibín – *Vanellus vanellus*

FOLK BELIEFS AND CUSTOMS

Various beliefs surrounded the plover's mournful cries.[1] In Ireland when the plover was heard at night or seen standing quietly in a field, this was taken as a sign of frost. The arrival of the migratory grey plover in coastal areas was also taken as a sign that biting winds were on the way. In Scotland the cry of the plover at night was supposed to portend death or some other evil. Similarly, in Wales the cries of a golden plover near a house where there was a sick person was an omen of death. A traditional Irish saying was: 'it's a long way from home that the plover cries.'

The lapwing, peewit or green plover is noted for its habit of feigning injury to draw potential predators away from its nest before flying away. This led to the traditional Irish expression *'cleas an philibín'* or 'to act the lapwing', meaning to deliberately mislead or lay a false trail. In European folklore generally, the lapwing is regarded as a deceitful bird.[2] In Sweden a folktale relates how the lapwing was once a handmaid to the Virgin Mary. One day the maid was discovered stealing a pair of scissors, and as punishment she was turned into the lapwing, which has a forked tail that looks like it has been snipped by scissors. Ever since, the lapwing has been compelled to cry, '*tyvit, tyvit*' ('I stole, I stole'). Another European tale has it that the lapwing was present at the crucifixion. Unlike other birds, such as the swallow or stork, which tried to help Jesus, the lapwing flew around the cross, shrieking: 'Let him suffer! Let him suffer!' As a result, while the stork and swallow were blessed by Jesus and so are loved by all mankind, the lapwing is condemned for all eternity.

MYTHS AND LEGENDS

In one Irish folktale, the cry of a plover keeps many warriors in a state of enchanted sleep for thousands of years.[3] Diarmuid of the Fianna was warned about this, however, and wore a collar with twelve sharp spikes around it. When he heard the plover cry and started to fall asleep, his head lolled onto the spikes which pricked him awake. He was thus able to reach the plover and take its egg. The plover immediately stopped singing and the spell was broken.

The plover was also believed to be a very wary bird, which cried out at the first sign of danger.[4] It was said that Brian Boru first introduced the plover into Ireland on account of its great wariness, and that the great king trained them to give the alarm if any enemy approached his camp. An Irish folktale features twelve plovers which stand guard at a castle and scream to alert the inhabitants if any intruder approaches. However, the young hero on his magical steed clears the walls in one bound and so is inside before they can react. In the story *Suibhne Geilt* or Mad Sweeney, one of the signs of approaching danger Sweeney watched out for was the cry of a plover being woken from its sleep.

NOTABLE FACTS

Lapwings and plovers were traditionally highly regarded as food.[5] The flesh of lapwings was highly prized in both Britain and Ireland, and was both sold in city markets in Ireland and exported to British markets in Liverpool and elsewhere, as late as the nineteenth century. Lapwings' eggs were also considered valuable: for example, in 1776 the price was three shillings a dozen, and by 1812 it had risen to four shillings a dozen. The golden plover was also traditionally considered a delicacy in Britain, and the L'Estrange *Household Book* published in 1520 recorded the price of golden plovers at twopence each, a considerable sum at the time. Plovers' eggs were also relished and were widely eaten, and thousands would appear for sale in nineteenth-century Irish markets in the spring. Similarly, in Britain the tradition of selling plover eggs was wide-spread for centuries, and continued until the Second World War.

Robin – Spideog
Erithacus rubecula

Wren – Dreoilín

Troglodytes troglodytes

Kingfisher – Cruidín
Alcedo atthis

Herring Gull – Faoileán Scadán
Larus argentatus

Oystercatcher – Roilleach
Haematopus ostralegus

Lapwing – Pilibín

Vanellus vanellus

Mallard – Lacha Fhiáin

Anas platyrhynchos

Domestic Chicken – Cearc

Gallus gallus domesticus

Duck — Lacha — *Anas* spp.

The duck, both wild and domestic, was seen as a blessed and good-natured bird. It was noted above all for its affinity with water and tolerance for wet weather. This led in folklore to a belief in its ability to forecast rain, and in Celtic myth to an association with water goddesses and healing springs.

Domestic Duck – Lacha tí – *Anas platyrhynchos domesticus*

Mallard – Lacha Fhiáin – *Anas platyrhynchos*

Teal – Praslacha – *Anas crecca*

Wigeon – Rualacha – *Anas penelope*

Pintail – Biorearrach – *Anas acuta*

Shoveler – Spadalach – *Anas clypeata*

FOLK BELIEF AND CUSTOMS

In Ireland almost every movement of the duck was said to forecast rainy weather.[1] It was believed that the loud quacking of ducks was a sure sign of rain, or else when they flew, or flapped their wings up and down. A duck waddling was also a sign of rain, and if the ducks sheltered from the rain, it was a sign that no fair weather would arrive that day.

The duck was also said in some Irish tales to be the first to announce the day.[2] In Kerry it was said the fox and the duck had a competition to see who could announce the day first. The duck lay down, put its head under its wing and went to sleep. The fox stayed up all night waiting quietly, and when morning came he called to the duck: '*Ó lacha, lacha!*' However, the duck woke up and immediately called out '*Lá, Lá*' ('Day, Day') in response. So the duck won, because he was still the first to announce the day. From Donegal a similar story related that a duck and a seagull had a bet to see which of them would be first to see the day. The duck was the first to wake and simply said, 'Wác! Wác! Wác.' 'Hó,' said the seagull sadly in response, 'that's the day – I'm too late!'

A few folk tales relate how the duck compared favourably to the hen.[3] A Mayo tale tells of how Christ was passing where a hen and a duck were feeding. It was raining and so Our Lord went under the hen's wing (presumably miraculously!) to shelter until the shower passed. However, the hen picked at him and he was forced to go under the duck's wing. The duck allowed him to shelter until the rain ended, and in gratitude he made her feathers grow in such a way that they would not let the water touch her skin. Similarly, a story from Scotland tells how Christ was hidden from his enemies by a good crofter under a heap of grain. Hens and ducks then came and fed on the grain. The duck trampled down the grain as it fed, but the hen scattered it about, thus revealing Christ. So the hen was condemned from then on to be confined to land, to dislike hail, rain, sleet or snow, to dread thunder, and to use only dust for her bath. The duck, on the other hand, was blessed with the ability to swim, to bathe in water and to have a liking for all kinds of bad weather. Another version of this, also from Scotland, was that the duck was considered blessed because it sheltered Christ under straw when he was being pursued by his enemies.

Various other traditional beliefs surrounded the duck.[4] In Ireland a traditional belief was that it was wrong to hunt wild ducks or other birds flying at night, because they were the souls of the dead travelling. In Scotland it was considered taboo to hunt a duck that was swimming with her young (as opposed to a duck flying), as such a duck was sacred to the Virgin Mary of Peace. In Scotland it was also considered lucky to see a wild duck on New Year's Day, especially for sailors, as it ensured safety from drowning. However, for some reason it was considered bad luck in Scotland to see a duck and a swan swimming together on Easter Monday. In Scotland it was also said that the raven is the first bird to nest, and the mallard the second.

MYTHS AND LEGENDS
The duck appears in many Irish folktales and legends.[5] A common motif in folktales is that the soul of a giant, witch or other enchanted

being is inside a duck egg hidden away from sight. As long as the egg is not harmed, the being cannot be killed, no matter what injuries they receive. Inevitably, the hero of the tale must carry out a series of complicated tasks to retrieve the duck egg, destroy it and thus defeat his enemy. For example, in one tale the hero Blaiman, son of Apple, can only kill a giant by destroying just such an egg. To get the egg he must first catch a ram with the help of a particular hound, then with a particular hawk catch the duck that flies out of the ram, and then retrieve the egg that the duck lays into the sea with the help of a particular otter. Even when he finally has the egg, Blaiman's task is not finished, because he must throw the egg at the giant and smash it on his bare breast. Only then will the giant finally die. Needless to say, Blaiman manages to perform these tasks and the kingdom is freed of the giant's oppression. Similarly, in another tale the hero can only kill a fairy queen by getting an egg, which is inside a duck, which is inside a wether (a castrated ram), which lives inside a holly tree.

The duck also appears in Irish legends.[6] For example, the first hunt of the hero Fionn Mac Cumhaill was to kill a wild duck, when he was still only a small boy. Later the cackling of ducks was said to be one of the sounds of nature that helped the adult Fionn to sleep. In the *Life of Saint Máedoc of Ferns*, the parting of the saint from his close friend St Dallán is described as like 'the parting of a woman from her son, or a cow from its calf, or a bitch from her pups, or a duck from its pond'. In an Irish legend concerning the exiled Scottish king, Cano son of Gartnán, the king has bad luck hunting some swans, failing to kill any of them. Shortly after, he decides not to hunt some ducks on a nearby lake, saying: 'I shall not harm a feather of the birds of the Son of the Living God.' Whether because of his mercy or not, the king later gains the throne of Scotland. In the ninth-century text *Cormac's Glossary* it said that poets' cloaks were made of the skins of birds, white and many coloured from their girdle downwards, and from mallards' necks and their crests upwards to their neck.[7] Also in *Cormac's Glossary* the origin of the Irish word for duck, *lacha*, is given as *lichiu í* 'wetter is it'. In the *Book of Invasions of Ireland* or *Lebor Gabála Érenn*, it was said that the Milesians came to Ireland from Spain in their ships over 'a plain of many ducks' (*lár il-lacha*).

Usually when ducks appear in stories the particular species is not mentioned, but Gerald of Wales recounts a tale concerning a flock of teal sacred to St Colman, which lived in a lake in Leinster.[8] The ducks were almost tame and took food from the hand of anyone who approached them. If any injury happened to the church or clergy of the saint the birds would fly off, and not return until due satisfaction had been given on the matter. In their absence, the water that was normally pure and clear would become dirty and brackish, and unfit for use by man or beast. Gerald goes on to relate how one of the teal was accidentally taken up with water for cooking meat. The meat would not cook despite every effort, and the bird was at last discovered swimming around in the water unharmed. As soon as the bird was brought back to the lake, the meat was cooked immediately. The birds remained sacred to the saint long after he was gone, and Gerald tells of an archer in the time of the Norman Robert Fitzstephen who killed one, and failing to cook it after many efforts, died soon afterwards.

Domesticated ducks were kept in early Ireland, though they seem not to have been very prominent.[9] It seems that in early Ireland wild birds were eaten more often than domesticated ones, and wild ducks were among the species of birds hunted.[10] Ducks were also kept on farms and hunted in Celtic Britain and Gaul, and sometimes appeared in burials and sacrifices as food in a ritual feast.[11] In Europe from the Bronze Age to the Celtic Iron Age, water birds, especially ducks, appear with solar imagery. Sun wheels and ducks appear together on bronze vessels, armour and jewellery, or else solar symbols appear on boats with water-bird heads.[12] For example, in Gaul ducks were particularly associated with the goddess Sequana, the personification of the River Seine. At the sanctuary dedicated to her at Fontes Sequanae (the source of the Seine), a bronze image of the goddess was recovered, depicting the goddess standing in a boat in the form of a duck, the prow fashioned as its beaked head and its tail forming the stern. The duck head of the boat is depicted holding a ritual pellet of cake in its mouth, which may signify fertility or sacrifice. Some of the gifts left by pilgrims for the goddess also took the form of ducks. In this case the duck clearly symbolised Sequana's aquatic identity and the spring's healing powers. The duck may also have been seen as a suitable solar emblem because it was able to both swim and fly, thus uniting sky and water and their healing powers.

NOTABLE FACTS

The mallard is the origin of almost all domesticated ducks, with many different breeds developed since the fourteenth century, when ducks began to be domesticated seriously in Europe for the first time (the exception is the Muscovy duck, which was domesticated in Latin America by Native Americans).[13] Some of the main breeds of duck kept for their eggs include the Buff Orpington, the Campbell, the Dun and White, the Magpie and the Welsh Harlequin; some of the main breeds of duck kept for their meat include the Aylesbury, the Muscovy, the Duclair, the Pekin, the Rouen, the Saxony and the Silver Appleyard. Many of these domesticated ducks escape back into the wild, with the result that many wild mallards are in fact hybrids.[14] This mixing is also helped by the mallard's willingness to nest in many urban environments where there is water nearby, such as parks and along canal banks. In the wild, the mallard will nest near the water in rough vegetation or in available nooks and crannies under rocks and trees, but in cities it is willing to adapt and use any suitable corner it can find. This regularly leads to the amusing spectacle of the mother duck leading her newly hatched ducklings across streets and busy roads to get to the nearest pond or water. For example, for several years a female mallard regularly nested in the grounds of Leinster House in Dublin, and each year was escorted to safety by gardaí who held up the traffic as she led her young to the pond in St Stephen's Green.[15]

Domestic Chicken — Cearc — *Gallus gallus domesticus*

The domestic chicken has been one of our most-valued domestic animals since ancient times, providing us with meat, eggs and feathers. The hen is a much-loved bird, even if it is seen as rather picky and crotchety. The cock or rooster, which crows at dawn and so signals the end of darkness, became a symbol of the resurrection of Christ and a powerful source for banishing evil.

FOLK BELIEFS AND CUSTOMS

In many parts of Ireland, 11 November or St Martin's Eve was marked by the killing of livestock for the winter, and the sprinkling of their blood on the threshold and in the four corners of the house to keep away evil spirits. Those who were better off killed a cow or sheep, while the less-well-off killed a hen or a rooster on the day.[1] In Galway it was believed that the rooster should be killed before sundown, and the rooster that fathered the most chicks should be the one chosen. The blood should then be spilled in the four corners of the house, proceeding in a clockwise direction, and the last of the blood should be used to form a pool in the centre of the kitchen. In the west of Ireland it was believed that what was in the craw of a rooster killed on St Martin's Eve should be kept, as it had the power to keep a child from being taken by the fairies. Another belief in Ireland was that a cloth soaked in the blood of the rooster killed on St Martin's Day (or else the previous evening) and kept in the rafters had the power to stop bleeding.

Many superstitions surrounded the behaviour of hens.[2] In Ireland hens picking at their feathers was a sign of rain, and it was also a sign of bad weather if the hens went to roost too early in the evening. In Mayo and Donegal, to see hens staying out in a shower of rain meant that the day would remain wet. In Donegal, if hens stayed out until late at night scratching for food, it was a sign that the next day would be wet and windy. To see a hen with a straw on its tail was a sign of a funeral, while a sop across her back meant that someone in the house would die soon, and the coffin would be shouldered to the cemetery. Also in Donegal if a hen or rooster was seen dragging a wisp of grass after them, it meant that a stranger was coming to the house, and the size of the wisp indicated the size of the person. If a hen crowed like a rooster that was a sign that someone would die soon, and an old saying went: 'a whistling woman and a crowing hen, there is no luck in the house they're in.' Traditionally, the way to deal with such a hen was to abandon it at a crossroads. However, in Mayo, to dream of hens was very lucky.

A number of stories exist in Ireland to explain why hens are continually scratching at the ground with their feet.[3] In one such story Jesus was fleeing from his pursuers and hid in an underground cave. The soldiers were on the point of passing over the cave without seeing him when they noticed some hens scratching at the earth. The hens had already cleared away enough earth to reveal the entrance to the cave, and so the soldiers searched the cave and captured Jesus. From that time onwards, it was said that the hen could not find a single bite to eat without first having to scratch away at the earth. Another popular belief in Ireland was that hens had been brought to Ireland by the Norsemen, and that every night they decide to fly back to Scandanavia in the morning. First thing every morning, they are still determined to go, but they decide to eat something first before the journey. However, the moment their beaks touch Irish ground they forget their plans and carry on feeding all day. When the evening comes, they remember their decision and once again firmly decide to leave first thing the following morning. Despite forgetting each day, they continue to harbour hostile feelings towards the Irish people, and their scraping on the floor of the kitchen is a vain attempt to set the house on fire.

Many beliefs also surrounded the crowing of the rooster.[4] In many parts of Ireland it was believed that if a rooster crowed at night it meant bad news was on the way. If it crowed three times at night, that was especially bad news, as it meant there would be a death in the family. In Mayo and Donegal it was believed that if a rooster crowed in the doorway of the house, it was a sign of good news. However, elsewhere in the country, if a rooster crowed through a window or door of a house it was a sign of a death in the family. In Ireland it was believed that the rooster was overwhelmed with joy at Christmas and would crow at unusual times, and to hear him crow at midnight was a particularly good omen. However, in Donegal it was believed that hearing a cock crow in the middle of the night meant that a member of the McBrearty or Cassidy families was about to die.

The crowing of the cock or rooster was traditionally associated with the resurrection, perhaps because it heralded the dawn. A popular Irish story about Christ's crucifixion illustrates this. The story goes that shortly after the crucifixion, a group of non-believers were talking around a pot that had a rooster boiling in it. 'We have buried Christ now,' the people said, 'and he has no more power to rise from the dead than the rooster that is cooking in this pot.' Immediately the rooster leaped onto the rim of the pot and crowed twelve times, saying: *'Mac na h-Óighe slán!'* ('The Virgin's Son is saved!'). It is said that from then on, this is what the rooster is saying when it crows. Versions of this story were so popular in medieval

Ireland that a cook and cooking pot appear on many Irish tombstones of the time. In County Clare the rooster was also said to cry: '*Agha na h-anachaine i bhfad uainn!*' ('May calamity stay far away from us!').

The crowing of the rooster was also said to have a powerful effect against spirits and fairies.[5] In one story, the people of a house were able to detect a woman ghost who was haunting it by waiting until the rooster of the house crowed three times. When this happened they were able to see the woman, who was the first wife of the man of the house, standing in the loft. Having confirmed that the house was haunted, they asked a priest to say Mass to lay the woman's spirit to rest. In one folk tale the hero is being pursued by a hag, wielding a sharp axe, and a venomous hound. However, just as the hag is about to kill the hero with the axe, a cock crows, and the hag, axe and hound each turn into beautiful women and walk away, leaving the hero unharmed.

It was widely believed in Ireland that, when the cock or rooster crowed first thing in the morning, the fairies ceased their wanderings and had to return to their fairy mounds and forts. Many stories exist which illustrate this belief: for example, in one story a man's wife was taken by the fairies, but she was able to return for a while to the house one night. Seeing his chance, the man grabbed her and held her until the cock crowed in the morning, and after that the fairies had no more power over her. In another story a woman spinning flax late at night was visited by a fairy who wished to take her away. He could not take her while she was spinning, and so the woman carried on spinning all night until the cock crowed. The fairy's power was ended and it had to go, and so the woman was saved.

Much folklore in Ireland surrounds the 'March Cock', that is, a cock or rooster born from an egg laid on the first Tuesday in March, and hatched out on a Tuesday of the same month.[6] The March cock was all black in colour and its crowing was believed to have greater powers to drive away evil spirits than roosters born at other times of year. For example, in one story a man walking home late at night was followed by a fairy woman. The man kept walking, afraid to stop, until at sunrise he at last heard a cock crow. 'There's the cock crowing,' he said relieved. 'That's only a weak cock of the summer,' the fairy woman replied. Soon after, another cock crowed, and the fairy woman undaunted remarked, 'That's only a poor cock of the harvest.' However, soon after, a third cock crowed and this time the woman said, 'That's a cock of March,' and left the man alone. It was generally believed that, if a householder was going to leave the house at night, a March cock would crow to warn if any bad spirits were waiting outside.

Various tales relate how the March cock protected the house from harm. One Irish tale concerns a man who took a skull from a graveyard for a bet, and kept it with him in his house. The man got married and one night six years later, the March cock the man owned gave a crow outside the door at midnight. The skull let out a laugh at this, and when the cock crowed a second and a third time, the skull also gave a laugh each time. The man picked up the skull and with some fear asked it why it was laughing. The skull explained that the devil was trying to enter the house to bring trouble between him and his wife, but each time the March cock crowed the devil was put out on the top of his head. After the third time, the devil went away and did not return. Another folk tale concerns a man who saw a coffin descend from the sky each morning towards his house. However, the March cock he owned would rouse itself and begin to crow until the coffin disappeared. The man's wife could not see the coffin, however, and one morning, sick of the loud crowing, she threw a mallet at the cock and killed it. The man was furious with her saying, 'My seven thousand curses on you! You killed the cock and you killed me too!' He took to the bed and three days later he was dead.

The March cock could also act against other misfortunes. A legend found in many Irish coastal areas tells of how a sea captain once saw a March cock at a farmhouse near the shore. As he was looking, he saw a thunderbolt heading for the house, but the cock crowed and deflected the disaster away. Realising the worth of the bird, the sea captain offered a substantial amount of money to the woman of the house, who foolishly accepted it. As soon as the captain had taken the rooster away, a fire broke out and consumed the house. Unlike other roosters, the March cock was said to crow regularly at night.

The powers of roosters were not always benign, however.[7] It was said in County Clare, for example, that those practising witchcraft would sacrifice black roosters to the devil. Carnelly near Clare Castle was said by tradition to have been the scene of such a sacrifice, when a black rooster with one white feather was offered to the devil on a so-called 'druid's altar' there. It was further said that the intent of the sacrifice was to bring vengeance on an enemy, but the result was only to bring misfortune on the sacrificer himself. Also, in Kilkenny in 1325 Dame Alice Keteler was tried as a witch, on the grounds that she had sacrificed nine red roosters to an imp or familiar spirit called Robyn Artysson. Dame Alice avoided burning only by escaping to England. However, it was traditionally believed in Ireland that to have a white rooster in the yard was very lucky.

A lot of folklore surrounds eggs in Ireland.[8] Eggs were marked with a cross for good luck when the egg began to hatch, and those wishing to bring bad luck to a neighbour would put rotten eggs in their haystacks. A widespread custom was to crush eggshells or throw them on the fire after the egg had been eaten, in the belief that otherwise they would become the home of the fairies. This is a very ancient belief as the Roman author Pliny recommended that eggshells should be broken after eating, so that they could not be used to bind the person in spells. In Beara in County Cork it was believed that the first egg laid in the morning by a black chicken was good for the voice. If a person drank the egg cold, without boiling, for three mornings in a row, they would acquire a singing voice. In Kerry it was believed that, if the first egg laid by a little black hen was eaten first thing in the morning, it would prevent fever for the year. In west Cork it was believed that eggs should be put under a hen for hatching only when the tide was coming in, otherwise they would not hatch. In County Laois it was believed that a horseshoe nail should be put in with the eggs, to ensure good results, and to prevent harm from thunder. In Donegal it was believed to be very unlucky to bring an egg on board a boat. A similar belief existed in Scotland, where it was thought that eggs caused contrary winds.[9] In Yorkshire fishermen considered it unlucky even to use the word 'egg'.[10]

In Ireland, as elsewhere in Western culture, eggs are associated with Easter.[11] While there is much speculation by writers that the reason for this is due to the egg being a symbol of resurrection and the life force, the most likely reason is that it derives from the Christian custom of abstaining from meat and eggs during Lent. This meant that there was a large accumulation of eggs by the coming of Easter that had to be eaten, thus providing an excuse for feasting. In Ireland the traditional custom was to eat as many boiled eggs as possible for breakfast on Easter Sunday, with a competition to see who could eat the most. Anything less than four or five was seen as a very poor effort, with the household 'egging' each other on to eat more. Often eggs were coloured or decorated with natural dyes and given to children as presents. Sometimes children would make the rounds of the neighbourhood collecting eggs, sweets and cakes to have as a feast. In many parts of the north of Ireland, the game of egg rolling was practised, a custom which was probably introduced from Britain. This involved each child having a different coloured or marked boiled egg and rolling them down a slope. If two eggs collided, the child whose egg did not crack could claim the other cracked egg, and the game naturally ended with the eating of the eggs.

A very ancient belief throughout Europe concerns the small yolkless eggs that are sometimes called 'cock's eggs', in the mistaken belief that they were laid by cocks.[12] They were considered very unlucky to bring into the house, and on no account should any attempt be made to hatch them, as the creature that hatched out would be a monster called a 'cockatrice'. The cockatrice was a mixture between a cock and a serpent that breathed fire, and could kill with a single glance.

Finally, some traditional beliefs concerned feathers.[13] It was widely believed that having hen feathers in the bed prolonged the death throes of a dying person. Feathers would be removed from the bed of a dying person so that death would be relatively quick and easy. On the other hand, it was believed in Donegal that putting hen or chicken feathers on a wound would stop it from bleeding profusely.

MYTHS AND LEGENDS
An Irish tale recounts how St Colmcille was leaving Derry for Scotland, and on the night before his departure he instructed a fellow monk to wake him at cock crow.[14] However, the cock did not

crow at daybreak that morning, but later at breakfast time. When Colmcille realised he had missed his early start, he cursed the roosters of Derry, saying none of them would ever crow until ten o'clock in the morning. A similar story from Donegal tells of a place called *Gort na Coileach* (Field of the Roosters). According to the story, Colmcille was very weary and stopped there to spend the night. He was woken by first cockcrow and was furious to discover that it was still the middle of the night. The saint cursed the roosters of the area so that they would never crow again. The Irish hermit Mo Chua (or Mac Duach) was said to have a rooster which helped him by keeping matins for him at midnight.

According to the twelfth-century Norman writer Gerald of Wales, the roosters of Ireland crowed differently from their English counterparts, by only crowing in daylight. In Britain and elsewhere, according to Gerald, roosters crowed at regular intervals throughout the night, but in Ireland they only first began to crow at daybreak.[15] Gerald puts this down to Ireland having shorter nights due to it being closer to the setting sun in the west. As this is something which has no astronomical basis, it is wisest to be sceptical of Gerald's claim regarding the roosters of his day.

Chickens were very highly valued in early Ireland, as a tenth-century saying makes clear: *fó cía beith cerc i trebad* ('it is good that there should be a hen on a farm').[16] A laying hen was valued at two bushels of grain, and a sexually active rooster valued at one bushel. When the rooster was no longer capable of siring fertile eggs, its value was reduced to half a bushel, and it was considered only fit for the cooking pot. However, the rooster had other virtues, as under Brehon Law the size of the green of a farm could be measured as far as 'the sound of a bell or the crowing of a cock reaches'.

Archaeological remains of chickens have been found at Celtic sites in Britain and the continent, for example, as food offerings in Gaulish graves.[17] Despite a remark by Julius Caesar that the Britons did not keep chickens, remains of chickens killed for food have been found in Iron Age domestic sites in Britain. Eggs have also been found as part of the grave goods of a Gaulish warrior chieftain in Marne. Chickens also appear in the art of the Celts.[18] For example, a silvered metal model of a cockerel was found at the Gallo-Roman sanctuary of Estrées-Saint-Denis, and a coral-inlaid brooch in the form of a hen was found in a princess's grave at Reinheim. Some Celtic deities are also depicted with eggs. For example, the healer-goddess Sirona at Hochscheid in Germany is depicted carrying a bowl containing three eggs, and three fertility gods called the Genii Cucullati are portrayed in Gloucester as carrying eggs. In Roman myth the rooster is linked to the god Mercury, perhaps because of its role in heralding the day. The link was retained with the Celtic Mercury who is depicted in several places accompanied by a rooster, for example at Gloucester and Reims. At Nîmes, the Gaulish hammer god is accompanied by a rooster, perhaps as a symbol of the welcome daylight and of spring. The link with the rooster is maintained in France to this day, as it is the symbol of the country, probably due to the similarity in sound between its Latin name *Gallus* and Gaul.[19]

The rooster also appears in other European mythologies.[20] In Norse myth a rooster clad in gold, called Vidofnir, sits at the top of the world tree Yggdrasil; and at Ragnarok, the twilight of the gods, a rooster called Fjalar will wake the giants, a rooster called Gullinkampi will wake the gods, and a third unnamed fiery red rooster will raise the dead in Hel. In Classical lore, as well as to Mercury or Hermes, the rooster was sacred to the sun god Apollo, as its crowing heralded the sunrise and its red comb symbolised the sun. It was also sacred to Ares, the god of war, because of its reputation for vigilance and valour.

NOTABLE FACTS

The domestic chicken originated several millennia ago from the red junglefowl *Gallus gallus*, which still exists as a wild bird in the rainforests of India, Burma, Malaysia, etc.[21] Over the centuries many different breeds of domestic chicken have developed, with complex histories and variations, but the main breeds of domestic chicken are generally categorised into five groups.[22] First are the Hard-Feather Large Fowl and Hard-Feather Bantam breeds, which are the old fighting-cock breeds, nowadays bred for exhibiting. These include the Asil (the most ancient fighting breed in the world, originally from India), Old English Game, Modern Game, Indian Game, Cornish, Malay and Shamo. Next are the Heavy Soft-Feather

Large Fowl and Heavy Soft-Feather Bantam. These started as either table breeds or dual-purpose farm breeds, and include the Orpington, Rhode Island Red, Brahma, Cochin and Dorking. The third group are the Light Soft-Feather Large Fowl and Light Soft-Feather Bantam, which were originally bred for egg production. These include the Silkie, Ancona, Dutch, and Scots Grey. Fourth are the True Bantam breeds, which include the Serbright, Pekin and Rosecomb. Lastly, there are also many different kinds of rare breeds which are exhibited in Poultry Club competitions, and which are too numerous to list here.

The habits of domestic chickens have given a few phrases to the English language, with their very strict 'pecking order' (one for the hens and one for the cocks), while the dominant cock 'rules the roost'.[23] Chickens were traditionally kept for their eggs, while cocks or roosters were usually the ones who were eaten. As well as being kept for their flesh, cocks were bred for fighting, and cockfighting was a traditional pastime throughout Europe. Cocks or roosters are known for their aggression towards rivals, and this usually meant that fights ended with the death of the loser. This was especially so as fighting cocks were habitually equipped with metal or bone spurs placed on top of their natural ones, in order to inflict maximum damage. In Ireland, cockfighting normally took place during holidays such as Ascension Thursday, Michaelmas, and St Stephen's Day;[24] but thankfully this cruel tradition no longer applies as cockfighting was made illegal in Britain and Ireland in the nineteenth century. Cockfighting is still very popular today in many parts of the world, however, such as Latin America and Southeast Asia.

Skylark — Fuiseog — *Alauda arvensis*

The skylark is well loved for its beautiful soaring song and flight, and is seen as a sign of spring and good weather. For this reason, the lark was considered a blessed bird, and a bird of cheerfulness and high spirits, but it was also sometimes seen as rather fickle and unreliable.

FOLK BELIEF AND CUSTOMS

Hearing the lark sing was traditionally a sign of the arrival of spring and good weather.[1] A widespread Irish belief was that if the lark sang on St Brigid's Day, 1 February, it was an omen of a good spring. It was also a sign that St Brigid's Day itself would be sunny, and that those who heard it on that day would enjoy good fortune throughout the year. Similarly, in Scotland it was believed that from St Brigid's Day the lark sang with a clearer voice. Seeing the lark flying high in the sky was also a sign of good weather. Seeing it fly high early in the year was a sign that spring had finally arrived, while in Donegal it was said that hearing the lark early in the morning meant it would be a good day. In Donegal where the lark built its nest was also an indicator of the weather ahead. If the lark built its nest in the hollows left by cattle on the mountain, then dry weather was on the way. However, if the spring and summer were going to be wet, it would nest on the sheltered side of the hill or in a hole in a ditch.

A story from Kerry casts doubt, however, on the skylark's power to foretell the weather.[2] The story goes that three or four people were out saving the hay when a lark rose up in the afternoon and began whistling and singing. The women said that there was no further need to save the hay that day, as the lark singing meant the following day would be fine. The father then spoke to his son: '*Ná creidse an fhuiseóigín riamh, a mhic, mar is comhrá gan chiall a bhíonn age mná. Pé an áit a n-eireóig a' ghrian, is mar toil Dé do bheig a' lá!*' ('Don't believe the skylark, my son, don't mind what women say. Wherever the sun rises, it's God who decides the day!').

The skylark has always been cherished for its beautiful song.[3] It was said in Ireland that the lark flew so high that she reached Heaven's Gate and brought back the beautiful music she heard there. In Britain some rhymes tell of what the lark says in its song. In Scotland one version says: 'Larikie, larikie, Lee! Wha'll gang up to heaven wi' me? No the lout that lies in his bed, no the doolfu' that dreeps his head.' Another tradition from Scotland and the north of England says that to hear what the lark is saying you must lie on your back in a field, and then you will hear it say: 'Up in the lift go we / tehee, tehee, tehee, tehee / There's not a shoemaker on the earth / can make a shoe to me, to me. / Why so, why so, why so? / Because my heel is as long as my toe.' The last line is a reference to the lark's long hind claw. The difference in the lark's song rising and descending was noted as well. In France it was said that the lark in her upward flight implores St Peter to take her into paradise. But the apostle refuses and so as she descends she begins to curse.

One Irish folktale describes how the lark's song came to the aid of a piper. Two pipers were in a challenge to see which of the two of them was better. Each played a tune in turn, and a time came when one of the pipers had no more tunes. His turn came to play, and he did not know what to do, so he went out into the street just as dawn was breaking. What happened to be outside but a lark, singing to herself. The piper listened to the tune she was singing – 'The Lark's March' – and went into the house again. He began to play the tune that the lark had been singing, and when he finished, it was the turn of the other piper, who had no tunes left to play and so lost the challenge. The winning piper had the lark to thank for his success, and that tune, 'The Lark's March', has been played ever since.

The lark was generally considered to be a blessed bird. In Ireland it was said to be sacred to St Brigid for its song awoke her every morning to her prayers.[4] In Scotland the lark was called 'Mary's bird', and it was considered unlucky to harm a lark's nest, on account of its blessed nature.[5] The three spots on its tongue meant three curses on anyone who would interfere with its nest.

However, in Donegal a rather fickle and unworthy side to the skylark is revealed in the story of a war between a mouse and a lark.[6] A mouse was living in a stack of oats one spring day. A lark came along and asked the mouse to sweep out some oats for him during the spring and when summer came, the lark would repay the mouse by getting food for him in return. The mouse agreed, but when summer came and the mouse asked for the lark's help, the lark replied that she had plenty to eat, gave a whistle and said she did not care about the mouse. The mouse was furious and replied that they were now at war, to which the lark replied that she could not care less. The mouse then gathered together all the four-legged creatures, while the lark gathered all the birds. The two sides fought outside the door of the High King of Ireland, and the fighting was heavy until the afternoon. The king decided that enough was enough and gave three whistles. A great eagle came along and killed the poor mouse, and the king declared that the lark had won the war. The moral of the story appears to be that might is right.

Some sayings exist about the lark.[7] Perhaps the best known is to describe an early riser as 'up with the lark.' Another used in Ireland expressed scepticism about some extravagant plan that will never happen: 'When the sky falls we'll all catch larks.' Another Irish expression declared the belief that a person's nature was innate and could not be changed: 'Every bird as she was reared, and the lark for the bog.' In Donegal children up to seven years old were called by the names of birds in order to confuse the fairies and so prevent them from taking the children. Girls were called *Spideog*, *Eiseog* and *Cuach* (Robin, Lark, and Cuckoo) and boys were called *Colmán* (Dove).

MYTHS AND LEGENDS

The lark's reputation as an early riser was not always seen as a good thing. A popular tradition holds that no skylarks ever sing in Glendalough because St Kevin forbade them from doing so.[8] The saint did this because he was aggrieved at them for causing the workmen of his cathedral to rise too early in the morning and thus feel listless and tired at their work. The lark is also mentioned in some early Irish poems and stories.[9] In a poem about summer, Fionn Mac Cumhaill says: 'the lark is singing clear tidings; May without fault, of beautiful colours.' In *The Cattle Raid of Cooley* there is a mention of the lark's soaring flight. While Cúchulain is lying recovering from his wounds he hears fighting in the distance. Deciding he will join the fight, he unfastens his wounds, and the dry wisps that plugged them spring up as high as a lark soars in the air.

The lark features in some Classical lore also.[10] In Classical medicine the flesh of the lark was supposed to strengthen the voice and increase its singing power. Writers such as Dioscorides and Galen also said that larks should be eaten roasted to assuage colic pains. In Greek myth the lark and its song were said to exist not only before the earth, but before Zeus and Kronos. A Greek myth recounted by the poet Ovid tells of Nisus, King of Megara, whose daughter Scylla, for love of Minos, betrayed her father and country. Afterwards, in despair she flung herself into the sea and was changed into a lark. However, she was doomed to be pursued forever by her father who had been changed into a hawk.

NOTABLE FACTS

The skylark was traditionally seen as a delicacy in Britain and Ireland and was a very popular dish until modern times.[11] For example, in Britain in 1854, approximately 400,000 larks were sent up to the London market alone, mainly from Dunstable in Bedfordshire, north of London, which was famous for its larks 'for the table'. In 1890 the dinner for the opening of the Forth Bridge included an immense pie of 300 birds. Fortunately for the lark, the custom of eating it has been outlawed, in these islands at least. The lark was also very popular as a caged bird, and in Britain a strong-voiced individual could sell for as much as 15 shillings.[12] Irish emigrants if they had a captive lark would take it with them when leaving, with a sod of Irish earth placed beneath it, so that one day a portion of clay from the 'old land' might cover them in their grave.[13]

Swallow — Fáinleog — *Hirundo rustica*

The swallow heralded the return of summer and good weather and was believed to bring good luck to the homesteads it visited each year. The swallow was also thought in ancient times to have the power to cure blindness, perhaps because its speedy and skilful flight was taken as a sign it had superior eyesight.

FOLK BELIEFS AND CUSTOMS

In Ireland some weather lore surrounded the swallow.[1] It was generally believed that swallows flying high was a sign of good weather, and flying low of bad weather. Also, the sudden appearance of an agitated flock of swallows meant that rain was on the way. In Donegal it was believed that swallows arriving early was a sign of a good summer, but if they did not come in large flocks and build their nests early, it was a sign that the summer was going to be very mixed. In Donegal a very hot summer's day was also called *Lá na nÁinleoige* (Swallows' Day), and it was believed that the swallows got together and talked to each other on that day. In County Clare it was customary to make a wish or prayer on seeing the first swallow of summer.

There were also various Irish superstitions about the swallow.[2] It was believed that when someone had their hair cut the clippings should never be left lying about, for if the swallows found them and used them in their nest, the one whose hair had been cut would be prone to headaches all summer. Furthermore, it was said that on everyone's head there was a certain hair which, if plucked by a swallow, doomed the loser to irretrievable misfortune. A similar belief about swallows appears in an Irish folktale. According to the tale, the daughter of a rich man became sick and fell into a trance. No one could help her until a poor farmer's son found a cure – the girl was under enchantment because a lock of her hair was stuck in a swallow's nest in a nearby barn. The youth retrieved the lock of hair, put it into the girl's hand, and she woke up as lively as ever she had been. The farmer's son and the girl were married and lived happily ever after. Despite these beliefs about swallows and hair in Ireland, it was nevertheless considered to be a very good omen if a swallow flew into the dwelling house. In Donegal this was thought to signal a great change for the better, perhaps the arrival of money. In Ireland it was also believed that if a farmer harmed a swallow that he would soon notice blood in the milk his cows gave, and farmers very much disliked anyone interfering with swallows on their land. In Donegal it was said that if a swallow was knocked to the ground, bad luck would follow for the animals on the farm – a cow, calf or horse would die.

Various superstitions also concerned the swallow in Britain.[3] As in Ireland it was thought in many parts of England that to harm the swallow and destroy its nest would cause the cows to give blood, but also it could cause them to cease giving milk altogether, or bring rain that would destroy crops, or generally bring bad luck to the family. Even for those who were not farmers, destroying the nests of swallows would bring bad luck. It was also considered lucky generally in England to have swallows or martins nesting in the eaves of the house, and it was said that they would never come to a house where there was strife. However, the swallow was not always such a lucky bird in Britain. If a swallow fell down the chimney and flew around the room of a sick person, it meant that they would soon die. In Norfolk it was said that when swallows sat together in long rows that they were deciding upon who was next to die. Also in Norfolk, an unusually large gathering of swallows around a house meant the death of an occupant, whose soul would follow the swallows in taking flight.

In many parts of Europe the swallow was welcomed as a herald of spring.[4] In Greece, bands of boys and girls would parade on 1 March with a pole surmounted by an image of a swallow carved in wood. This appears to be a custom with very deep roots, as the Roman writer Claudius Aelianus reported that a song to welcome the swallow each spring was a custom on the island of Rhodes. In Westphalia in Germany, farmers and their families would wait at their gates and throw open their barn doors to allow the swallows to enter. Also in Germany, in Hesse, a watchman would be stationed on a high tower to signal the arrival of the first swallow, whereupon the news would be announced to the public by the magistrates. In Scotland, it was said to be lucky to see the first swallow but only, for some reason, if you were sitting down. In Brittany it was said that the swallows would be sure to arrive before Maundy Thursday so as to be present at the commemoration of the Crucifixion on Good Friday. This was probably related to the belief in France and other parts of Europe that it was the swallow that removed the crown of thorns from the head of Jesus when he was crucified. As it was doing so, the sharp thorns pierced the swallow's breast and gave it its red colour.

A widespread belief throughout Europe was that the swallow had the power to cure blindness.[5] In Normandy it was believed that the swallow had the ability to go to a beach and find a pebble with the power of restoring sight. The rather cruel way of procuring this stone was said to be to put out the eyes of the female swallow's nestlings. The swallow would go out and find the stone, cure her chicks, and then, if a red blanket was left under her nest she would drop the stone onto it, thinking it was fire. Similarly, in Brittany it was said that swallows kept certain stones in their nests which would cure diseases of the eye. In Austrian Tyrol, these stones would only be found in nests that had been occupied for seven consecutive years. These beliefs are probably developments of similar ideas held by writers in ancient Greece and Rome (see below).

MYTHS AND LEGENDS

The swallow appears as a symbol of speed in several Irish legends.[6] In a tale about the Irish warrior band the Fianna, a messenger hastens to them 'with the swiftness of a hare, or of a fawn or a swallow'. In another tale, a messenger from Fionn Mac Cumhaill, leader of the Fianna, travels with the 'quickness of a swallow or a weasel [stoat] or a blast of wind over bare mountaintops'. In the Irish tale *Táin Bó Cuailnge* or *The Cattle Raid of Cooley*, the hero Cúchulainn fights another warrior Ferdia, leaping up 'with the quickness of the wind, the readiness of the swallow, and with the fierceness of the lion'. In another version of the same tale, Cúchulainn meets a warrior called Fannell (*fáinle* or 'swallow') at a ford and kills him after combat. Fannell was said to have got his name because he could 'skim over water as lightly as a swan or a swallow'. In the same version of the *Táin*, Cúchulainn's scythed chariot was said to move 'as swiftly as a swallow, or as the wind, or as a deer across the level plain'. In one Irish folktale, the hero of the tale turns himself into a swallow to escape a pursuing giant and his twelve sons, but his pursuers turn themselves into hawks and harry him mercilessly. Fortunately, he is quick enough to escape them by flying into a summer house and landing on the lap of a princess. The swallow is also mentioned in an early Irish poem about May and the arrival of summer: 'light swallows dart on high, brisk music encircles the hills, tender rich fruits bud.'

In ancient Greece and Rome, it was believed that the swallow could cure blindness.[7] The Classical herbalist Dioscorides wrote that the plant *Chelidonium majus* (Greater Celandine), whose name comes from the Greek word for swallow, got its name either because it flowered at the coming of the swallow, or because mother swallows employed the plant to give sight back to their blinded nestlings. The sap of *Chelidonium* was traditionally considered by medieval herbalists to be good for eye ailments, sharpening the sight and removing cloudy spots upon the eyeball. The Roman writer Pliny the Elder wrote that a stone that could cure blindness, the *chelidonias* or 'swallow stone' could be found in the stomach of the eldest of a brood of swallows, provided that it was collected before, or at the time of, the August full moon. Why the swallow was associated with curing blindness is not known, but perhaps it was thought that a bird that could fly so quickly and skilfully to catch insects on the wing had to have special powers of sight. Whatever the reason, the swallow's aerial skills continue to delight us today.

NOTABLE FACTS

Like the house martin and swift, the swallow was probably originally a cave-nester that adapted to man-made structures thousands of years ago, when the first agricultural buildings appeared.[8] The swallow will nest in a wide range of outbuildings, and in porchways, towers, the undersides of bridges, and even garden sheds; and a swallow's nest can last for ten to fifteen years and be reoccupied continuously.[9] Nowadays it is known that swallows migrate each year to southern Africa for the winter, but formerly it was a mystery as to what happened to them. A very popular theory among early naturalists was that swallows, swifts and martins hibernated in trees, burrows, and even at the bottom of lakes! This question particularly obsessed the famous naturalist Gilbert White, who often addressed the topic in his classic work *The Natural History of Selborne* published in 1788. White went as far as hiring locals to scour the winter bushes for sleeping birds, and although his notes report that he heard many third-hand tales of hibernating birds being found in church towers and cliffs he (naturally) never found any hard evidence of this.[10] Nevertheless, he never gave up hope, and his notes show that to the end, he was convinced that a more thorough search of the countryside than he could manage would someday unearth the mystery location of the hibernating birds. In recent years in Ireland the swallow has declined in numbers, probably due to changed agricultural practices reducing the numbers of prey insects such as hoverflies, bluebottles and horseflies.[11] A lot of modern buildings are also less accessible for swallows to nest in than their older, more open equivalents. This decline is a great shame, for the swallow is surely one of the iconic sights of our countryside.

SIMILAR BIRDS

Swift – Gabhlán gaoithe – *Apus apus*

House Martin – Gabhlán binne – *Delichon urbica*

Sand Martin – Gabhlán gainimh – *Riparia riparia*

The swift was widely called 'Devil Bird' on account of its black plumage and habit of flying screaming around buildings during late spring and early summer evenings.[12] For this reason swifts were generally considered in England to be unlucky birds. The Latin name *Apus* means 'no feet' because it was thought in ancient Greece and Rome that the swift stayed permanently on the wing and did not have any feet at all. While this of course is not true, the swift does spend so much time in the air that its legs are weakened, and it can only take off with difficulty if forced to land on the ground. The swift flies a staggering 800 kilometres a day on average (including their migration to and from Africa), and feed in the atmosphere up to 3 kilometres to catch higher-altitude insects.[13] In Dublin city centre, as late as the mid-nineteenth century, swifts were a common sight, and their shrill cries were even known to startle horses in the street as they swooped down to catch insects.[14] Also, many of the windowsills of the principal houses in the streets and squares of Dublin had two or three pairs nesting in the crevices underneath.

Unlike the swift, the martin was viewed in a similar light to the swallow as a blessed bird.[15] For instance, in England it was said to be unlucky to kill a swallow or martin, as they were in mourning for the death of Our Lord. A traditional English saying declared that 'the martin and swallow / were God Almighty's bow and arrow'.

Cuckoo — Cuach — *Cuculus canorus*

The cuckoo's distinctive call after its arrival in April made it a harbinger of love and summertime. However, its habit of laying its eggs in the nests of other birds and fooling them into raising its offspring as their own made it a symbol of adultery and being 'cuckolded', and of deception and foolishness.

Folk Beliefs and Customs

Across Europe, including Ireland, a myriad of superstitions surrounded hearing the cuckoo for the first time.[1] For example in Britain, Ireland and mainland Europe, if you heard the cuckoo and had money in your pocket, it meant that you would never be without it for the rest of the year. In Britain and Ireland if you first heard the cuckoo with your right ear you would have good luck for the year, while if you first heard it with your left ear you would have bad luck. In Ireland, the Scottish Highlands and Germany it was unlucky to hear the cuckoo on an empty stomach or before breakfast, as it meant that you would have a hungry year. In England and Ireland it was believed, if you took off your shoe or boot when you first heard the cuckoo and found a hair on your foot, that a black hair meant bad luck for the year, while a white hair meant good luck. The colour of the hair could also indicate that you would marry a person with hair of the same colour. In Britain and in Donegal, it was thought that whatever activity you were doing when you first heard the cuckoo would be what you would do for the rest of the year.

Some superstitions seem to be peculiar to particular countries. For example, in Ireland if you first heard the cuckoo when you were stooping, or in a graveyard, it meant a death in the family. Also in Ireland, to be indoors and hear the cuckoo call through an open window or door meant very bad luck. Where you were when you heard the cuckoo was also important in Ireland, because it meant that you would spend the rest of your life in that place. In west Cork it was lucky to hear the cuckoo call in front of you, and unlucky to hear it from behind. In Clare it was good to make a wish or prayer on hearing the first arrival of the cuckoo. In Wales it was believed that hearing the first cuckoo's call while standing on grass or something green would bring good luck, while hearing it on rocky or stony ground meant you would not live to hear the cuckoo call the following year. In Denmark, for a man to see the cuckoo for the first time while hungry meant that he would never find anything that he sought, while a woman would have to guard against being deceived by men. In Perigord in France to hear the cuckoo on an empty stomach meant that you would be an idle layabout for the rest of your life.

Across Europe the cuckoo was expected to arrive on a particular day in spring, which varied from country to country.[2] In medieval Ireland it was thought that the cuckoo appeared first on St Patrick's Day, when it sat on the spire of the cathedral at Armagh and first sang at the rising of the sun. In the Scottish Highlands, the arrival of the cuckoo was looked for on May Day and boys went around in groups shouting: 'Cuckoo! Cried the gowk on yellow Beltane Day' ('gowk' is the Scots word for the cuckoo). In Ireland by contrast, to hear the cuckoo on May Day was a bad omen. In Cornwall the inhabitants of the village of Towednack held a cuckoo feast each 28 April. According to local lore, the feast first began long ago when the winter lasted that long into the year, and on that date a villager lit a fire and placed the stump of a tree in it. As the villagers were drinking and singing around the blazing fire, a bird suddenly flew out of the stump crying, 'cuckoo, cuckoo'. The story reflects an early belief that cuckoos hibernated in old hollow trees for the winter. Various parts of England had different dates when the cuckoo's arrival was expected. In Herefordshire it was 23 April to coincide with Orleton Fair, while in Worcestershire it was 20 April, the date of Tenbury Fair. In the south of France the date was the feast of St Benedict on 21 March, while in many parts of Germany it was the feast of Ss Valerian and Tiburtius on 14 April.

The cuckoo was also noted for disappearing equally suddenly once late summer arrived.[3] One Irish tradition explained why the cuckoo was no longer heard after 29 June, because the day before

St John was about to be martyred, the cuckoo was cooing incessantly all day long, and in the evening St John said: 'Shut up, we are bothered from you.' Closer to reality, if still inaccurate, was the widespread belief that the cuckoo had ceased to call because it had flown away to Spain (the cuckoo in fact flies all the way to Africa). In medieval Ireland it was traditionally believed that the cuckoo disappeared at the rising of the Dog Star, Sirius (around the time of the summer solstice on 21 June). In Scotland the cuckoo was said to have entered its winter house on St John's Eve (23 June) and it was not natural to hear it after that date. In Germany it was believed that cuckoos became sparrowhawks after St John's Day (24 June), while in France it was though that the cuckoo became a hawk on St James's Day (25 July). These superstitions about hawks reflect Classical beliefs.

The cuckoo's regular migratory habits were the subject of much folklore in Ireland.[4] A popular rhyme explained the cuckoo's habits: 'In April, come he will / In May he sings all day / In June he alters his tune / In July, he prepares to fly / In August go he must.' It was believed by many people in Ireland that when the cuckoo was flying to Ireland, it brought a stick on its back, and when it felt tired, it placed the stick beneath its breast and floated on it. In Britain and Ireland the cuckoo's arrival was so regular that it marked the time for planting crops. The following rhyme instructed the farmer in how to react to the cuckoo's arrival: 'If a cuckoo sits on a bare thorn / You may sell your cow and buy corn. / But if she sits on a green bough / You may sell your corn and buy a cow.' In Ireland oats sown after 1 April were derided as 'cuckoo oats' and thought to yield only a very poor crop. In addition, it was thought in Ireland that all corn should be sowed before the cuckoo's first call. In Galway anyone who sowed corn on May Eve or May Day was known as *Leadaí Leisce na Cuaiche* – 'the Lazy Cuckoo Lad', and the 'cuckoo goods' sown on that day would be worthless and without nourishment.

In Ireland the cuckoo was also thought to be a good indicator of the weather.[5] It was considered to be very bad luck to kill the cuckoo or to break its eggs, because the cuckoo brought fine weather with it. In west Cork the last three days of April and the first three days in May were called the 'Cuckoo Days', and a storm at that time was

called a 'cuckoo storm'. In Donegal it was believed that if the cuckoo called with a clear, sweet voice it meant good weather was on the way. If the cuckoo only called intermittently in a hoarse voice, it meant that the weather prospects were not good.

In Britain a common superstition was that the number of years a person had left to live could be counted by listening to the number of times the cuckoo called.[6] More cheerfully, it could also mean the number of years until the hearer was married. In England the cherry tree is also associated with the cuckoo. An old English proverb states that the cuckoo never sings till he has thrice eaten his fill of cherries. In Yorkshire children sang around a cherry tree: 'cuckoo cherry tree, come down and tell me how many years I have to live.' Each child then shook the tree and the number of cherries which fell symbolised the years of his or her future life. In the north of England generally, on hearing the cuckoo the following was said: 'Cuckoo, cuckoo! Cherry tree, good bird, tell me how many years before I die?' Alternatively the questioner asked: 'how many years shall I be, before I get married?' Cherry stones were used by children in a counting rhyme to foretell when a wished-for event would come to pass: 'This year, next year, sometime, never'. A traditional English ballad called 'The Cherry Tree Carol' sheds some light on this connection with the cuckoo. The carol tells of St Joseph and the pregnant Mary walking through a cherry orchard. Mary asks Joseph to pick a cherry for her and Joseph bitterly replies, 'Let him pluck thee a cherry that brought thee with child.' At this the infant Jesus speaks from within his mother's womb and commands the tallest tree to bow down to Mary's hand so that she can gather the fruit. At the sight of this Joseph repents of his harsh words. The clear implication is that Joseph is bitter because he feels cuckolded and this suggests that the cherry, like the cuckoo, is a symbol of love outside marriage.

There are some other beliefs and customs which involved the cuckoo.[7] In Donegal, to hear the cuckoo calling sweetly at night meant that you would marry someone from the area soon. In Scotland to hear the cuckoo calling from a house-top or chimney was very bad luck, as it indicated a death in the household within the year. In Donegal children up to seven years old were called by the names of birds to confuse the fairies and so prevent them from taking the children. Girls were called *Spideog, Eiseog* and *Cuach* (Robin, Lark and Cuckoo) and boys were called *Colmán* (Dove). In addition, in Donegal an only child was called *Éan na Cuaiche* (the Cuckoo Bird).

The cuckoo also appears in a few traditional sayings.[8] In Donegal anything, strange, rare or unexpected was called a 'winter cuckoo'. In Scotland to say, 'You'll get it when you find the cuckoo's nest' meant, of course, that the person would never be able to get it; while to 'send someone to chase the cuckoo' meant to send a person on a fool's errand or April Fool. In Scotland 1 April was often called 'Cuckoo Day' or the 'Day of Tricks'. In the Scottish Highlands the cuckoo was generally seen as a silly bird, going about all day aimlessly uttering its peculiar note.

The cuckoo also appears in some Irish place names.[9] In County Longford there is Drumacooha (*Droim na Cuaiche* – Ridge of the Cuckoo); County Tipperary has Knocknagoogh (*Cnoc na gCuach* – Hill of the Cuckoos); and County Limerick has Knockaunnaguagh (*Cnocán na gCuach* – Hillock of the Cuckoos). County Carlow has its Cuckoo Corner and Dublin has its Cuckoo's Nest; while the Cuckoo's Stone (*Cloch na Cuaiche*) is found in County Donegal.

MYTHS AND LEGENDS

The cuckoo appears in early Irish poetry and stories as a symbol of summertime and beauty.[10] In a poem about summer the warrior Fionn Mac Cumhaill mentions the cuckoo: 'The hardy, busy cuckoo calls, welcome noble summer!' The outcast hermit Mad Sweeney in his description of his life in the wild wood declares in one poem that sweeter to him 'than the grig-graig of the church bell / is the cooing of the cuckoo of the Bann'. Similarly, the warrior Oisín of the Fianna proclaims: 'The music of the woods is best to me, the sound of the wind and of the cuckoo and the blackbird, and the sweet silence of the crane.' A poem in praise of a fortress called *Druim den* says 'pleasant the calling of cuckoos that dwell with thee'. In the story of the doomed lovers Deirdre and Naoise, Deirdre declares in one poem: 'sweet the cuckoo's note on bending bough / on the peak above Glen Daruadh.'

The cuckoo appears as a symbol of female beauty in some Irish legends, probably from a play on words due to the Irish word *cuach* meaning both 'cuckoo' and 'curl, ringlet'.[11] In one story the daughter of a pagan king from Greece travels to Ireland to hear about God, and is baptised by St Patrick. As it is summer, she hears a cuckoo calling among the trees and remarks how lovely it is. In response Patrick calls the cuckoo, and it lands in the palm of his hand. He makes a cage of wood for the cuckoo and gives it to the girl to keep as she returns to Greece. In another story a very beautiful princess called Crédhe, daughter of King Cairbre, was described as 'Crédhe, for whom the cuckoo calls'. A fifteenth-century poem makes the wordplay explicit: 'in your bright-braided tresses there is a flock of cuckoos . . . a bird flock which does not sing, yet torments all men.'

The Classical writers Aristotle and Pliny both believed that the cuckoo turned into a species of hawk in the winter, and as seen in the superstitions mentioned above, this belief persisted in Europe until recent times.[12] Other authors thought that it was the offspring of the mating of a hawk and a dove.[13] However, the most famous Classical reference to the cuckoo appears in the comedy *The Birds* by the ancient Greek writer Aristophanes. The play concerns a plan by the birds of Greece to better their lot by constructing a 'cloud-cuckoo town' between heaven and earth, which will intercept all communications between men and the gods, and thus force the gods to take notice of them. Even though in the play their efforts are successful, and they win concessions from the gods, ever since the idea has come to mean any fantastical or illusory plan that has no hope of success. This reflects the perception of the cuckoo as the master of deception, getting others to serve its own ends by subverting their good efforts.

NOTABLE FACTS

The exact method used by the cuckoo to replace the host bird's egg with its own was the subject of great controversy among ornithologists.[14] A particular mystery surrounded how the cuckoo was able to get its egg into nests built by much smaller birds, which had tiny openings or were hidden in tree hollows and so on. A widely held theory was that the female cuckoo laid her egg on the ground, swallowed it, and regurgitated it quickly into the host nest while the host bird was away. It was not until the 1920s that ornithologist Edgar Chance settled the matter with the use of film. After close observation Chance managed to capture the answer on camera, which is that the cuckoo is able to remove the host's egg and lay its own egg (in the normal manner) into the nest in a matter of seconds. Each season the female cuckoo is capable of laying between ten and twenty eggs in this manner. In Ireland the meadow pipit is the chief host species, and some of its names in Irish reflect this: *banaltra na cuaiche* ('nurse of the cuckoo') and *giolla na cuaiche* ('servant of the cuckoo'). Once hatched, the naked and blind baby cuckoo ejects all the other eggs, and so claims the attention of its foster parents. Another remarkable and mysterious aspect of the cuckoo's habits is that the young when reared have the navigational ability and instinct to fly to the cuckoo's winter grounds in Africa, despite never having been shown the way before.[15]

Dove — Colm — *Columba* spp. / *Streptopelia* spp.

The fact that doves mate for life, and the affection both male and female show to each other, has made them a symbol of love and faithfulness. The pigeon was also valued as it was domesticated for food and for carrying messages. In European Christian tradition the souls of those who were without sin, or heavenly beings such as the Holy Spirit or angels, were often said to appear in the form of a white dove. This also made it a symbol of purity and peace, and a messenger of divine inspiration.

Domesticated Dove – Colm tí – *Columba livia domestica*

Rock Dove – Colm aille – *Columba livia*

Woodpigeon – Colm coille – *Columba palumbas*

Turtle Dove – Fearán eidhinn – *Streptopelia turtur*

Stock Dove – Colm gorm – *Columba oenas*

Collared Dove – Fearán baicdhubh – *Streptopelia decaocto*

FOLK BELIEFS AND CUSTOMS

Some superstitions surrounded the pigeon or dove in Ireland.[1] For example, to see a pigeon enter the dwelling house was very bad luck, and it was held to be very unlucky if a pigeon flew into a farmyard where there were not pigeons already. In Ireland it was also believed that pigeons sometimes accompanied funerals to graveyards. In Donegal it was said that the soul of a child would take the form of a dove, and a dove would often be seen leaving a house where a child had died. In Donegal it was also said that the soul of a person who had died without sin would take the form of a dove. In Donegal children up to seven years old were called by the names of birds to confuse the fairies and so prevent them from taking the children. Girls were called *Spideog, Eiseog* and *Cuach* (Robin, Lark, and Cuckoo) and boys were called *Colmán* (Dove). In

94

Donegal a woman who did not bother much with making beds was said to 'make a dove's nest'. This is because the dove does not make a very tidy nest, or make a great effort in building it. In Ireland, a wild pigeon crooning in a tree was an indication of mild weather.

Similar beliefs were held in Britain.[2] In England to see a rock dove or pigeon settle on a chimney was a bad sign, as it meant one of the occupants would die before long. In Scotland to hear the stock dove calling from the top of a tree was considered to bring bad luck for the next year. However, in Scotland and northern England it was a sign of peace to a parting soul if a white dove or pigeon came to the window, or was seen flying over the house of a dying person. A common European tradition was that the dove perched in the neighbourhood of the cross as Christ was dying, wailing 'Kyrie, Kyrie' ('Lord, Lord'), to alleviate the agony of his final moments.

In England the pigeon also featured in some rather gruesome folk cures.[3] It was believed that fevers, headaches, frenzy and madness could all be cured by taking a live pigeon, cutting it in half, and applying it to the feet of the sufferer. Similarly, the medieval German herbal *Hortus Sanitatis* declared that the fresh flesh of a dove was a remedy against serpents. Strangely, it was also believed in England that people near death could not die if they were lying on pigeon feathers, but would linger on suffering until the feathers were removed.

The Irish folklore about pigeons or doves probably refers either to the woodpigeon or 'woodquest', which is a long-standing native bird, or to the domesticated dove. The stock dove and collared dove are both recent arrivals to Ireland, the stock dove arriving in the second half of the nineteenth century, and the collared dove recorded first in Ireland in 1959.[4] The rock dove, meanwhile, is rare nowadays and is generally found around coastal cliffs, while its descendant, the feral pigeon, is usually found in towns.[5] The rock dove was also noted for nesting inland in crevices and trees around the mouth of caves, and the place name Pollnagollum (*Poll na gColm*, Hole of the Doves) appears frequently to describe caves in places such as Marble Arch, County Fermanagh; Slieve Elva, County Clare; Slieve Rushen, County Cavan; and Drumshanbo, County Leitrim. The domesticated dove is also descended from the rock dove, and was traditionally reared in Ireland in dovecotes for eating since at least the Norman invasion.[6] The turtle dove is a rare passage migrant to Ireland, found mainly around the south coast during the spring and autumn,[7] although it is more common in Britain and features in folklore there, in songs such as the two turtle doves in the Christmas song 'The Twelve Days of Christmas'.

MYTHS AND LEGENDS

The dove appears in some Irish folktales, usually as a person or fairy in disguise.[8] In one story a fisherman is told by a giant that he can save his son from captivity if he can pick him out of twelve doves the next morning. The fisherman's son comes to him in the night and tells him to watch for a dove that has a spot under one wing and walks in a ring around the other doves. The next morning the giant throws some grain on the ground and calls the twelve doves to feed. The fisherman watches them closely and successfully identifies his son, and the giant is forced to let him go free. Similarly, in another tale, after completing a series of tasks, a prince is told by a farmer that he can pick one of his daughters to marry, but he can only choose when they are in the form of pigeons. The prince is already in love with one of them, who has helped him complete the tasks, and she tells him to look for the pigeon with the black quill in one of its wings. Watching carefully, the prince chooses the right daughter and they are happily married. In one story from Mayo, doves overcome a hostile fairy host.[9] According to the tale, the fairy hosts of Connacht and Munster were fighting each other at Moytirra near Nephin. The host of Munster made flying beetles of themselves and began eating up every green thing they came upon. They were destroying the whole country until they came to Cong. There out of a hole in the ground arose thousands of doves who swallowed down all the beetles and put an end to them. The hole has been called *Poll na gColm* (The Doves' Hole) ever since.

The dove appears in association with several Irish saints in various Irish legends, often as a symbol of divine help or favour.[10] A story in Keating's *History of Ireland* explains how St Colmcille got his name. The saint's baptismal name was Crimthan, but as a child when he left the monastery to play with the other children of the village, they used to declare, 'here comes the *Colm Cille* (Dove of the Church). When the teacher heard that, he declared that was the name by which he should be known henceforth. A Donegal folktale recounts how a dove also showed Colmcille where to build his church. According to the tale, Colmcille and his servant went to build a church in a particular spot, but each day when they returned, they found that the previous day's work had been scattered. The third time this happened, the two men sat nearby and discussed what to do. Then Colmcille noticed a white dove arrive, take three pebbles from the foundation stones into its beak and fly off. The dove returned and took some lime in its beak and again flew off, and a short time later it returned and took three splinters in its beak. Colmcille realised there was something miraculous about this, and he and his servant followed the dove. They arrived at a particular spot and saw the pebbles, lime and splinters lying on the ground. Colmcille decided to build his church on that spot instead, and succeeded in building it without any further difficulty.

In another story in Keating's *History of Ireland*, St Patrick prayed to Michael the Archangel to save the life of Lugaidh, son of King Laoghaire, who was choking to death. The Archangel appeared in the form of a dove and took a morsel of food out of the child's throat, allowing him to breathe again. Out of thanksgiving, the boy's mother, the queen, declared that she would give a sheep out of every flock she possessed to the poor on the Archangel's feast day, thus beginning the custom of giving alms to the poor every Michaelmas. In a more modern folktale, the ailing daughter of an Englishman finds the prayer book of her Catholic maidservant and reads it. She is taken miraculously to Rome and meets St Patrick (presumably in spirit form) and is baptised. The sick girl dies immediately and ascends to heaven in the form of a white dove. Another folktale about St Patrick concerns the period he spent on Croagh Patrick. The saint was being assailed by demons, and when his prayers did not get rid of them he threw his bell at them. This overcame them successfully, but the bell fell into a hole called *Log na nDeamhan* (the Devils' Hole). However, a dove from God retrieved the bell and brought it back to St Patrick. In the story of the *Life of St Moling*, the infant Moling was born in the snow, but his mother would not come to his aid due to her shame at having conceived him with her sister's husband. However, a dove came down to earth to protect the infant, putting its wings about the child to keep him warm.

In several early Irish legends and poems the turtle dove is praised for the beauty of its crooning, purring call.[11] The turtle dove is now a relatively rare visitor to Ireland, and its appearance in Irish works suggests it may have been more common in earlier times. Alternatively the reason may be due to the influence of the Bible, where the call of the turtle dove is mentioned several times, such as in Jeremiah 8:7, and the Song of Songs 2:11–12. In the story of the hermit *Suibhne Geilt* or Mad Sweeney, a poem describing his life in the wild declares: 'Once a sweeter sound to me / Than local people's quiet speech / Was the rustling by the pool / of turtle doves that call and croon.' An early Irish poem in praise of the mountain Beann Ghualann states that 'the turtle doves (*feáráin*) of your sheltering trees / lift sorrow from your womenfolk.' A tenth-century poem about the hermit Marbán speaks of the 'music of the bright, red-breasted turtle doves' around his hut in the woods. In the tale of the two lovers, the poets Liadain and Cuirithir, when Liadain arrives for a tryst, a servant tells him that Cuirithir is waiting for him at the well outside the court, saying: 'It is a fitting place to wait / the well before the house's gate / fair doves (*ferait*) flutter all around it / little birds gladly surround it.'

In Celtic Gaul, doves were associated with peace, harmony and good health, and images of doves were offered to the presiding deities at several curative thermal springs, particularly in Burgundy.[12] At springs such as Nuits-Saint-Georges, Beire-le-Châtel and Alesia, pilgrims offered multiple stone figures of doves in groups of two, four or six; while at springs like Essarois and Fontes Sequanae, pilgrims dedicated images of themselves carrying doves as gifts to the presiding gods. The deity most associated with these springs was the Celtic Apollo who was both a healer and prophetic god, and doves may have been linked to him in part because of their distinctive voices. As well as cures, the springs were places where prophecies would take place, as visions and dreams were seen as part of the healing process.

In ancient Greece and Rome doves were said to be associated with the goddess of love, Aphrodite or Venus, on account of the fact that doves are forever caressing each other.[13] To the Greeks, the dove represented both kinds of love, Aphrodite Urania, the goddess of pure love, but also Aphrodite Pandemas, the goddess of sensual, lustful and venal love and the patroness of prostitutes. One version of the birth of Aphrodite is that she was hatched from a dove's egg in the sea and brought ashore by a fish. The Greek shrine at Dodona was said to contain an oracle in the form of a dove, who spoke with a human voice. In Virgil's *Aeneid*, the hero Aeneas is led by two doves sent by his mother Venus to a tree where he is able to pluck the Golden Bough. The Classical belief that the dove paired for life made it a model of conjugal fidelity, and it was believed that if one partner died, the other remained single and gave itself over to lamentation. For this reason doves were often considered chaste birds, despite their reputation for love. Those seeking chastity, moreover, could also eat the flesh of the woodpigeon because it was said to inhibit sexual desire. The Roman writer Martial declared: 'Wood pigeons make the private parts sluggish and weak, let the man not eat this bird who desires to be lecherous.'

The use of the dove or pigeon to carry messages appears in the Old Testament story of Noah, who sent the dove out from the ark to see if the flood sent by God had receded.[14] The dove came back with an olive branch, which showed that it had reached dry land. This meant that God must have forgiven mankind, and so the olive branch became a symbol of peace and friendship. The Irish *Lebor Gabála Érenn* or *Book of Invasions of Ireland* contains a version of the story of Noah, where the raven was once white, and the dove black. At the end of forty days in the ark Noah released the raven to look for land, but it did not come back. Then he released the dove. The first time it came back because it could find nowhere to land, but the second time it came back with an olive twig in its beak. Then Noah blessed the dove and cursed the raven, so God gave the colour of the dove to the raven, and the sheen of the raven to the dove, on account of the raven's insubordination.

The dove also appears in the New Testament, when the Holy Spirit appeared to the apostles in the form of a dove. This led to it being seen as a symbol of innocence and purity among Christians.[15] The dove therefore appears in Christian iconography countless times as an image of the Holy Spirit, hovering over the head of Jesus or the Virgin Mary or descending from the clouds in a shaft of heavenly light. The Holy Spirit in the form of a dove also appears in later European legends. According to legend a heavenly dove appeared to the French king Clovis, at his coronation on Christmas Day 496 in Reims, carrying a vial of chrism (a mixture of consecrated oil and balm) with which to anoint him. This image of the white dove as a symbol of love and peace has spread out from its original Christian context and appears in countless works of art and imagery today.

NOTABLE FACTS

Rearing doves for their flesh and eggs goes back as least as far as Roman times.[16] For example, the Roman author Varro in his work on agriculture *De Re Rustica* gives detailed instructions for how to raise pigeons in dovecotes, similar in design to the ones used in modern times. In Britain and Ireland, doves raised for food were also traditionally kept in dovecotes, where the young, known as 'squabs', were regularly harvested as a major food source. The traditional design of a dovecote was of a multistorey building, with its interior walls lined with alcoves or ledges to mimic the conditions of the wild doves' caves. The ledges were high up the walls to be out of reach of predators, and access to them was generally by a ladder. Some of the large dovecotes in Britain could hold as many as 1,500 nests. As doves can breed as many as six times throughout the year, the dovecotes provided a continuous source of food, and also feathers, which were used for stuffing mattresses, pillows and so forth.

Pigeons have also been valued for their use as messengers since ancient times.[17] For example, a frieze in the Egyptian temple of Medinat built in the time of Rameses III (*c.* 1297 BC), shows a priest sending out four pigeons to convey the news of the coronation of that pharaoh. The Romans used pigeons to carry the news about the outcome of chariot races, so that owners would know how their entries had done. Pigeons were particularly valued as messengers in times of war, and were noted for their feats of flying. One message-bearing pigeon of the Duke of Wellington was reputed to have dropped dead one mile from its loft, having allegedly flown 7,000 miles in 55 days. However, the carrier pigeon really came into its own in the Siege of Paris in 1870 during the Franco-Prussian war, when 409 pigeons were used to send messages for the besieged citizens. Of the 409 pigeons used, 73 returned safely, braving cold, fatigue, falcons and Prussian bullets. Pigeons were used to carry messages as late as the Second World War, and twenty-six received the Dicken Medal during the conflict, the animal equivalent of the Victoria Cross. Pigeons were also used for commercial messages. For example, the famous Reuters News Agency, founded in 1849 by Paul Julius Reuter, began with messenger pigeons flying with news of stock prices between the German town of Aachen and Brussels.

Modern pigeon racing by 'fanciers' originated in Belgium in the early nineteenth century, with the racing pigeon the Homer, but many different breeds of 'fancy' pigeons have now been developed. The grouping of fancy pigeons has become complex and varied, but there are eight main categories of pigeon.[18] The first category is the original Homer or Homing Pigeons, which were bred for their homing abilities, but can also be bred for showing. These include the English Carrier, the Dragoon and the German Beauty Homer. Next are utility pigeons that were bred for meat, such as French Mondain and the King. Third are Flying Tumbler and Highflier pigeons bred for show purposes, but which also can be used in flying competitions. These include the Tumbler, the Tippler and the Roller. Another group are the Asian Feather and Voice pigeons, bred for their showy feathers and laughing or 'trumpeting' voice. These include the Fantail, Trumpeter and Jacobin. The fifth group are the Exhibition Tumblers originally bred for their acrobatic abilities. These include the Nun, the English Short-Faced Tumbler and the Magpie. Sixth are Colour Pigeons bred for their colourful feathers and markings. This group includes birds such as the Archangel, the Swallow and the Danish Suabian. Seventh are the Pouters and Croppers, bred purely for their ability to inflate their crops with air. This group includes the English Pouter, the Norwich Cropper and the Pigmy Pouter. Eighth and last are the Frills and Owls, bred for their extraordinary chest feathers and stunted beaks. These include the Old German Owl, the Oriental Frill and the Aachen Shield Owl. Pigeon racing and fancying remain popular pastimes in many countries around the world, including the UK, United States, Canada, Australia, Belgium, Turkey and South Africa.

Several wild species of pigeon have notable features.[19] For example, woodpigeons are unusual among birds in that both adults feed the young on 'pigeon milk' produced by special cells in the crop. Woodpigeons are a serious pest of arable farming, consuming large amounts of cereal crops, brassicas and peas. Despite various attempts, no satisfactory method has been found to control their numbers. The collared dove is a common bird throughout Europe nowadays, but its spread across the continent is notable for being the most rapid of any recorded species. At the beginning of the twentieth century it was found only in the Balkans; by 1931 it had reached Hungary, and by 1940 it was in Poland. By 1955 it had crossed into Britain, and had spread throughout Britain and Ireland within a few years. The exact reasons for this extraordinary spread are not fully understood, and remain a subject of debate among ornithologists.

Blackbird — Lon Dubh — *Turdus merula*

The blackbird was much loved in ancient Ireland for its melodic song, being praised in many poems and stories as a symbol of the beauty of nature, especially of the woods. The blackbird's striking combination of black feathers and golden beak has also inspired much folklore. For example, the blackbird is linked to blacksmiths in some tales, perhaps because the colours of its feathers and beak are reminiscent of black soot and golden fire. The blackbird's habit of calling loudly in alarm at the slightest threat also adds to its fiery reputation.

FOLK BELIEFS AND CUSTOMS

A large amount of weather lore was associated with the blackbird.[1] In Ireland generally, it was thought that when the blackbird whistled, or sang loud and shrill, rain was on the way. In County Tyrone it was said that a blackbird or thrush which sang before Candlemas (2 February) would be sure to mourn for many days afterwards. Similarly, in County Meath it was said that 'if the blackbird sings before Christmas she will cry before Candlemas', and the same belief was held in Scotland. Presumably these sayings meant the blackbird sang in good weather and mourned in bad. In Donegal the blackbird was also known as the Snow Bird. It was a sure sign that snow was on the way to see a blackbird appear at the door of the byre, feed on scraps in the farmyard or forage under a tree or in a ditch in open country. In addition, if a group of blackbirds formed together, then a storm was thought not to be far away. In Mayo if a blackbird was chirping at night it was a sign of snow.

A common notion in Ireland was that of 'The Borrowed Days', namely the first three days of April.[2] It was said that the weather was always very bad on those days, as March vengefully borrowed them from April to kill and skin an old brindled cow that had boasted it survived the rigours of March. In Ulster the tradition was more elaborate, as March borrowed nine days from April to carry out its revenge. The first three days of April were called *Trí Lá*

Lomartha an Loinn – 'Three days for skinning the blackbird' (presumably for making a similar boast). There were another three for the bird called the stonechat, and the last three for the old brindled cow. In Scotland the same tradition existed of *Trí Lá Lomaidh an Loin*.

A certain amount of folklore surrounded the occasional appearance of a blackbird with white feathers.[3] An old Irish saying asserted that there would be white blackbirds before an unwilling woman tied the knot (the fact that white blackbirds do, in fact, exist shows that there are always grounds for hope!). In Donegal the appearance of a white blackbird was a sign that some huge change was on the way – usually a death in the house, especially of a woman. In Moycullen in County Galway, a tradition existed of a white blackbird which appeared around the locality. The blackbird was held to be the soul of a drowned man, who had to spend a certain amount of time in that form close to where he died before his soul could be let into heaven. Historically, white blackbirds have also drawn the attention of naturalists. O'Sullivan Beare in his *Natural History of Ireland*, written in 1625, stated that white blackbirds were sometimes seen in Ireland, and that they were smaller in size than ordinary blackbirds. In ancient Greece Aristotle described white blackbirds living in Arcadia that had a wider range of notes than other blackbirds and appeared only by moonlight. In fact, the appearance of blackbirds with part or all-white feathers is not uncommon, and is due to a condition known as 'leucism', but there is no evidence that they differ from ordinary blackbirds in any other way. Leucistic blackbirds are far more common than albino blackbirds, which also exist and can be distinguished by their pink eyes.

Various European folktales relate how the blackbird got its present distinctive appearance.[4] According to a French tale, the blackbird was once as white as snow, until one day it was told by a magpie where it might find hidden treasure. To get the treasure the blackbird had to seek out the Prince of Riches underground, offer his services, and in return he would be rewarded with as much treasure as his beak could carry. The blackbird entered the cave which the magpie had shown him, and soon came upon a cavern full of silver. Mindful of the magpie's advice, the blackbird carried on without touching it. Next the blackbird came to a cavern full of gold. This was too much for the blackbird, which plunged its beak greedily into the gold on the floor. Immediately a terrible demon appeared vomiting fire and smoke and made for the blackbird with lightning speed. The blackbird escaped just in time, but its feathers were all blackened by the smoke forevermore, and its beak had turned to gold from the gold it had unsuccessfully tried to take. In Italy it was said that the blackbird was once white in colour, but during a cruel and cold winter it was forced to take shelter in a chimney, where it became blackened by soot. In commemoration, the last two days of January and the first of February became known as *i giorni della merla* – 'the blackbird days'. A tradition from Scotland simply says that the blackbird's beak became yellow after it dug its beak into a mass of gold in an enchanted cave.

Some other folklore also involved the blackbird.[5] In Donegal if a blackbird entered the house it was a sign that good news would follow. In Carmarthenshire in Wales it was the custom to break the eggs of magpies, crows and blackbirds on May Day, the eggs having been collected for the purpose. The point of this exercise is not explained, but it is worth noting that the birds concerned all have black feathers. In Germany the blackbird was called *Gottling* – 'little god' – and was said to protect against lightning if kept in a cage.

MYTHS AND LEGENDS

The blackbird appears in some Irish folktales.[6] In one tale the hero Fionn Mac Cumhaill had been mortally wounded after a battle and lay at the bottom of a boat with his entrails hanging out. A blackbird appeared and began to pick at Fionn's entrails, before saying: 'Many a long day have I watched and waited for this chance, and glad I am to have it now.' The blackbird then turned into a little man not more than three feet high. He had been under a druidic spell to be a blackbird until he could get three bites of fat from the entrails of Fionn Mac Cumhaill. Having regained his true shape, the little man is able to cure Fionn's wounds, by putting his entrails back into their proper place and rubbing him with an ointment. Another tale describes a hero going through his enemies 'as a hawk through a flock of small birds on a March day, or as a blackbird . . . between two thickets'. A flock of blackbirds with fiery beaks appears in a story concerning a battle between the Fianna and the Tuatha Dé Danann. The blackbirds are let out by the Tuatha Dé Danann and land on the breasts of the people, burning them. In another tale a blacksmith's apprentice called Lun Dubh Mac Smola (Blackbird son of Thrush) vied for the blacksmith's daughter with another apprentice Césa MacRí. Although the maiden favoured Lun Dubh, Césa tricked him out of her hand by driving a spike through Lun Dubh's finger and fastening him to an anvil until he promised to let Césa have her. But Lun Dubh had his revenge later by killing Césa with one blow of his hand.

A connection between the blackbird and blacksmiths appears in other tales.[7] One such tale concerns the question of the coldest night in Ireland. According to the story there was a night many years ago that was so cold that an eagle went about the next morning, asking various ancient creatures if they had ever seen a colder one. One of the creatures he asked was the Blackbird of the Forge, who was standing on an iron rod which was nearly worn through. The rod was once very long and thick, but it was worn down by the blackbird rubbing its beak against it once every seven years. In all the time it had taken to wear down the rod, the blackbird had never seen a colder night. Eventually the eagle finds a salmon who tells him that once there had been a colder night, thousands of years ago. A similar story appears in the Welsh tale *How Culhwch won Olwen*. In the tale the hero Culhwch must find the hunter Mabon, who was taken from his mother when he was three nights old. He went to various ancient creatures to ask them if they had ever heard of Mabon or where he was. One of the creatures he asked was the Blackbird of Kilgowry. The blackbird had been in Kilgowry so long that the smith's anvil it stood on was now nothing more than an iron nut. In all that time, the only thing wearing down the iron anvil had been the blackbird's own beak rubbing against it each night. Perhaps the connection between the blackbird and blacksmiths in these tales derives from an association between the blackbird's black feathers and gold beak and the black soot and bright fire of the blacksmith's craft. Interestingly, in Scotland another name for the blackbird or ousel was the 'blackbird-chacker' or 'blackbird-smith'.

The most famous Irish myth about the blackbird concerns St Kevin of Glendalough.[8] The saint lived a hermit's life close to nature, and it was said that while he prayed, little birds would often perch on his hands and shoulders. It was also his custom while praying to raise his hand and put it out through the window of his cabin. On one occasion during Lent, while St Kevin was praying in this fashion, a blackbird came and landed on his palm, and proceeded to make its nest there and to lay its eggs. The saint was moved with such pity and was so patient, that he kept his hand in the same position until the blackbird's eggs were completely hatched out.

In Ireland blackbirds and thrushes were sometimes hunted for food when meat was scarce, and this practice continued up until modern times.[9] An incident in the tale of *The Colloquy of the Ancients*, which involves Oisín of the Fianna returning to Ireland from *Tír na nÓg*, the Land of Youth, illustrates this. Oisín had gone there long ago, where he had spent several hundred years as if they were a few weeks. When he returned to Ireland he found that the rest of his warrior comrades in the Fianna were long dead. Now a decrepit old man, he spent the rest of his days with St Patrick debating the merits of Christianity and paganism. One day Oisín complained that he was not getting enough to eat and Patrick responded by saying that, on the contrary, he got a quarter of beef every day. Oisín replied with contempt that the quarter was miserable in comparison to the old days of feasting with the Fianna, and that in those days he often had a quarter of a blackbird bigger than Patrick's quarter of beef. Patrick did not believe Oisín and told him that he was lying. This put Oisín into a rage, and one day afterwards he went with his serving boy and a hound to a particular place and retrieved a great sounding horn of the Fianna. When he blew the horn, a great flock of blackbirds appeared and the serving boy released the hound, who attacked one of the birds and managed to kill it. Oisín asked the boy to cut off a quarter of it with his sword, and they returned to Patrick with the quarter which was bigger than any quarter of a bullock. When Patrick saw the blackbird's quarter he was forced to withdraw his words and admit that Oisín had told no lie. Another reference to the blackbird that seems to relate to its use as food appears in the early Irish saga *The Cattle Raid of Cooley*. In it the hero Cúchulainn warns another warrior that if he bothers him again: 'I shall cut off your head as the head is cut off a blackbird.' The custom of eating blackbirds was also found in Britain, which is reflected in the old nursery rhyme about 'four and twenty blackbirds / baked in a pie'.

The blackbird appears in some other tales in various guises.[10] In one story, *Finn and the man in the tree*, the blackbird appears as a sort of spirit of the woods, along with the stag. In the tale the hero Fionn Mac Cumhaill went in search of a servant of his whom he had previously exiled. He found him sitting in the top of a tree, a blackbird on his right shoulder and in his left hand a vessel of white bronze filled with water, in which was a skittish trout, and a stag at the foot of the tree. The servant Derg Corra would crack nuts, eat one half himself, give the other half to the blackbird, then take an apple out of the bronze vessel, split it in half, eat one half himself, and give the other to the stag. Then all three, man, bird and stag, would take a sip out of the water together. The stag and blackbird also appear together in Gráinne's lay to her lover Diarmuid: 'The stag in the east is awake / Loudly he roars without cease / Though with blackbirds among the oaks / He has no mind to sleep.' The soul of a warrior appears to take the form of a blackbird in another early Irish tale. In the tale the severed head of a warrior called Fothad begins to sing to his former lover: 'It is the dusky ouzel [blackbird] that laughs / a greeting to all the faithful / my speech, my shape, are spectral / – hush woman, do not speak to me!'

Above all, however, the blackbird is praised in numerous early Irish poems and stories for its beautiful song.[11] In the old Irish work *Cormac's Glossary* a poem states: 'Sweet was the voice of the wood of blackbirds, round the rath of Fiacha son of Moinche.' Oisín, in his lament for the old days of the warrior Fianna, states that he prefers 'the chatter of the blackbird of Leitir Laoi' to the music of the clergy, and later says: 'Blackbird of Doire an Chairn, your voice is sweet; I never heard on any height of the world music was sweeter than your voice, and you at the foot of your nest.' Fionn Mac Cumhaill, the hero of the warrior band the Fianna, praises the song of the blackbird in a poem about summer: 'May-time, fair season, perfect is its aspect then; blackbirds sing a full song, if there be a scanty beam of day.' The tenth-century poem about the hermit Marbán describes his simple hut in the woods, surrounded by nature: 'the she-bird in its dress of blackbird colour sings a melodious strain from its gable.' Another early poem compares the blackbird itself to a hermit: 'Ah, blackbird, it is well for you where your nest is in the bushes; a hermit that clangs no bell, sweet, soft, and peaceful is your call.' Another hermit, Sweeney, mentions the blackbird several times, for example, saying: 'sweet I think the blackbird's warbling, and to listen to mass.' Finally, a well-known eighth- or ninth-century poem vividly describes the blackbird of Belfast Lough and his song. It has appeared in many translations, and here is another by the author:

THE BLACKBIRD OF BELFAST LOUGH

The wee bird
Softly flutes
With his peaked bill
Orange gold.

Skilfully sounds
Over Belfast Lough
Bird on the branch
A golden horn.

NOTABLE FACTS

The blackbird was once a bird of dense woodland, but over the eighteenth and nineteenth centuries it has been venturing into urban gardens across Britain and Ireland, to the point where it now outnumbers the thrush by a ratio of about 4.5 : 1.[12] In Ireland it is one of the most common birds, and has been extending its range west into more open and barren countryside. While the blackbird is well loved for it melodious song, it is also famous for its highly strung temperament, and tendency to shriek raucously and chatter with alarm at the slightest hint of a threat.[13] The blackbird was also disliked by some country people in Ireland on account of its habit of ripping thatch off the roof in search of insects.[14]

SIMILAR BIRDS

Song Thrush – Smólach ceoil – *Turdus philomelos*

Mistle Thrush – Liatráisc – *Turdus viscivorus*

Despite being one of our best-known garden birds, there is surprisingly little folklore about the thrush.[15] Nevertheless, it appears in some early Irish poems and legends on account of its song, which is almost as melodious as that of the blackbird. For example, the poem 'Crédhe's Lament' concerning the death of the warrior Cael states: 'Pitiful the cry, pitiful the cry the thrush is making in the pleasant Ridge, sorrowful is the cry of the blackbird in Leitir Laeig.' Oisín of the Fianna, when recounting the glories of nature in his youth, mentions: 'The sweet-voiced thrush of Gleann an Sgáil.' Also, a poem lauding the natural beauty of Beann Ghualann speaks of 'the sweet singing of your thrushes'. O'Sullivan Beare in his *Natural History of Ireland*, written in 1625, stated that in Ireland thrushes became famous in 1621 by dying after starting bloody fights among themselves.

The song thrush is well known for its habit of eating snails by catching them by their shells and smashing them open by knocking them against a stone. This trait of the thrush appears in the book *The Hobbit* by J. R. R. Tolkien. In the book the dwarves must find the secret door into the Lonely Mountain by waiting for the last rays of the setting sun to illuminate the keyhole of the door 'when the thrush knocks'. In British folklore, a curious superstition held that thrushes acquired new legs and cast out the old ones when they were about ten years old. The mistle thrush is only a recent arrival in Ireland, having first come here in numbers in the early nineteenth century. It gets its name from its habit of spreading mistletoe by feeding on it, and is also called the 'storm cock' from its habit of singing immediately before stormy weather or high winds.

Eagle — Iolar — *Accipitridae*

The eagle with its majestic wingspan, noble appearance and ruthless power made it a symbol of the strength and authority of kings. The eagle was traditionally believed to be able to look directly into the rays of the sun, which was seen as a sign of its just, righteous, but also fierce nature. It was also believed to live an extremely long time, making it a bird of wisdom and prophecy, as well as strength.

Golden Eagle – Iolar Fíréan – *Aquila chrysaetos*

White-tailed (Sea) Eagle – Iolar mara – *Haliaetus albicilla*

FOLK BELIEFS AND CUSTOMS

Although the eagle became extinct in Ireland at the beginning of the twentieth century, some folklore about them remained.[1] In Kerry a traditional belief was that the eagle was a very long-lived bird, with a life span of three *crí*. A *crí* was the length of time it took to dig a field, put in potatoes, then put in oats, then let it rest so long that it was not possible to tell that anything had ever been planted there. It was also said in Kerry that the eagle's beak would grow too long for it to eat anything, so the eagle would have to break its beak against a rock by swooping down on top of it. The eagle then had to do without food for a while until its beak grew back to a normal size again. The eagle was traditionally regarded with suspicion by Irish farmers for stealing lambs, but another tale from Kerry cast the eagle in a more useful light. According to this story a poor man was able to feed his family during a summer famine by climbing up to the Eagle's Nest in Killarney and robbing the eaglets of part of the food brought to them by their parents. The man was able to prolong this food source by clipping the wings of the eaglets, thus retarding the time when they would leave the nest. An old Irish tradition held that Adam and Eve still exist as eagles on the island of Inisbofin, at the mouth of Killary Harbour in Galway.

Some humorous Irish stories involve the eagle.[2] One such story concerns the adventures of a Daniel O'Rourke from Bantry in County Cork. In the story O'Rourke was coming home drunk one night and fell into a river, and after that became lost in a bog. An eagle came along who told him he would rescue him if he got up on his back. Daniel got up on the eagle's back, but the eagle flew to the moon and dumped him there. When Daniel indignantly asked why the eagle had done this, he replied that it was in revenge for Daniel robbing his nest last year. Then the eagle flew off laughing and abandoned him. Daniel was then thrown off the moon by the Man of the Moon and fell straight down. Luckily he managed to break his fall by grabbing hold of the leg of a gander. The gander was not stopping, however, but was migrating to Arabia, so Daniel was forced to let go and fall into the sea. Then he was splashed in the face by a whale, but it wasn't a whale, only his wife who was throwing water over him to wake him out of his drunken stupor. The whole thing had been a dream!

Another humorous story, concerning the eagle protecting its nest, comes from Kerry. In the story a soldier decided he was going to steal the young from a nest on the aptly named Eagle's Nest in Killarney. As soon as the mother eagle had flown away, he let himself down by a rope from the top of the cliff. However, the mother eagle returned unexpectedly and asked the soldier to explain his presence. The soldier replied that he had merely come to pay his respects to the eagle and her family. Unconvinced by this, the eagle asked the Echo of the Mountain if the soldier had come to rob the eagle's nest. 'To rob the nest, to rob the nest,' the Echo replied. The soldier immediately began to climb up the rope again as fast as he could, but the eagle said, 'As you have come to pay me a visit, it is only fair that I show you the shortest way home.' She then caught him a blow over the head with one of her wings, and kicked him with her claw down the cliff. The soldier fell into a river, which was lucky for him, otherwise he would have been smashed to bits.

The eagle does not come out so well in another story, again in Killarney, about how she was outwitted by a fox.[3] The story tells of a very lean time when a hungry fox wandered about the Lakes of

Killarney looking for something to eat. The fox spied three ducks swimming in the lake and devised a plan to catch them. Using a plant with very big leaves, he was able to swim out and grab one of the ducks before they realised what was happening. He left the first duck on the shore and decided he would try to grab the other ducks too. He went out a second time, and again a third time, but when he returned to shore the third time the first two ducks were gone. Greatly perplexed by this, the fox looked around and spied the eagle's nest high up above him. He concluded that he had found his culprit and plotted his revenge. The fox noticed a fire smouldering in the distance and, taking the duck he had left, he dragged it back and forth through the embers. Then he left the duck on the shore and concealed himself in some bushes. Sure enough, before long the eagle swooped down and snatched the duck, bringing it to her nest. But the feathers of the duck had been reddened from the fire, and the nest was ablaze in a matter of seconds. The burning nest tumbled down the mountainside, and the fox not only got his three ducks back, but also three dead eaglets for his larder.

Some superstitions surrounded the eagle in Britain.[4] In Scotland eagle feathers were traditionally worn in the cap of a clan chieftain. They were the only ones considered suitable, as the eagle is the king of the birds. A traditional charm was said on St Brigid's Day in the Scottish Highlands to ask for the saint's protection of the livestock: '. . . from the blue peregrine of Creag Duilion / From the brindled eagle of Ben-Ard / From the swift hawk of Tordun / From the surly raven of Bard's Creag'. Similarly on the quarter days of Bridget's Day, May Day, Lammas and Halloween, special cakes called bannocks were eaten, and a piece thrown over each shoulder alternatively as a gift to the wolf, fox, eagle, raven, marten and harrier to spare livestock. In Wales the eagles of Snowdon were regarded as oracles; their cries were held to predict calamity and their appearance over the plains to foretell death. Also, when it was stormy in Wales, people would say: 'the eagles are breeding whirlwinds on Snowdon.'

MYTHS AND LEGENDS
One of the most persistent legends about eagles is the notion that they will snatch away human babies if they have the chance.[5] One

such tale from Scotland concerns a crofter called William Anderson on the island of Unst in Shetland, who left his child wrapped in a shawl in a field while he worked. Suddenly he saw a huge eagle swoop down, grab the baby in its talons, and fly away to the south. He and his wife frantically pursued the bird, and followed it out on a boat to the island of Fetlar. Locals told them a sea eagle's eyrie was on the high cliffs and a local youth managed to climb down to it and rescue the child, still wrapped in its shawl, and nestling between two eaglets. The baby was then reunited with its relieved parents, quite unharmed. An Irish version of this story concerns a baby taken from a woman in Achill, County Mayo. According to this tale, a woman laid her young child on the ground in order to chase a fox that was trying to get her chickens. When she returned, she discovered a large eagle making off with the child, heading for Clare Island, 5 miles away. She soon rounded up some local fishermen, and they headed out to the island in hot pursuit. The men discovered the eagle's nest on a cliff ledge, and after some men were lowered down with ropes, they managed to retrieve the child. To their amazement, they found the infant completely unharmed, sleeping right next to the young eaglets who were feeding on a fresh lamb carcass. The child was quickly returned to its mother, still warmly wrapped in thick red flannel. What is notable about these stories is that the eagle appears to have no intention of killing the child as prey, but seems rather to want to care for it along with its own young. Also, despite the vividness of these stories, no account of eagles snatching babies in this way has ever been properly verified.

In reality, the stories of eagles abducting children probably developed out of widespread legends of royalty or nobility finding children in the nests of eagles and adopting them.[6] For example, a legend about King Alfred the Great relates how he was hunting in the forest one day when he heard the sound of an infant crying from the top of a tree. He sent his huntsmen to investigate, and they discovered at the top of the tree, in an eagle's nest, a beautiful child clothed in purple with gold bracelets on its arms. Alfred commanded that the child should be cared for, baptised and educated, and in remembrance of the manner of its discovery he ordered that it be called Nestingus. A similar story explains the crest of the Earls of

Derby, the Stanley family, which features an eagle and child. According to the story, a fourteenth-century ancestor of the Stanleys found a child at the foot of a tree underneath an eagle's nest, and decided to raise it as one of his own. A cynical interpretation of this story is that the Stanley concerned had found a clever way to pass off one of his own illegitimate children as a foundling. The Stanley crest is commemorated in the large number of pubs named 'The Eagle and Child', which still exist in England, many of which are located close to Stanley lands.

One folk tale provides an Irish version of the same story. According to the tale, a king was walking with his retinue near Slieve League in Donegal when he saw an eagle flying overhead. This made the king sad, as it reminded him of the fact that he and the queen had no child, despite being married for ten years. The previous night the queen had dreamt that she had a beautiful baby boy and that she was sitting with it outside in the sun. Suddenly a huge eagle swooped down and grabbed the boy with its claws and flew off with it. The queen was very upset with this dream because it felt like she had lost a child after waiting so long for one. The king was thinking of this dream when he heard a child's cry, and at the same time the cry of an eagle. After a search he saw a child lying in an eagle's nest halfway down a cliff; despite the danger, the king climbed down and rescued the child. The child was a baby boy wearing purple clothes and gold bangles on his arm. The king took the child home and sent out messengers throughout the land to find his parents. No parents were found, so the king and queen raised the child as their own. The queen was overjoyed and thanked heaven for her gift, but at the same time she was careful never to let the child out of doors until he was too big for eagles to take.

One Irish tale explains how the eagle was outwitted by the Old Crow of Achill.[7] According to the tale there was a night in Ireland many years ago that was so cold that the Old Crow did not know how he would survive it. The Old Crow found an eagle's nest, killed the fledgling inside and hid in the nest. The eagle then came along and sat on the crow, not realising that her fledgling was gone. While sitting on the nest, the eagle complained of the bitterly cold night, and the crow told her that there was once an even colder night long ago – on Old May night (11 May). The eagle did not believe him, but the crow said to go and check with the Blackbird of the Forge. The next morning the eagle went to see the blackbird to see if what the crow had said was true. The blackbird said that the previous night was the coldest it had ever felt, and the blackbird had been at the forge for so long that the iron rod it was standing on was worn through. It was once many inches long and thick, but every seven years the blackbird rubbed its beak on it and wore it down a little. In all that time there had never been a colder night. However, the blackbird told the eagle to check with a bull in a nearby field. Although the bull had been in the field for thousands of years, it too had never seen a colder night. The bull told the eagle to check with the oldest creature known, the salmon of Assaroe. The eagle went to the salmon to ask, and the salmon replied that yes, there had once been a night colder long ago. It was so cold that when the salmon jumped out of the water, it was frozen when it came back down. The Old Crow of Achill had come along and pecked out its eye, and had also pecked out a hole in the ice that the salmon used to escape back into the water. The salmon added that the only living thing that could know about this night was the old crow itself, so it could not have been the eagle's fledgling that told him the story. The eagle returned to her nest in a rage to find it empty and the Old Crow gone.

The eagle is mentioned many times in early Irish literature, usually in association with warriors and kings.[8] In the saga *The Cattle Raid of Cooley* one of the men of Ulster is described as 'The awe-inspiring eagle. He is the strong spear. He is the goring beast.' In one story concerning the warrior band the Fianna, a hero called Labhrán turned himself into an eagle in order to fly swiftly across the sea to another country to urgently obtain a magical shield and sword. Despite being weak to the point of death, he successfully brought back the arms in time for the Fianna to use them in a major battle. In another tale, a queen lamenting her husband's death states that she knew harm had come to him, as she had seen an eagle flying every evening for his fort. The warrior Oisín, speaking about his time with the Fianna in the beauty spot of Beann Ghualann, says: 'Listening to the chatter of your eagles / caused our spirits to rise.' A poem about the beauty of nature in the time of the Fianna states that dear to them was 'the scream of the eagle on the edge of the wood'. A poem about winter states 'the eagle of brown Glen Rye gets affliction from the bitter wind; great is its misery and its suffering, the ice will get into its beak.'

The eagle also appears several times associated with Irish poets or seers.[9] For example, the legendary seer Fionntan Mac Bóchna was said to have lived for thousands of years, giving him detailed knowledge of past events and Ireland's lore. He achieved this feat by transforming himself into a one-eyed salmon, an eagle and a falcon before eventually returning to his own shape. Similarly, another legendary seer called Tuan Mac Cairill was said to have owed his long life to his various transformations. Originally the nephew of Parthalán, the first settler in Ireland after the Biblical Flood, he survived by transforming himself in turn into a stag, boar, eagle and salmon. Eventually as a salmon he was eaten by Caireall's wife, who gave birth to him, and so he resumed a human form. Similarly, the eagle appears in British stories as a bird of prophecy. In Geoffrey of Monmouth's *The History of the Kings of Britain*, Loch Lomond in Scotland is described as having sixty islands in it, with sixty crags, upon each of which is an eagle's nest. The eagles would flock together each year and prophesy any important event that was about to occur in the kingdom. They did this by emitting at the same time a shrill, high-pitched scream. The same work also described how, when the palace of Shaftesbury was being built by the British King Hudibras, an eagle had spoken and made prophecies, which were collected into a book called *The Auguries of the Eagle*.

The eagle appears in some early Welsh legends and poetry.[10] In the tale *Math son of Mathonwy*, Lleu Skilful Hand was turned into an eagle when he was struck by a spear by his rival Goronwy, who had conspired with Lleu's wife Blodeuedd to kill him. Concerned for Lleu's fate, his uncle Gwydyon went searching for him, and found a badly injured eagle sitting in the top of an oak tree. Convinced it was Lleu, Gwydyon sang to the eagle and it consented to fly down and sit in his lap. Gwydyon was then able to use his own magic to return Lleu to his human form. When Lleu had recovered from his injuries some time later he sought revenge. Blodeuedd was turned into an owl for her adultery and Goronwy was killed with a spear thrown by Lleu himself. The name Lleu means 'brightness' and he may have a celestial or solar aspect, while his association with the eagle and the oak link him closely with the symbolism of the sky god Jupiter. A Welsh triad called *The Three Powerful Swineherds of Britain* describes a supernatural sow Henwen (Old White) giving birth to some very curious offspring, including a wolf-cub, an eagle, a bee, a kitten and a grain of wheat. In the Welsh myth *How Culhwch won Olwen* the hero Culhwch encountered the Eagle of Gwernabwy, the oldest animal in the world, and the one that had travelled the most. A Welsh medieval poem features a dialogue between King Arthur and an eagle, formerly Eliwlat, his own nephew, who gives him advice on Christian beliefs. A ninth-century elegy on the death of King Cynddylan portrays the eagle as a bloodthirsty creature, feasting on the flesh of men:

> The eagle of Eli, loud is his scream tonight;
> he swallowed gory drink,
> the heart's blood of Cynddylan the fair...

> The eagle of Penngwern, grey crested, uplifted is his cry,
> greedy for the flesh of Cynddylan.

> The eagle of Penngwern, grey-crested, uplifted is his claw,
> greedy for the flesh I love.

The reference to the eagle's grey crest suggests the white-tailed eagle was the species in mind.

The eagle was associated with the Roman sky god Jupiter or Jove, as its majestic size and noble bearing made it an appropriate emblem of the sky god.[11] In Roman-Celtic culture the symbolism of Jupiter was merged with the Celtic sun god, and so eagles began to appear in Celtic imagery of the sun god alongside the usual solar wheel in locations such as Alesia in Burgundy, Alzey in Germany and Willinghan Fen in Cambridgeshire. The eagle also appears on other Celtic objects.[12] For example, a gold neck ornament from Besseringen in Germany is decorated with a pair of wedge-tailed eagles, while a pair of eagles also appears on the famous Gundestrup cauldron from Denmark. Some coins from Armorica (modern Brittany) depict a giant wolf about to swallow the sun and moon, while beneath his paws are an eagle and a snake. The coins may depict a struggle between the forces of earth and sky. Two bucket mounts combine the eagle and bull in their imagery. One from Thealby in Lincolnshire shows a bull's head surmounted by an eagle, while in an example from the River Ribble in Lancashire, the heads of a bull, an eagle and a man are combined. Bulls were companions of the sky god along with eagles, so the imagery is probably an intensification of the theme of the sky god.

The eagle also appears several times in Norse myth.[13] An eagle sat at the top of the highest branch of the world tree Yggdrasil, with a hawk on its brow; and another eagle called Hraesvelg, the Corpse Eater, was said to sit at end of the world. When Hraesvelg flapped his wings, he caused the wind to move over the world of men. An eagle was said to hover over Gladsheim, the hall of the god Odin. In one Norse myth, Odin stole the Mead of Poetry from the giant Suttung by swallowing it all down in three huge gulps. Then he took the form of an eagle and flew back to Asgard, hotly pursued by Suttung, also in the form of an eagle. When he reached Asgard, so closely was he followed by the giant that Odin was forced to spit all the mead into crocks the other gods had assembled for him. A small portion of the mead spilled outside the walls of Asgard into the mortal world, and the gods decided to let it be the portion for human poets. In another myth, a giant in the disguise of an eagle hid in an oak tree, and was able to trick the god Loki into bringing him the goddess Idun, whose apples kept the gods young. When the other gods found out, they were furious with Loki, and he was forced to don the falcon skin of the goddess Freya to fly to the giant's house to take Idun back. He succeeded in rescuing Idun by turning her into a nut, and carrying her off. However, the giant in his eagle form pursued Loki and nearly caught him, but the other gods were ready, and lit a fire of shavings that leapt up and burnt the eagle's wings as it approached Asgard. It is worth noting the link made between the eagle and both the oak tree and fire.

As stated above, the eagle was sacred to the chief of the gods, Jupiter or Zeus.[14] In one Greek myth, Zeus punished the Titan

Skylark – Fuiseog
Alauda arvensis

Swallow – Fáinleog
Hirundo rustica

Cuckoo – Cuach
Cuculus canorus

Collared Dove – Fearán Baicdhubh
Streptopelia decaocto

Blackbird – Lon Dubh
Turdus merula

Golden Eagle – Iolar Fíréan
Aquila chrysaetos

Sparrowhawk – Spioróg
Accipiter nisus

Curlew – Crotach
Numenius arquata

Prometheus for giving fire to mankind by chaining him to a rock, and having an eagle eat his liver every day. As Prometheus was immortal, his liver would grow back each night so that the eagle was able to feast again each day. This lasted for twelve generations until Heracles freed Prometheus by shooting the eagle with an arrow. Various beliefs were also held about the eagle in ancient Greece and Rome.[15] One such belief was that the eye of the eagle was so strong that she could gaze upon the sun without being dazzled, and she would compel her young to stand the same test when they were fledglings, to prove whether they were degenerate or not. Another Classical legend held that when the eagle felt old, it placed itself in a particular way to the sun so that it set its wings on fire. When its old feathers were consumed, it then plunged into the sea, or into a fountain, from which it arose with new life and strength. But if the eagle left it too late to 'take the plunge' it would be too weak and drown. The Roman writer Pliny stated that a stone taken from the nest of an eagle had many medicinal properties, and was proof against fire, but only after it has been immediately taken from the nest. It was also later believed that an eagle's stone had the power to help women who were having a difficult birth, to make the birth swift and easy. Pliny also stated that there was a traditional antipathy between the eagle and the wren, on account of the wren having usurped from it the title of the king of the birds (see Wren).

The eagle surmounted the standards of Roman legions, and so became a symbol of the power of Rome.[16] Naturally, this also made the eagle the symbol of the Roman emperor, and during the ceremony to deify a dead emperor, a caged eagle would be released to symbolise the emperor's soul ascending to heaven. The emperor Constantine the Great later introduced the double-headed eagle ensign to symbolise the twin sovereignty of Church and state in the Byzantine Empire. This in turn lead to later European rulers adopting the eagle as an emblem to claim legitimacy as the heirs of the Roman Empire. For example, the emperor Charlemagne adopted the eagle as his emblem; later on, the Prussians and other German kingdoms retained on their shields the semblance of a Roman eagle. The Russian czars also used the eagle in the same way, and in fact the name 'czar' (or tsar) is itself a version of 'caesar'.

NOTABLE FACTS

Both species of eagle became extinct in Ireland around the beginning of the twentieth century, due to widespread persecution at the hands of farmers, gamekeepers, egg collectors and trophy hunters.[17] The white-tailed eagle was extinct by 1900, the last breeding pair being recorded in 1898. The golden eagle persisted longest in remote parts of Donegal and Mayo, but by the mid-nineteenth century it was reported to have long deserted the famous Eagle's Nest in Killarney. The last breeding pair of golden eagles was recorded in County Mayo in 1912. Golden eagles will hunt a variety of birds and animals, and are indeed big enough to take small lambs, but despite their notoriety in this regard, such episodes are rare.[18] Also the vast majority of those lambs would be already dead or sickly, and the impact upon numbers is marginal. White-tailed or sea eagles prefer fish, but will also take birds and small animals. They will eat carrion, including fish, birds, cetaceans and seals and, like the golden eagle, will also eat lambs with the same limited impact. As has been seen in some of the legends mentioned above, eagles were also happy to feed upon human carrion if the opportunity arose, but thankfully this is no longer really a concern in modern Europe!

Efforts are under way to re-establish both the golden and the white-tailed eagle in Ireland by the Golden Eagle Trust.[19] The golden eagle reintroduction began in 2001 with the release of Scottish birds in Glenveagh National Park in Donegal. As of 2013, there were two active breeding nests of golden eagles in Donegal and several other sites occupied by pairs or single birds. The white-tailed eagle re-introduction began in Killarney National Park, with the release of 100 young Norwegian birds between 2007 and 2011, and as of 2014, eagles are nesting in Counties Kerry, (west) Cork, Clare and Galway. Despite setbacks due to natural deaths of young birds, bad weather and deliberate poisoning by a hostile minority, the programmes are gradually succeeding.

Hawk — Seabhac — *Falconiformes*

The skill of the hawk or falcon in its mastery of the air and ability to swoop and strike its prey made it the basis of the sport of falconry and a symbol of the noble skills of the knight. Its ruthlessness and efficiency in hunting down and killing its victims also made it a symbol of strength and war.

Sparrowhawk – Spióróg – *Accipiter nisus*

Peregrine Falcon – Fabhcún gorm – *Falco peregrinus*

Kestrel – Pocaire gaoithe – *Falco tinnunculus*

Merlin – Meirliún – *Falco columbarius*

Buzzard – Clamhán – *Buteo buteo*

Hen Harrier – Cromán na gcearc – *Circus cyaneus*

FOLK BELIEFS AND CUSTOMS

The hawk or falcon (folklore makes no distinction) features in some Irish folktales.[1] For example, a hawk appears in a story about Gearóid Iarla, the famous Third Earl of Desmond of the Fitzgerald family. The Earl was said to be an expert in magic and all the black arts. His wife was curious about this, and persisted in asking him to use his powers to take any form he pleased. In the end, despite his reluctance he agreed, but warned her that if she showed any fear he would not be able to return to his human form. So one summer evening he used his powers to turn into a goldfinch and began flying about the room. He perched on his wife's shoulder and entertained her by whistling a lovely tune. Then he flew out into the garden, but instantly returned with a hawk pursuing him. His wife screamed in fright, but the hawk dashed itself against a table and was killed. However, when she turned to look for her husband, the Earl was gone, and did not return again in either bird or human form.

Another Irish folktale tells of how a hawk was outwitted by a hooded crow. According to the tale, a hawk stayed with a crow for a year to learn all its tricks, and things went very well. The hawk learnt many tricks, and at the end of the year said that it was ready to go. However, the crow persuaded him to wait another year, because there was one more trick to learn which was better than the rest. So the hawk stayed, but at the end of the year he said that he had learned nothing more than what he had previously known. The hooded crow then finally told him about the trick: 'When you are out with another bird, fly out in front of it, turn around beneath it with your belly facing up, and attack the other bird from below'.

Then the two birds flew out together, and before the hawk realised what was happening, the crow played the very same trick and killed him.

The hawk or falcon appears in some Irish place names.[2] For example, a County Wexford townland called Shouks derives its name from *Cnocán Seabhac* (hill of the hawk), while Hawkswood is a townland in County Offaly. On the Iveragh Peninsula in County Kerry is *Cuas na Seabhac* (the hawk's cave); while in County Galway is found Srashouke (*Sraith seabhac* – the river-meadow of the hawk).

Some superstitions surrounded hawks and falcons in the Highlands of Scotland.[3] On New Year's the Hogmanay rhymers would sing the following verse to those who had been inhospitable: 'The curse of God and Hogmanay upon you / and the scath of the plaintive buzzard / of the hen harrier, of the raven, of the eagle / and the scath of the sneaking fox.' ('Scath' or 'scathe' means an injury or harm). A traditional charm was also said on St Brigid's Day to ask for the saint's protection of the livestock (see Eagle). Similarly on the quarter days of Bridget's Day, May Day, Lammas, and Halloween, special cakes called bannocks were eaten, and a piece thrown over each shoulder alternatively as a gift to the wolf, fox, eagle, raven, marten and harrier to spare livestock.

MYTHS AND LEGENDS
Hawks or falcons appear in many Irish myths and stories, usually only called *seabhac* or 'hawk', so generally it is not possible to tell what species of hawk is being referred to. In some tales the hawk or falcon appears connected to Irish saints.[4] In the life of St Finian of Clonard, the hawk fulfils a curse made by the saint. In the tale Finian asked Bresal, prince of Leinster, for a field to build his church, but Bresal refused him. Finian cursed him, saying: 'Before this hour has come tomorrow, the hand that was stretched forth to refuse me shall be in a hawk's talons and laid before me.' The following morning Bresal marched out to defend his lands against a raid by the men of Ossory and was slain. A hawk then came and took his hand and laid it down in front of Finian. Seeing that the curse had come to pass, Bresal's father Muiredach gave Finian the land he needed for his church. The motif of a hawk taking up the

severed hand of a warrior also appears in the poem about the Hawk of Achill. This motif may have developed out of falconry, where the hawk grasps the outstretched hand or arm of the falconer.

A falcon appears as a friend to St Brigid in a tale told by Gerald of Wales. In his work *The History and Topography of Ireland*, he tells of a falcon that lived on the top of a church in Kildare from the time of St Brigid onwards. The falcon was called 'Brigid's bird' by all the townspeople, and was respected by them. It would do their bidding, and that of the soldiers of the castle, exactly as if it had been tamed and trained in hunting, and would force ducks and other birds onto the ground. A remarkable feature of the bird is that it would never mate in the precincts of the church, but would respect its sanctity by flying off to the mountains near Glendalough each year to find a mate. According to Gerald, the bird lived for many generations until the time of King John, when its trusting nature towards humans led to it being killed by a countryman with a stick as it was on the ground with its prey.

Given their skill and speed as ruthless hunters, it is not surprising that hawks are frequently compared to warriors and heroes in various tales.[5] For example, the warrior Oisín, as an old man lamenting the end of his days of hunting and fighting with the Fianna, described his leader Fionn as a 'clean hawk of the air'. In the tale *Deirdre and the Sons of Uisneach*, when Deirdre lamented the death of the three sons, she described them as 'the three darlings of the women of Britain, three hawks of Slieve Cuilenn'; and in the tale *The Wedding of Maine Morgor* the warrior Donall is described as a 'hawk of valour'. In the legend *The Cattle Raid of Cooley* the warrior Cúchulainn is described as having seven fingers on each hand, with the grasp of a hawk's claws. In some legends the warriors literally become hawks. In the tale *The Sons of Tuireann*, the three sons are turned into hawks in order to fly swiftly and skilfully into a garden and capture some golden apples that have magical powers of healing. Although the gardens are well guarded, and they are attacked by spears and darts, they are able to dodge them to achieve their objective. However, the king who owns the gardens sends three of his daughters in the form of ospreys to pursue the brothers, who only escape them by changing into swans.

In one Irish tale the childhood feat of a warrior called Fiachna son of Baeton involves a hawk. Fiachna was hated by his father Baeton for his dour nature and likeness to his mother, and when he was still a child Baeton tried to kill him. What happened was that one day Fiachna came to his father's royal dwelling with a piece of meat on a spit for some of the other boys. Seeing him approach, his father unleashed a savage hound, and at that exact moment a hawk swooped down to snatch the meat. Fiachna deftly met the challenge of both hound and hawk. He thrust the spit, meat and all, down the hound's throat to the heart; and with his other hand he grasped the hawk and held it tight. This act of skill and bravery was the first sign that Fiachna would go on to become a great warrior.

Although the evidence points to the sport of falconry or hawking being practised in Ireland only after the Norman invasion, it is mentioned in some Irish tales.[6] In the tale *Deirdre and the Sons of Uisneach*, when Deirdre laments their death, she says: 'their three hounds, their three hawks, will be from this time without huntsmen.' Similarly, when Gráinne laments the death of her lover Diarmuid, she says: 'I am looking at the hawk and the hound my secret love used to be hunting with, she that loved the three [herself], let her be put in the grave with Diarmuid.' One Irish story concerns the dangers of keeping a hawk for hunting. According to the tale, the nobleman Mossad son of Maen found a hawk on Magh Eoin and decided to keep it for hunting. He fed it and nourished it, till it used to eat herds of horses and droves of cattle and even humans by twos and threes. When at last it could find nothing else to devour, it turned against its fosterer Mossad and ate him too! The story is probably a humorous comment on the voracious appetites of hawks kept for hunting.

The evidence is that falconry was introduced to Britain in the ninth century, so it naturally appears in some Welsh stories also.[7] In the Welsh tale *How Culhwch won Olwen*, the maiden Olwen is praised for her beauty. She is praised for her hair yellower than broom, and her skin whiter than sea-foam, and 'neither the eye of a mewed hawk, nor the eye of a thrice-mewed falcon was fairer than hers'. ('Mewed' means 'moulted' in this context.) The Welsh tale *Gereint and Enid* describes the procedure for a tournament in which a kestrel is the prize: 'They place in the meadow two forked sticks, and across the sticks a silver rod and on the rod a kestrel, and there is a tournament for the kestrel.' Whoever wins the kestrel three years in a row is given it to keep and is known as the Knight of the Kestrel.

While the general word *seabhac* or 'hawk' is usually used in Irish stories, sometimes the behaviour described can give a clue to which species is meant. For example, the sparrowhawk is known for its tactic of flying low and hidden, and emerging suddenly to ambush its prey, sometimes pouncing on flocks of small birds. Some of the references in various stories appear to describe this behaviour, suggesting that the sparrowhawk is the species being referred to.[8] In the tale *The Cattle Raid of Cooley* the warrior Cúchulainn warned his rival Fergus to stand aside or he would 'swoop on you as a hawk swoops on little birds'. In the same tale Cúchulainn was goaded that his rival Ferdia 'darts on you as the hawk darts on little birds'. Similarly, in the tale *The Pursuit of Gruaidhe Griansholus*, Laoi, Cúchulainn's attendant, attacked warriors 'as a hawk attacks little birds', so that he made a hacking slaughter, and scattered them all into bits. In another story, when Diarmuid of the Fianna fought his enemies 'he went through them and over them like a hawk would go through little birds, or a wild dog through a flock of sheep, killing all before him.' In one folk tale the hero went through his enemies 'as a hawk through a flock of small birds on a March day'; while in another tale Diarmuid of the Fianna went through them like 'a hawk through a flock of starlings on a chilly March morning.'

Another species suggested is the peregrine falcon, also known in Irish as the *seabhac seilge* or 'hunting hawk', which is known for hunting from cliffs, and there are several references in stories to hawks on a cliff.[9] For example, the warrior Diarmuid of the Fianna is described as wrestling with another warrior 'like two daring hawks on the edge of a cliff'. In the tale *The Cattle Raid of Cooley* the warrior Cúchulainn is described as driving his chariot 'like a hawk sweeping from a cliff on a day of hard wind'. In a folk tale *Blaiman, Son of Apple*, the hero is given help by the 'Hawk of Cold Cliff' who catches a duck that had flown out over the sea carrying an enchanted egg.

The peregrine falcon is also mentioned in the most famous example of poetic seership, that of the poet Amairgen, who according to legend became the first person of the Irish race to set foot in Ireland. As he did so he recited a famous and extraordinary poem in which he proclaimed, through the power of his poetry, the ability to take on different natural forms and exercise various powers. In the poem Amairgen spoke of being a stag, hawk, boar and salmon, and different elements of nature such as wind and water. His form as a hawk is described as *seabhac ar aill* – 'a hawk on a cliff', which implies a peregrine falcon.

The hawk or falcon also appears associated with the legendary seer Fionntan Mac Bóchna.[10] He was said to have lived for thousands of years, giving him detailed knowledge of past events and Ireland's lore. He achieved this feat by transforming himself into a one-eyed salmon, an eagle and a falcon before returning to his own shape. Furthermore, a famous ninth-century poem recounts Fionntan's conversation with the Hawk of Achill (Achill, County Mayo), which tells him that it is also very old, and has witnessed all the major events of the country's history. The Hawk emerges as a bloodthirsty and ruthless creature, witnessing many battles and ruthlessly feasting on the flesh of fallen warriors, including Fionntan's sons. The Hawk recounts the various adventures of its life with a *Grand Guignol* relish, for example telling how it was responsible for plucking out one of Fionntan's eyes when he was a salmon, and how it took the hand of Nuadu, the king of the Tuatha Dé Danann, when it was severed at the first Battle of Maigh Tuireadh. The Hawk continued in its blood-thirsty way until it attempted to pluck out Cúchulainn's eye as the hero was dying, strapped to a pillar. This time the Hawk had met its match, as Cúchulainn pierced it with a javelin and it was forced to flee with a grievous injury that would ultimately cause its death. Although the bird is clearly described as a hawk, its taste for carrion on the battlefield gives it some of the characteristics of the raven or crow, which is probably due to 'poetic licence'. The poem is too long to translate in full here, but parts of it have been translated below by the author.

The poem begins with Fionntan and the Hawk greeting each other, and Fionntan asking the Hawk why it stayed in Achill. The Hawk replies by praising Achill's beauty and rich hunting grounds.

Fionntan then tells of his great age and how the loss of his sons caused him such grief that the Lord put him into the shape of a salmon. He recounts all the rivers and estuaries he stayed in, until his arrival in Assaroe in Donegal, where he leapt out of the water and landed back on ice as it was so cold.

Fionntan
A bird of prey from Achill cold
Came over the harbour of Assaroe
No need to hide it, no reason why
He stole away one of my eyes.

Blind One of Assaroe was my name
From that night on, and bitter the fame.
With only one eye to see the way
No wonder I am old and grey.

Hawk
It was I who swallowed your eye
O Fionntan of the manner kind.
I am the Hawk grey and strong
I live in the heart of Achill alone.

Fionntan
If you are the one who wrongly
Left me so blind and lonely
As is the just and legal way
Compensate me for my eye.

Hawk
A small fine I'd give to you
O Fionntan Mac Bóchna true
That one eye in your ancient head
Was just a morsel when I fed.

Fionntan then rebukes the Hawk for its harshness and then tells of how he later took on the forms of an eagle and a hawk before taking the shape of a man once more. He goes on to recount the many kings he has seen in his long life and how he acted as a judge for them, staying youthful and vigorous until the death of his son Illain caused him to age. The Hawk in reply recounts its knowledge of the First Battle of Maigh Tuireadh between the Tuatha Dé Danann and the Fir Bolg, and how it feasted on the flesh of Fionntan's sons after they had fallen in the battle. There follow two verses where the hawk describes the battle field and those who fell there. The Hawk then tells of how it took away with it the arm of Nuadu, king of the Tuatha Dé Danann after it had been severed in the battle.

> Among the slaughter on every side
> In one corner a hand I spied
> A red gold ring, a scarlet band
> On every finger of the hand.
>
> Fit for a hero its mighty size
> Alas for him of it deprived.
> Noble its shape, its length and span
> Its ruddy nails, so fine and grand.
>
> A sleeve of glossy satin bold
> And inside it a sleeve of gold.
> With this the arm was finely dressed
> Its whole length up onto the breast.
>
> I lifted it, no little feat
> The hand, heavy with blood and meat.
> I carried it with me a long way
> To Drum Ibar of the many bays.
>
> The hand of Nuadu I did bring
> The Tuatha Dé Danann's great high king.
> In my bird's eyrie for seven years
> O Fionntan, so my story hear.

The Hawk then explains how Nuadu was rescued from the battlefield and fitted with a silver arm, but was nevertheless killed at the Second Battle of Maigh Tuireadh, and how the god Lugh achieved victory for the Tuatha Dé Danann against the Fomorians by retaliating with tremendous slaughter. Fionntan angrily replies that it is bitter to hear him talk of gnawing on the bones of his family, and it would be fitting for his cruel deeds if the Hawk's blood flowed onto the ground to nourish it. Undaunted, the Hawk asks Fionntan to recount more of his deeds and knowledge of the Milesians. Having made his protest, Fionntan now seems happy to comply and tells of the coming of the Milesians to Ireland and how they defeated the Tuatha Dé Danann to claim Ireland for their own. He also tells of the coming to Ireland of a magical character called Tréfuilngidh who carried a magical branch of nuts, apples and sloes with various wonderful properties. The Hawk then replies with its own adventures, feasting on the flesh of many warriors until Cúchulainn dealt it a terrible blow.

The Hawk relates how it paused before Cúchulainn as he was dying, strapped to a stone pillar.

> I paused before the champion great
> A dark expression on his face.
> To pluck his eyes, not make him die
> I lowered my head amid his cries
>
> He felt my wings upon his face
> And with his shaking hand he raised
> His warrior javelin sure and just
> To pierce my flesh with a single thrust.
>
> I flew up bloodily to flee
> To Inishkea over the tossing sea.
> I wrenched from me, a cruel task
> A hard and rigid javelin shaft.
>
> The head of it stayed within my flesh
> Tormenting my heart whene'er it pressed.
> Since that day I am not whole
> I tell the truth, you who are old.

Despite its wound, the Hawk went on to kill various birds, including cranes, eagles and blackbirds, and was able to carry off deer and pigs in its talons. After many years it grew old and weary, however, and retired to the west. In the end it asks Fionntan to seek for it God's pardon as tomorrow its life will end. The poem ends on a tone of forgiveness, with Fionntan telling the Hawk not to worry as it will soon be in heaven, and that he, Fionntan, who is also ancient, will soon be joining it.

The hawk or falcon appears in some Norse myths.[11] An eagle with a hawk on its brow sat at the top of the highest branch of the world tree Yggdrasil, while the goddess Freya had a falcon skin that the trickster god Loki borrowed on several occasions to travel in speed and in disguise. For example, he used the falcon skin to fly to the abode of the giants to rescue the goddess Idun, and bring her safely back to Asgard. Loki also used the skin to fly in falcon form to the land of the giants to search for Thor's hammer, which had been stolen. In Classical myth the hawk was sacred to the Greek god Hermes, messenger to the gods; and to Apollo the god of the sun. The enchantress who changed Ulysses' men into swine was called Circe which means 'hawk'. The hawk is also famously associated with the Egyptian gods Ra, the god of the sun, and Horus, the sky god.

NOTABLE FACTS

Falconry was known all over the old world, and was first practised in China 4,000 years ago.[12] It was known in Japan, India, Persia, Arabia and Syria from at least 600 BC. The Classical writers Pliny, Aristotle and Martial all state that falconry was practised in Europe in their day. There is also evidence that the Continental Celts of the Iron Age engaged in falconry. Bronze brooches dating from the fourth century BC found at the hillfort of Durnberg in Austria depict birds of prey wearing collars. It appears that hawking was only introduced into Britain in the ninth century from France, and there is no clear evidence of hawking or falconry in Ireland before the Anglo-Norman invasion.[13] On the contrary, the Early Irish Brehon Laws only mention hawks as vermin, stating that anyone is entitled to trap hawks on another's land without permission. Heroes of the earlier Irish eighth- and ninth-century sagas are depicted with horses and hounds, but not hawks, which only start to appear in post-Norman literature. For example, in the twelfth-century *Life of Saint Colmán* there is a reference to two hunting hawks belonging to a king.

For falconers the favourite bird was the peregrine falcon, on account of its relative docility and ease of capture.[14] The female was called the falcon and usually flown at herons and rooks on account of her greater size. The male was called the tiercel and was more frequently flown at partridges and magpies. The fourteenth-century Red Book of Ormond also specifies the sparrowhawk, goshawk and osprey as birds used in hawking in Ireland. The male sparrowhawk was called the musket and was traditionally the hawk kept by priests. The word musket was later used for a crossbow bolt and later still for the new invention of the handgun. Kestrels were the lowliest of falcons, used only by knaves or servants. Nevertheless they had a use, as they were traditionally kept near dovecotes to scare sparrowhawks away, because they would not bother the doves themselves. It was even said that pigeons would seek out a kestrel for protection if a sparrowhawk was about. The merlin was considered a lady's falcon on account of its small size, and was the favourite hunter of monarchs such as Mary Queen of Scots and Catherine the Great.

All the indications are then that falconry arrived in Ireland with the Anglo-Normans, as a prestigious sport among the aristocracy.[15] An example of this is found in an incident in early fourteenth-century Dublin. While being bathed in a stream near College Green, the falcon of the Chief Justice of Ireland was frightened by an eagle, and flew away. It flew to Castleknock, where it was detained by the sixth Baron, despite its loss being solemnly proclaimed, and the considerable sum of twenty shillings being offered for its recovery. Learning of this, the Chief Justice took the Baron of Castleknock to court, looking for damages of £20. However, the Baron appeared at the trial and undertook to return the falcon. This proved to be a wise course of action, as when it was delivered to the Chief Justice he decided to drop the case. As well as demonstrating the value of falcons, the incident is noteworthy for the casual aside that eagles frequented College Green in Dublin. The laws of Henry IV dating from 1481 show that falconry was still important in Ireland a century later. They state: 'whatsoever merchant shall carry any hawk out of Ireland shall pay for every goshawk 13s 4d; for a tiercel 6s 8d; for a falcon 10s; and the poundage upon the same pain. And the person that bringeth any such hawk or hawks to the king shall have a reasonable reward, or else the same hawk or hawks for his trouble.' Similarly, in Britain, in the reign of James I, Sir Thomas Mason is said to have spent £1,000 in obtaining two falcons, a fortune in those days. Most European falconers in recent centuries came from the Dutch village of Falconswaerd or Vaalkenswaard in North Brabant. In the seventeenth century in Ireland the nobility used sparrowhawks to hunt blackbirds, and there are records of this taking place in the Phoenix Park in Dublin.

However, from the seventeenth century onwards the attitude of the nobility towards birds of prey changed dramatically. As fashions changed and the sport of hunting game with guns began to grow, raptors were increasingly seen as vermin, and a centuries-long persecution at the hands of gamekeepers began. Just as the ruthless campaign of extermination began to ease in the mid-twentieth century, birds of prey were hit by another threat, as the build-up of pesticides like DDT in their systems poisoned them and caused them to lay eggs with shells that were too thin to incubate properly. Numbers plummeted, until the problem was understood and the harmful pesticides were withdrawn. Numbers of birds of prey have substantially recovered since, but loss of habitat and continuing persecution from a small minority of landowners mean the status of most raptors from a conservation point of view is still a cause for concern.

Curlew — Crotach — *Numenius arquata*

The curlew was famous for its whistling and screeching calls, which were believed to foretell the arrival of rain or stormy weather. It was also noted for its shy and wary nature, and its ability to hide its nest from approaching enemies.

FOLK BELIEFS AND CUSTOMS

In Ireland there was a long-established belief that the curlew was said to whistle for rain.[1] For example, writing in 1625, O'Sullivan Beare stated that: 'it foretells rain by a frequent, plaintive cry.' Sometimes it was thought that only certain calls of the curlew had this ability. For example, it was thought by some that a sign of approaching rain was when the curlew produced a double whistle. In County Donegal a sure sign of rain was hearing the curlew at night; and it was also said that when the farmer heard the curlew screeching he knew that rain was on the way. In County Mayo it was also thought that when curlews screeched loudly it was a sign of broken weather to come, and that when the curlew cried and flew towards the hills, stormy weather was on the way. Another Irish belief was that a flock of curlews, rising in the east and flying to the west, was a sign that frosty weather was at hand.[2]

The curlew is a famously wary bird, flying away at the approach of people, and this naturally led to the belief that it had a great ability to hide its nest.[3] Various Irish folk tales tell of how Jesus gave the curlew this gift. According to one story, Our Lord went into a cave to rest and fell asleep. After some time the enemies of Jesus came looking for him. When they were near the cave the curlew began to scream, and woke Our Lord who was able to escape. In gratitude Jesus blessed the curlew and gave it the instinct to build its nest in such a way that no man could find it. Another story has it that Christ was escaping from his enemies by walking along a strand. However, Jesus was leaving footprints behind him, and his pursuers were hot on his trail, following the footprints in the sand. The curlew then came and walked behind Christ, destroying the trace of his footprints and allowing him to escape. In thankfulness the Saviour gave the curlew the gift that no one would ever be able to find its nest. Another version of the story states that when Our Lord was fleeing from his enemies, a great tiredness came upon him and he lay down on the mountainside. The curlews were beside him and when they saw his enemies approaching they began to whistle. Our Lord was alerted and so was able to escape in time. In thankfulness, he gave the curlew the gift that no enemy would ever be able to approach it unawares.

A similar version of the tale is found in the Isle of Man. According to the Manx version, when St Patrick first visited the Isle of Man he heard the shrill cry of the curlew warning that a kid goat had fallen down the rocks. He blessed them both and, from that day, no man was ever to find a curlew's nest, or see a goat giving birth. In Scotland too the curlew was considered famously wary, and only a good hunter was able to kill it.[4] In Scotland the curlew was known as a 'whaop' or 'whaup', which was also the name of a goblin with a long beak supposed to go about under the eaves of the houses after nightfall. In the Shetland Islands the idea of eating such an uncanny bird was regarded with horror. In some parts of England, the wailing cry of the curlew while on the wing in the dark nights of winter was said to resemble the moans of wandering spirits, and was believed to be a death warning called the 'Cry of the Seven Whistlers'.[5] Also, because their cry was said to be like the yelping of hounds they were also known in England as 'Gabriel's Hounds', the hounds of a ghostly huntsman travelling through the air at night.

NOTABLE FACTS

The curlew was traditionally regarded in Britain and Ireland as an excellent bird for the table when young.[6] Indeed, many were prepared to pay good money for the curlew, as an old Suffolk rhyme declared: 'A curlew, be she white, be she black / she carries twelve pence upon her back.' In Dublin markets a similar nineteenth-century rhyme about the curlew went: 'Be she white or be she black / she carries tenpence on her back.' The curlew can produce at night a long-drawn-out whistle, so intense and low that coastguards have mistaken it for an alarm call of a shipwreck. For example, the coastguard in the Martello Tower in Malahide, County Dublin, reported that he had been started from his bed regularly by the cry.[7] Yet the sound of the curlew could also evoke feelings of joy.[8] An eleventh-century English poem declares that: 'I took my gladness from the cry of the gannet / and the sound of the curlew instead of the laughter of men'; while the poet Robert Burns wrote that he never 'heard the loud solitary whistle of curlew on a summer noon . . . without feeling an elevation of soul.' The curlew has a very soft pliable bill that it can manipulate under the mud to grasp its prey, in a similar fashion to an elephant's trunk. It shares this ability, called 'rhynchokinesis', with the woodcock and some other waders.[9]

SIMILAR BIRDS

> Snipe – Naoscach – *Gallinago gallinago*
>
> Woodcock – Creabhar – *Scolopax rusticola*

The snipe is noted for making a unique drumming or bleating noise during the breeding season of March to mid-June, produced by the rapid vibration of the outer tail feathers during a steep downward dive.[10] This is the source of many local names, such as 'heatherbleat', 'airy goat', and in Irish *gabhairín reo* ('little goat of the frost'). Alongside this unique noise, the snipe would call out a distinctive *chip-er, chip-er* note. In west Cork it was said that in May the snipe were saying: '*Megigigé, Gobhairín a 'Reótha / glanaidh na meadaracha / Tá na ba 'breith'* (Megigigé / the heatherbleat / clean out the churns / the cows have given birth). The local children would call this out to the snipe flying above, in the belief that it could understand them. The snipe is also a bird that lives in marshlands and damp pastures, which explains why the ninth-century Irish work *Cormac's Glossary* gives the origin of the Irish name for snipe as *naoscach as én uisce* – 'water bird.'[11] Some other superstitions surrounded the snipe.[12] In Scotland it was thought that to hear the kid-like cry of the snipe while bent over would bring bad luck for the year, and that to hear the snipe on a Tuesday would bring bad luck. It was also thought to be bad luck in Scotland to raise a snipe before cattle when driving them to pasture. In Germany the snipe was the weather bird, storm bird or rain bird, and its flight was said to betoken an approaching thunderstorm.

In both Britain and Ireland snipe and woodcock were hunted as game.[13] In Britain snipe were such popular birds for shooting that they are the origin of the word 'sniper'. Both snipe and woodcock appear as game birds in early Irish literature. For example, one text mentions that woodcocks were among the birds eaten by the warrior band, the Fianna. Writing in 1625, O'Sullivan Beare stated that the flesh of the woodcock was valued as food in Ireland. Unlike snipe which prefers marshy ground, the woodcock, as its name indicates, is a woodland bird. The woodcock is unusual in its habit of refusing to walk over fallen branches or other obstacles on the forest floor, trying to go around them instead. Hunters exploited this to guide the birds easily into their snares, and so it gained a reputation among them as a foolish or naive bird. In Shakespeare's *Hamlet*, Polonius dismisses the prince's protestations of love for Ophelia as mere 'springes to catch woodcockes'. The Irish hermit Mad Sweeney also mentions this trait of the woodcock in his description of his life in the woods: 'The silly woodcock [*creabhar oscar an-tuisccseach*] does not know / Why before my step it flies.' The woodcock is also known for the extraordinary display flight of the male from mid-February to July known as 'roding'.[14] This involves the male flying a regular circuit over trees or open ground uttering two unusual calls, one a thin '*tsiwicck*' and the other a low frog-like croak. Finally, the 'pin-feather' of the woodcock was highly prized in earlier times.[15] This is the small, pointed plume at the base of the leading primary feather on each wing, which was used for detailed painting work, for example, by watercolour miniaturists.

Corncrake — Traonach — *Crex crex*

The corncrake with its distinctive rasping call was a much-loved feature of the Irish countryside. It was also noted for its shy and wary nature, which meant that it was often heard but rarely seen.

FOLK BELIEFS AND CUSTOMS

In Ireland it was widely believed that the corncrake made its familiar *crek-crek* sound by lying on its back on the ground and rubbing its legs together.[1] In west Cork it was further believed that the corncrake imagined, as it lay on its back, that its legs were keeping the sky and land apart. As it lay there the corncrake was believed to say: *'Tréan le tréun, tréan le tréun / dhá gháigín an éin / A' ciméad an aeir go léir / Uaidh suas, Uaidh suas!'* (Strength to the corncrake, strength to the corncrake / two slender legs of the bird / keeping up all the air / up with them, up with them!). There is a play on words in the verse between *tréan* 'strong' and *tréun* 'corncrake'. This belief also existed in Scotland, where it was said that when uttering its call the corncrake did so on its back, otherwise the heavens would fall.

The other notable feature of the corncrake was that it was a summer visitor, like the cuckoo, that appeared suddenly and disappeared just as quickly in the autumn.[2] This led to a variety of beliefs to explain this phenomenon, such as the notion in Ireland that the corncrake turned into a water hen (or moorhen) during the winter months; or in Scotland that the corncrake spent the winter under the water in lakes. In Scotland it was held that the three birds that appeared and disappeared mysteriously this way were fairy birds: the stonechat, the cuckoo and the corncrake. However, the corncrake was believed in Scotland to be a lucky bird: 'The lark, the corncrake or the grouse / will bring good luck to ilka house.' By contrast, in Ireland it was considered very unlucky to bring a corncrake, alive or dead, into the house.[3] An expression in Irish wishing someone bad luck was *Nár fheice tú an chuach ná an traonach arís'!* (May you never see cuckoo or corncrake again, i.e., may you not live to see another summer.)[4] In Scotland it was said that if the corncrake was heard calling frequently rain would follow; however, it was also said that the first call of the corncrake meant the danger of frost was past.[5]

In France a popular name for the corncrake was *Roi des cailles* or 'King of the quails', out of an old European belief that a corncrake was always chosen by the quails to lead them on their migratory flights.[6] This is a very old belief, as the Classical philosopher Aristotle called the corncrake the 'dam of the coturnices' (mother of the quails). However, it was said that the quails did this, not out of respect for the corncrake, but because they believed that the first bird to arrive on land after an arduous sea crossing would be the most likely to be taken by predators.

Donegal has always been a stronghold of the corncrake, so it is no surprise that it appears in two place names there: Carntreena (*Carn Traonach* – Cairn of the Corncrake) and Largatreany (*Learga an Traonaigh* – Slope of the Corncrake).[7]

MYTHS AND LEGENDS

A saying in early Ireland was that there were three tokens of a cursed site: the nettle, the elderberry and the corncrake.[8] This saying may derive from the corncrake's habit of choosing nettles to nest in, as well as the more usual hay meadow. However, the call of the corncrake also evoked the summer. Fionn Mac Cumhaill of the warrior band the Fianna, mentions the corncrake in an old Irish poem about Maytime: 'the corncrake clacks, a strenuous bard.'[9]

NOTABLE FACTS

Gerald of Wales, writing about Ireland in the twelfth century, stated that 'hoarse and noisy *ratulae* [probably corncrakes] are innumerable'.[10] The corncrake or landrail was prized as a delicacy in Elizabethan England.[11] A Dr Thomas Muffet writing on the subject at the time said that their flesh deserved to be placed next to the partridge. Mrs Beeton in her cookbook recommended it in a dish with four birds roasted on a skewer.

Although the corncrake was once a very common bird throughout Britain and Ireland, its numbers have declined disastrously since the nineteenth century due to modern techniques of agriculture.[12] The corncrake's habit of nesting in the middle of hay meadows meant that the change from hand-cutting with scythes to mechanised mowers did not give the chicks enough time to escape. Especially damaging was the habit of mowers starting at the edge of fields and working their way into the centre, so that the chicks were trapped in the last stand of hay. In addition, the switch to silage meant cutting the grass while it was still green, so that the chicks were even younger. It is estimated that the mortality rate for chicks when cutting silage is 95 per cent. It is no surprise then that the corncrake is critically endangered in Ireland, with only 132 male birds recorded calling in 2003. The situation has not improved since then, and the corncrake lingers on in only a few locations in Ireland, such as the Shannon Callows, and parts of north Donegal and west Mayo. Conservation measures are in place, such as grants to farmers not to cut their pastures early, and hopefully these will ensure that this iconic bird will continue to be heard somewhere in Ireland's meadows.

Crane — Corr Léana — *Grus grus*

The crane, with its long legs, neck and beak, is tall and erect, like a sentry standing to attention. This made it a symbol of watchfulness, vigilance and war. However, the crane was also loved for its beauty and ability to be tamed, even if its stabbing beak made it dangerous for the unwary. In addition, the crane's habit of living in mysterious watery places probably gave it the role in Celtic myth of a guardian of otherworld treasures.

FOLK BELIEFS AND CUSTOMS

A difficulty in writing about the crane in Ireland is that the same word *corr* was used in Irish to describe both it and the heron. In terms of folklore, as the crane has been extinct in Ireland for centuries, it is more likely that the heron is the bird that is meant. However, one aspect where the crane may still have a presence on the Irish landscape is that of place names. Research by Lorcán O'Toole and Ronan O'Flaherty has identified over 1,000 townland names and another 140 place names that include the word *corr* in one form or another.[1] A distribution of the names across Ireland shows a bias towards the north midlands, and areas of poor-draining soils and wetlands, in regions which would have been the favoured habitat for the crane. They argue that this would indicate that at least some of the names refer to the crane. In particular it is argued that the word *corrach*, meaning a marsh and usually anglicised as 'curragh', derives from 'crane-meadow'. One Irish place name definitely involves the crane: the Latin *Life of St Abbán* explains the Irish lake-name *Loch na Corr* as *stagnum gruum*, i.e. 'lake of the cranes'.

However, there are a number of difficulties with the word *corr*, not least of which is that it can have other meanings. In fact, a linguistic analysis by Padraic De Bhaldraithe of the names where *corr* occurs as an element indicate that the majority probably refer to the topographical meaning of the word, namely 'a round or conical hill'. A further complication, of course, is that some of the names may also refer to the heron. On balance, therefore, it would seem that the number of place names that can be ascribed to the crane with any certainty is quite small, and this is an area that will require further research. In any case, the role of place names is not central to proving the existence of the crane in Ireland, as there is other evidence pointing to their presence. It should also be remembered that the number of place names that involve birds such as the goose is also quite small, and this can hardly be taken as evidence that they were not prominent birds in the Irish landscape.

Whatever about the situation in Ireland, the crane is a common occurrence in many English place names, indicating it was once widespread there.[2] The more than 300 English names show a bias towards wetland areas such as Cranforth ('crane's ford') in Lancashire, Cranmere in Shropshire, and Cranborne ('crane's stream') in Dorset.

MYTHS AND LEGENDS

The same word *corr* was used in Irish to describe both the crane and the heron, and as most Irish legends predate the seventeenth century when the crane became extinct in Ireland, it is possible that *corr* could refer to either bird. However, examining the details of the bird's appearance in the stories can often provide clues as to which bird is meant. An example is in the story *Cath Finnthragha* (The Battle of Ventry) where Crédhe, wife of the warrior Cael, was searching for her dead husband on the battlefield.[3] As she searched, she noticed 'a crane of the meadows' (*corr léna*) and her two nestlings trying to keep away a fox. The fox was watching the nestlings, and when the crane tried to cover one to save it, the fox would make a dash for the other. As Crédhe looked at that, she declared: 'It is no wonder that I have such love for my comely sweetheart, when the bird is in that distress about her nestlings.' The significance of this incident is that herons nest in trees where foxes cannot reach them, whereas the crane nests on the ground, where it is more vulnerable to foxes. Furthermore, Crédhe then referred to the crane, saying: 'sweet-voiced is the crane, O sweet-voiced is the crane in the marshes of the Ridge of the Two Strong

Men; it is she who cannot save her nestlings.' It is possible to describe the bugling call of the crane as 'sweet-voiced', but hardly that of the heron.

Another story where the crane appears concerns St Kieran of Saighir in County Offaly.[4] In the story, Kieran's mother Liadain cared for a beautiful fosterling called Bruinnech, who was carried off one day by a king called Díma. Kieran went to the king to demand the maiden's return, but he refused, saying that he would not let her go unless he was awakened the following morning by the voice of a crane (*corrghlas*). As the story is set in winter, Díma thought he was asking the impossible. Therefore, the story only makes sense if the crane was meant rather than the heron, as the crane is normally only a summer visitor. The following morning there was a heavy fall of snow, but the voice of the crane was heard miraculously from every housetop in the precinct. Hearing the cranes calling, the king repented of his actions and returned the fosterling back to Kieran. Seeing Bruinnech approach heavily pregnant, Kieran made the sign of the cross over her, and her pregnancy disappeared.

Another story about the crane concerns St Kieran of Clonmacnoise.[5] According to the story, a mill servant had been taking bread secretly and when Kieran discovered this, he cursed him, saying: 'may a crane take your eye out of your head, and may it be on your cheek when you get home'. Sure enough, as the servant was going along his way, a pet crane picked the eye out of his head and it lay upon his cheek. The master of the mill and the servant prostrated themselves before Kieran, and promised to give him the mill and all its contents if he healed the servant. Kieran put the eye back in and blessed it, and the man was made whole again. Again, although the word *corr* is used, it seems likely that the crane is meant. There is evidence that cranes were kept as pets in Ireland (see below), and in modern times there have been documented reports of handlers losing the sight of an eye as a result of stabbing by cranes kept in captivity. It is interesting that both St Kierans should be associated with cranes, as they are both linked with midland sites close to bogs and marshland where cranes would have been a more common sight than elsewhere in Ireland. Another reference to cranes taking out an eye occurs in the description of the warrior Cúchulainn and his famous 'war spasm'. When the warrior entered this ferocious state, one eye was sucked so deep into his head that 'a wild crane could hardly have reached it to pluck it out from the back of his skull onto his cheek'. The other eye, however, sprang out of his head onto his cheek.

The crane also appears as a pet in the most famous of the stories surrounding it, namely the Crane-bag of Mannanán.[6] According to the story, Aoife, daughter of Dealbhoth, was turned into a crane by Iuchra, who was jealous of her love for his rival Ilbhreac. Iuchra beguiled Aoife to come swimming and then drove her forth in the form of a crane over the moorlands, saying that she would be 200 years in the house of Manannán, the Irish god of the sea: 'Thou shalt be always in that house with everyone mocking thee, a crane that does not visit every land, thou shalt not reach any land.' The reference to 'visiting every land' indicates that the migrating crane is the bird involved, rather than the more sedentary heron. When she died, Manannán made a 'good treasure of vessels' from her skin, which held every precious thing that he possessed. This included such things as his shirt and knife, the king of Lochlainn's helmet and the bones of Asal's swine. The Crane-bag had the peculiar property that when the tide was full, its treasures were visible in the middle of the bag, and when the tide ebbed it appeared to be empty. Ownership of the bag passed to Lugh and various other owners, until it came to Cumhall son of Trénmhór.

Sometimes it is not so easy to tell whether cranes or herons were meant, or whether a distinction was ever made between them. In Irish legend, the Tuatha Dé Danann god Midhir possessed three cranes or herons which guarded his *sídh* or otherworld residence of Brí Léith.[7] The cranes guarded his home against visitors, and had the reputation of robbing warriors of their courage and will to fight. Another story also relates how the poet Athairne took these three cranes 'of churlishness and denial', so that none of the men of Ireland would get a good reception if they came to his house. The first crane would say: 'Do not come, do not come', the second would say: 'Get away, get away', and the third would say 'Go past the house, past the house'.

Several stories concern cranes or herons living on offshore islands (see Heron).[8] The solitary nature of the birds would seem to indicate herons, but it is not possible to be certain. In one such story concerning the two herons of Scattery Island, County Clare, the she-heron would go on the ocean westwards to hatch her chicks, apparently to some otherworldly island that cannot be found by any boat. Another legend states that a heron lived on the island of Inishkea in County Mayo since the beginning of the world, and it will live there until the Day of Judgment.

The crane, heron or egret appears in two intriguing Gallo-Roman monuments, one in Paris and one in Trier.[9] The Paris monument is dedicated to Jupiter and one panel shows a bull standing in front of a tree with two cranes on his back and a third perched on his head. An inscription underneath says *Tarvostrigaranus* or 'the bull with three cranes'. An adjoining panel shows a wood-cutter named Esus (or 'Lord') cutting down the branch of a tree. The monument in Trier, in western Germany, is dedicated to Mercury and shows a woodcutter chopping at a similar tree, in which are a bull's head and three cranes. The symbolism is obscure, but the scholar Miranda Green argues that the motifs of tree, birds, bull and water are all related to life. The tree, which Green identifies as willow, could represent the Tree of Life, and its destruction by the woodcutter, could be the seasonal 'death' of winter and the departure of the tree's spirit in the form of birds. Cranes, egrets and willows all have water associations and the egret nests in willows. In addition, egrets feed on ticks and other pests in the hides of cattle and are often to be seen perching on their backs. The bull may represent new life and virility and the regenerating strength of spring, while the association with water also represents life force and fertility.

It is clear that a complex set of imagery and myth surrounded the crane and similar birds, such as the heron and egret, and it is worthwhile reviewing the evidence. In various stories the crane is depicted as guarding both treasure and the entrance to an otherworld dwelling; and it is known for living near watery places, such as marshes, ponds and islands. A long-standing custom throughout Bronze Age and Iron Age Europe was the depositing into water of ritual offerings such as weapons, jewellery, cauldrons, coins and other valuable objects. These offerings must have been a temptation to looters, whatever the religious taboo involved. Could it be that the crane was seen as standing guard over the valuables, watching for looters on behalf of the gods so as to ensure their vengeance? There could hardly have been a stretch of water without these tall birds, standing still, and watching all creatures that approached. Lakes, marshes and islands are also all locations with otherworld associations, so it may be that the crane was seen as a bird that guarded various watery entrances to the otherworld, warning away the unworthy with its forbidding presence. In Celtic myth the bull is a symbol of strength, fertility and prosperity, and so could represent these aspects of the tribal father-god or 'Lord'. The cranes may be an aspect of the war goddess, supporting and protecting the wealth of the tribe and its father-god, in a similar manner to the 'crow of battle' or Badhbh (see Hooded Crow). Cranes are often associated with women in various stories (see Heron).

A logical extension of this role is that the crane would act as a psychopomp, guiding those who were worthy on the path to the otherworld.[10] In this regard it is worth noting a scene from the base of the North Cross at Ahenny, County Tipperary, which shows a crane leading a procession of warriors on horseback and in a chariot. The scene is part of a frieze running around the base, which includes a funeral procession on the opposite side. Lorcán O'Toole and Ronan O'Flaherty argue that the role of the crane in this context is indeed as a conveyor of the spirit to the afterlife.

Cranes or herons also appear in a more directly warlike context. For example, the practice of a form of magic called *corrguineacht* or 'heron/crane slaying' appears in early Irish stories (see Heron). This involved the practitioner delivering a satire or malediction standing on one leg, with one arm outstretched, and with one eye shut, and apparently in the pose of a heron, with the implication that the destructive power of their satire would act to harm their enemy like the beak of a heron on its prey. Cranes also appear in some early Celtic artefacts, again usually with some connection to war or battle.[11] At Risingham, Bedfordshire, a stone depicts Mars and Victory accompanied respectively by a goose and a crane. Interestingly, the goose was another bird valued for its role in guarding against intruders. Cranes also appear on Celtic coins; for example, an Arvernian coin shows a horse accompanied by a crane, which is seemingly defending the horse from a ram-horned snake threatening its underbelly, while on a coin of the Lemovices, a crane perches on the back of a horse. A coin from Maidstone in Kent shows two cranes facing each other, while a stag and boar appear on the other side. Cranes also appear on Iron Age helmets, and on a shield depicted on a first-century monument at Orange in the south of France.

It has also been suggested by O'Toole and O'Flaherty that the earlier Bronze Age weapon, the halberd, was associated with a warlike crane cult. The halberd's pointed blade mounted on a long timber shaft bears a strong resemblance to the long neck and beak of a crane. Images of Bronze Age warriors in rock art, at Mont Bego in the Italian Alps, appears to show them dancing while holding their halberds aloft, perhaps in imitation of the jumping and flapping motions of the crane in its courtship dance.

Various beliefs were held by scholars in ancient times about the nature of the crane and its habits and properties.[12] According to Pliny the Elder, at the start of their annual migrations cranes would swallow stones as ballast in order to avoid being swept off course by changing winds. When their journey was done they would vomit up the stones, which then had the ability to identify gold-bearing rocks. Pliny the Elder also wrote that the fat of cranes eased hard swellings and other tumours. The *Iliad* mentions the crane, where it says that the bugling calls of the migrating flocks were like the sound of armies advancing into battle. The Greek scholar Aristotle wrote that, in the winter, cranes arrived at the Egyptian marshes at the source of the Nile where they engaged in battle against pygmies. Another well-known Classical belief about the crane was that the birds would post sentries to keep a lookout for attacks, and that these lookout birds would stand on one leg and hold a stone in the other. If they should happen to doze off, they would lose their grip on the stone, which would fall on the ground and wake them up. The crane, therefore, became a symbol of watchfulness and vigilance. The Roman author Gaius Julius Hyginus related another story about the crane by stating that the god Mercury invented the seven Roman letters of the alphabet A, B, H, T, I, Y from watching the flight of cranes, which when they fly, form letters. Gerald of Wales, writing about Ireland in the twelfth century, stated that the crane has such a warm and fiery liver that if it should eat iron, it would not let it through undigested.

NOTABLE FACTS
The evidence suggests that cranes were native breeding birds in Britain and Ireland up until the seventeenth century at the latest.[13]

In Ireland the bones of cranes have been found in excavations of crannógs in Ballinderry and Lagore dating from the early Christian period. Gerald of Wales, writing in the twelfth century, reported that flocks of cranes could be seen in Ireland, often up to 100 in number. A manuscript of his work *Topography of Ireland* written about 1200 illustrates this chapter with a drawing of what is unmistakably a crane. In the medieval Latin *Life of St Ailbe* there is also a reference to the destruction of grass and cereals by a flock of cranes (*grues*). Furthermore, writing in 1625, O'Sullivan Beare remarked in his work *The Natural History of Ireland*, that 'on this island cranes (*Grues*) are frequent'. He then went on to give an accurate description of a crane, and further remarked that 'when they are tamed they are so simple and stupid that they wheel about going ahead of and following a man'. He also described how they prepare themselves for migration, coming together in a line in military fashion, and selecting a leader to follow. However, cranes seem to have disappeared from Ireland sometime in the seventeenth century, probably due to hunting and loss of habitat. Writing just over a century later, Smith in his *Histories of the Counties of Waterford and of Cork* wrote that some few cranes were seen there during the great frost of 1739, 'but not since or before in any person's memory'. Again the reference to winter suggests that these were passage migrants making their way from Scandinavia to southern Spain or North Africa. Another crane was supposed to have been shot in County Galway in 1834, and this was probably also a stray passage migrant.

Similarly in Britain, cranes were also reportedly seen as late as the seventeenth century, but had possibly died out as a breeding species by 1600. Sir Thomas Browne of Norwich wrote in 1667 that cranes were often seen there in hard winters, which suggests they were passage migrants from Scandinavia rather than breeding birds. In 1678 Willughby in his book *Ornithologia* wrote that in the fen counties of Lincolnshire and Cambridgeshire there were still great flocks of them, but admitted that he did not know if they were breeding or not. The decline in numbers of cranes was similarly put down to the combined effects of drainage of marshes and hunting.

In Britain the crane was considered the ultimate prey for the falconer, and usually the prestigious gyrfalcon was employed, the only species with the size and strength to tackle it.[14] The gyrfalcon was reserved for royalty, and successive British kings kept them especially to fly at cranes. For example, as early as 754 King Ethelbert II of Kent wrote to Boniface, the Bishop of Mayence in Germany, asking to be sent a pair of gyrfalcons. The crane was also considered a prestigious dish, on a par with swan and peacock, and was usually roasted with a sauce of ginger, vinegar and mustard.[15] In 1465, 204 cranes were ordered for the banquet of George Neville, Chancellor of England, when he was made Archbishop of York. The English naturalist Edward Topsell considered the flesh of cranes an excellent remedy for cancers, palsy, ulcers, and 'wynde in the guts'. However, it seems that neither herons nor cranes were eaten in Ireland prior to the Anglo-Norman invasion. Indeed, Gerald of Wales, in his work *Expugnatio Hibernica,* wrote that the Irish had an abhorrence of crane flesh.[16] The Annals of the Four Masters mentions that crane or heron flesh was served at the banquets at Dublin Castle by Henry II to entertain the Irish kings who were invited. However, they were suspicious of the dishes and did not eat until the king himself had tasted them first.

In Ireland the Brehon Laws frequently mention the crane or heron as a pet, which was set at the same value as a kitten, puppy, cock or goose.[17] Although it is not possible to tell from the texts which bird is intended, there is modern information about the two birds as pets which sheds some light. The heron is a difficult pet that rarely bonds with a human. It is strongly territorial and tends to attack other domesticated birds, as well as dogs, cats and children. The crane, on the other hand, easily bonds with humans. This would seem to indicate that the crane was more likely to be the species that was domesticated. There is also evidence of the crane being used as a pet outside Ireland. The laws of the sixth-century Franks also mention the domestic crane, which was probably used in the training of hawks. In Britain cranes when taken young were regarded as amusing, albeit somewhat dangerous pets; and as long ago as 1500 in an inventory of a Sergeant Keble's goods, there were three cranes valued at five shillings each.

In Britain there is some good news in recent times regarding the crane, in that its long absence from the British countryside has ended.[18] A small breeding colony of cranes has successfully re-established itself in Norfolk since the 1980s. Also, a project to reintroduce the crane to the Somerset levels is ongoing, with seventy-seven birds released as of 2014, most of which have survived. Regarding the situation in Ireland, there is also good news. In 2011 the Golden Eagle Trust commissioned a report on the possibility that cranes might be reintroduced. The report, by the Swedish Crane Working Group, looked at various locations in the midlands, including cutaway bogs, and found that the possibilities of the crane once again becoming a breeding bird in Ireland were promising. This raises the hope that this magnificent bird will once again grace the Irish landscape with its presence.

SIMILAR BIRDS

Stork – Storc bán – *Ciconia ciconia*

The stork has never been native to Britain or Ireland, but as it is often confused with the crane, a few words about it should be said for the sake of clarity.[19] The stork is a widespread bird across the continent of Europe and was traditionally regarded as a harbinger of spring, when it arrives from its winter feeding grounds in Africa. The stork often builds its nest on the roofs and chimney tops of houses, and the presence of a stork's nest was believed to bring good luck to a house. This may be the origin of the widespread tradition that storks deliver babies. This tradition features in the folktale *The Storks* by Hans Christian Andersen. A tradition also arose that storks will only live in free states and republics, but how this story came about is not clear, as they must obviously have always nested in the territories of monarchies.

Heron — Corr Réisc — *Ardea cinerea*

The heron is noted for its patience and skill as a hunter, as it stands tall and erect for hours before suddenly attacking its prey with its stabbing beak. This made the heron, as with the crane, a symbol of watchfulness, vigilance and war. In addition, the heron's habit of living in mysterious watery places probably gave it the role in Celtic myth, along with the crane, of a guardian of otherworld treasure.

FOLK BELIEFS AND CUSTOMS

In rural Ireland the heron is more often called the crane, but as the crane has been extinct in Ireland for centuries, it is almost certain that the heron is the bird that is actually meant. A lot of Irish folklore surrounding the heron concerned the belief that it was a good predictor of the weather.[1] It was said that the weather followed the heron, so that when herons flew south it meant that cold weather was on the way, but when herons flew north it meant that warmer weather was in store. Similarly, when herons moved upriver it meant that the weather would be dry, but if they moved downriver, wet weather was to be expected. In Donegal it was also said that when the heron was seen flying with a wide wingspan spread over the water, good dry weather could be expected; but that when seen flying downstream, heavy rain and floods were on the way. It was also said in Donegal, when two herons were seen picking along a riverbank, or flapping their wings on the surface of the river, that a storm was coming. Another Donegal belief stated that seeing a heron flying up a mountain was a sign that a spell of warm weather was on the way. In west Cork it was said that a very cold day was one that felled even the heron.

In Ireland the fat of a heron was said to be good for various folk cures.[2] One folk cure stipulated that the body of a heron should be put in a container and buried somewhere like a manure heap. After a month, a greasy oil should have collected at the bottom of the container, and this was held to be a very effective cure for burns. In

the north of Ireland it was said that a common cure among old women for rheumatic pains was the fat of a heron killed at the full of the moon. This belief may have arisen from the fact that herons will feed at night during the full moon, but not during dark nights.

Various others folk beliefs surrounded the heron.[3] It was said in Ireland that dipping fishing bait into water in which the flesh of a heron had been boiled would confer a great power on it to catch fish. Among Irish Travellers it was said that if a heron flew near you or towards you, you would meet friends shortly afterwards. In Britain it was believed that a heron flying near the house or sitting on the roof was a sign of bad luck as it meant there would be sickness in the house. In the Scottish Highlands if an animal was reluctant to cross a ditch and stream, a remedy was to throw a stalk into a ditch and say a rhyme to encourage the animal to cross, which included the words *'casa curra fothaibh'* – 'heron's legs under you'.

MYTHS AND LEGENDS

The same word *corr* was used in Irish to describe both the crane and the heron, and as most Irish legends predate the seventeenth century when the crane became extinct in Ireland, it is possible that *corr* could refer to either bird. However, examining the details of the bird's behaviour or appearance in the stories can often provide clues as to which bird is meant. For example, some early Irish legends associate the heron with St Colmcille (or Columba).[4] A story about Colmcille, which appears in Geoffrey Keating's *History of Ireland*, concerns how he turned a queen and her handmaid into herons in retaliation for their lack of hospitality. According to the story Colmcille had arrived in Ireland from Scotland to attend the convention of Drum Ceat, hosted by King Aodh. Aodh's wife told her son Conall not to show any reverence to the 'crane-cleric' or his company, and in retaliation the saint turned the queen and her handmaid (who had conveyed the news) into herons. The two herons were fated to stay at the ford of Drum Ceat until Doom, and it was further said that, ever since then, the two birds were to be seen at the ford. This description of the two birds at the ford strongly suggests the traditional fishing activity of the heron along rivers. The taunt about Colmcille being a 'crane-cleric' appears to mean that he was a harbinger or bringer of war (see Crane), in a reference to a battle Colmcille was involved in starting, known as 'the battle of the book'.

In Adamnán's *Life of Columba*, there is also a story which seems to involve a heron (despite *'grus'* being used in the original Latin text). When the saint was in Iona, he called one of the brothers and told him that on the third day a heron would arrive from Ireland onto the beach on the western part of the island, wearied and fatigued from various winds. Colmcille instructed that it be treated tenderly and brought to a neighbouring house to be nursed and fed for three days and nights. At the end of the three days it would be refreshed and fly back with renewed strength to Ireland. Colmcille instructed that all this be done because the heron came from his native place. It came to pass exactly as the saint had predicted, and so the heron was cared for and flew back to Ireland as soon as it could, on a calm day. The heron is indicated in this story rather than the crane, as the crane would have no difficulty flying the distance between northern Ireland and Scotland, whereas a heron would; and also it is implied that the bird was sedentary like a heron, rather than migratory like a crane. In Donegal folklore Colmcille was said to have given the heron the ability to stand on one leg better than any other bird, and he gave to the other leg the ability to give a sweet sound to any fiddle that it was put into. It was traditionally said that the reason the foot of a heron gave a fiddle a sweet sound was because it contained the sound of the sea. This strongly suggests the heron, which often moves to the coast after breeding to fish along the seashore.

Several legends refer to cranes or herons living on offshore islands.[5] The solitary nature of the birds' life on islands suggests that the heron was more likely to be the bird intended. One legend concerns one of the Three Wonders of Connacht, which was the two herons of Scattery Island, County Clare. They would let no other herons onto the island, and the she-heron would go on the ocean westwards to hatch her chicks, and return to the island with her young. According to the legend, despite searches, no boats have ever discovered the place of hatching. According to a Scottish legend there was supposed to be a heron living on the island of Inishkea in County Mayo since the beginning of the world, and it will live there until the Day of Judgment. The heron was said to be a person under enchantment, doing penance. The ninth-century poem about the Hawk of Achill also mentions a heron on Iniskea, but says that the hawk killed it. Despite their differences, the two stories doubtless have a common tradition.

Cranes or herons were also associated with women in Irish legends, which often involve the women being transformed into the bird.[6] The most famous of these is the story of the Crane-bag of Mannanán Mac Lir, but it is more likely to be a crane that is meant in that story (see Crane). The warrior Fionn Mac Cumhaill also encounters cranes or herons in several stories. In one story he is saved as a child from falling to his death over a cliff by his grandmother, who is transformed into a crane; while in another story he encounters the hostile 'Hag of the Temple', whose four sons take the form of cranes. They can only be turned back into human form if the blood of an enchanted bull is sprinkled on them. In the story *Buile Shuibhne* or Mad Sweeney, the hermit Sweeney meets a hag in the wood, describing the pair of them as 'a couple of herons hard-shanked / I hard and ragged, she hard-beaked.'

The practice of a form of magic called *corrguineacht* or 'heron/crane slaying' appears in early Irish stories.[7] This involved the practitioner delivering a satire or malediction standing on one leg, with one arm outstretched, and with one eye shut. The practice appeared to involve the person adopting the pose of a heron, apparently with the implication that the destructive power of their satire would act to harm their enemy like the beak of a heron on its prey. It can be speculated that a knife or spear was held in the outstretched arm, and brought down suddenly in imitation of the heron's stabbing beak. Cúchulainn is described as adopting this pose in the *Táin Bó Cuailnge* (*The Cattle Raid of Cooley*) and appears to invoke the practice in another story when he warns an adversary that if he should torment him, 'I will make myself as long as a heron above you.'

The myths surrounding the heron, crane and similar birds are complex, and the evidence points to the heron and crane as guarding both treasure and the entrances to otherworld dwellings (see Crane). The birds are known for living near watery places such as marshes, ponds and islands, which were the focus throughout the Bronze and Iron Ages of ritual offerings such as weapons, jewellery, cauldrons, coins and other valuable objects. The heron or crane may have been seen as standing guard over the valuables, watching for looters on behalf of the gods so as to ensure their vengeance. It may also be that the heron was seen as a bird that guarded various watery entrances to the otherworld, warning away the unworthy with its forbidding presence. This role would perhaps be an aspect of the war goddess, supporting and protecting the wealth of the tribe, in a similar manner to the 'crow of battle' or Badhbh (see Hooded Crow). A logical extension of this role is that the heron or crane would act as a psychopomp, guiding those who were worthy on the path to the otherworld.

The call of the crane or heron is mentioned frequently in Irish tales.[8] The calls described seem to be harsh or unpleasant, or else in cold weather, so it is more likely that the heron is the bird that is meant. In the story *Buile Shuibhne* or Mad Sweeney, the hermit Sweeney, who has gone to live in the wilds to get away from people, mentions the heron's cry several times. For example, he talks of 'the herons a-calling / in chilly Glenn Aighle'. He also talks of fleeing in his disturbed state 'at the cry of the heron'. Later still on his travels, he warns against the cry of 'a heron from a blue-watered, green-watered lough'. Also, a poem about Beann Ghualann, a wooded glen beloved of the Fianna, mentions its 'clamour of herons at night'. There are also some references to the harsh call of the 'crane' in early spring or autumn, which can be more confidently ascribed to the heron, as the crane is a summer visitor only. A story about the poet Athairne states: 'raw and cold is icy spring – passionately wailful is the harsh shrieking crane [heron].' An early Irish poem about autumn declares: 'Sliabh gCua, haunt of wolves, rugged and dark . . . the crane [heron] screams over its crags.'

NOTABLE FACTS

For falconers in Britain the heron was a favourite bird for hunting, on account of the good sport it gave in trying to evade capture, and usually the more prestigious peregrine falcon was used in the hunt.[9] The heron was also said to make excellent food, the flavour resembling that of hare.[10] However, it was said by other sources that they were very variable in taste, and were often not good to eat. Nevertheless, in Britain in the reign of Edward I in the late thirteenth century, the heron was esteemed as food, and could fetch from sixteen to eighteen pence. A hundred years later in the reign of Richard II the value of a heron was similarly fixed at sixteen old pence. About 100 years later still in 1465, 400 herons were ordered for the banquet of George Neville, Chancellor of England, when he was made Archbishop of York. However, it seems that neither herons nor cranes were eaten in Ireland prior to the Anglo-Norman invasion.[11] Indeed, Gerald of Wales, in his work *Expugnatio Hibernica*, wrote that the Irish had an abhorrence of crane-flesh. In support of this, the Annals of the Four Masters mentions that heron or crane flesh was served at the banquets at Dublin Castle by Henry II to entertain the Irish kings who were invited. However, the native princes were unwilling to eat until the king himself had tasted some of the suspicious-looking dishes.

The heron is famous for its ability to catch fish, with its combination of patient, motionless waiting and lightning-quick stabbing with its bill when prey appears.[12] Various explanations have been put forward to explain its prowess, such as that its down is luminous, allowing it to fish at night; or that it contains a fish-attracting oil. None of these explanations have any basis in fact, however, as the heron's success is simply down to its patience and skill. This has always made it unpopular with fishermen, and in more recent times it has also attracted the ire of those who like to keep ornamental fish in their garden ponds. As well as catching fish, the heron will on occasion take ducklings, rats, mice and even stoats. Perhaps this opportunism explains why the heron is flourishing throughout Britain and Ireland with no threat to its numbers. Writing in 1625 O'Sullivan Beare stated that 'in Ireland the heron is very well known. His name is taken from his lofty, that is his high flight.'[13] This is a play on the heron's Latin name *Ardea* and the Latin for lofty *arduus*. In 2004 there were 3,650 breeding pairs in Ireland,[14] and so the heron continues to be a familiar and well-loved sight, not just in the countryside, but throughout our urban areas as well.

Swan — Eala — *Cygnus* spp.

*T*he *swan's grace, serenity and snow-white feathers give it the appearance of an almost otherworldly creature. This meant that in many traditional legends across Europe, swans appear both as maidens and youths under enchantment. Similarly, in folk belief swans were thought to represent the souls of the dead who were pure of heart, and so it was considered very bad luck to kill or harm them.*

> Mute Swan – Eala bhalbh – *Cygnus olor*
>
> Whooper Swan – Eala ghlórach – *Cygnus Cygnus*
>
> Bewick's Swan – Eala Bewick – *Cygnus columbianus bewickii*

FOLK BELIEFS AND CUSTOMS

In Ireland it was generally believed to be very unlucky to kill a swan, and many tales were told of the dire consequences for those who did so.[1] For example, the mysterious death of one of their farm animals often occurred soon afterwards. In County Mayo the whooper swan was never interfered with, on account of a tradition that the souls of virgins, who whilst living had been remarkable for the purity of their lives, were after death enshrined in the form of these birds. It was further believed that whoever meddled with them would pay with their life before the year was out. Similarly, in Donegal it was believed that swans were people under enchantment, so that bad luck would come to anyone who interfered with them or killed them. It was also said in Donegal that when a swan was killed it turned black immediately.

Not only was it considered unlucky to kill or harm a swan, but the body of a dead swan should also not be tampered with. This is illustrated in a story from Killorglin, which involved an old man whose wife was dead, and who had a lot of money but did not know where to hide it. He was walking alongside the River Laune one day when he saw a dead swan on the riverbank. He picked it up and saw an empty space inside it. He got the idea that he would put his treasure into the swan and bury her in the garden. He did so, but after one day, the swan rose out of the earth and flew away with his money. The old man was so angry that he died soon after and, ever since, the swan came to visit the spot in the garden where she had been buried. Although it does not say so, it is tempting to interpret from the story that the swan was the soul of his dead wife, returned to take revenge on her husband for his miserliness.

The swan was also revered in Scotland.[2] In the Scottish Highlands swans were said to be ill-treated ladies under enchantment, driven from their homes and forced to wander and dwell where they were most kindly treated and least molested. Therefore, they were regarded with love and veneration, and treating them well was thought to bring good luck. To see seven, or a multiple of seven, on the wing meant that peace was ensured for that number of years. In addition, for a person to hear a swan in the morning while fasting, especially on a Tuesday, was a thing much to be desired. It was also considered good luck to see a swan on a Friday: 'Shouldst thou see a swan on Friday / In the joyous morning dawn / There shall be increase on thy means and thy kin / Nor shall your flocks be always dying.' However, for some reason, seeing a duck and swan swim together on Easter Monday meant there would be no blessing that year. As in Ireland, there was a taboo on killing the swan, and in the Scottish Highlands a young man going hunting for the first time was blessed with the words: 'Thou shalt not wound . . . the white swan of the sweet gurgle.' During milking, a blessing was traditionally said which included the words: 'The calm Bride of the white combs / Will give to my loved heifer the lustre of the swan / While the loving Mary of the combs of honey / Will give her the mottle of the heather hen.' Another blessing from the Scottish Highlands was for those going to court to seek justice. It said: 'Black is yonder town / Black are those therein / I am the white swan / Queen above them.'

In England, the swan's status as a royal bird has given it a special place in English culture.[3] A great many streets, hotels and, above all, pubs are named after the swan. Over 770 pub names have been recorded with names like The Swan's Nest, The Swan & Cygnets, The Swan & Peacock, Ye Olde Swan and The White Swan. More mysteriously, a common pub name is The Swan with Two Necks. There are various explanations for this, one being that it was originally The Swan with Two Nicks, in a reference to the swan mark of the Vintners' company (see below about swan marks). Another explanation is that it derives from a heraldic symbol of two swan heads encircled by a coronet. The swan is a regular occurence in English heraldry, for example, the principal device on the badge of Henry IV was a silver swan.

Myths and Legends

One of the most popular motifs in European folklore is that of the swan maiden, a beautiful young woman who also takes the form of a swan.[4] An Irish version of the tale from County Clare tells of how a chief of the O'Quinns acquired a swan maiden for his wife. The story relates how the young chief was out hunting deer, and in his eager pursuit of a stag got separated from his companions. As he wandered along the shore of a lake, he saw five beautiful swans playing in the water. They came ashore, took off their plumage and became maidens of exquisite beauty. After a moment's amazement, he ran after them, but they threw on their feathered robes except one, and flew away. O'Quinn seized the one who had been slow to don her feathers, and took her back weeping to his castle. However, he comforted her and won her love. But before she married him she asked him to make two pledges, firstly that her identity should be kept a secret, and secondly that no O'Brien should be admitted under their roof. The young chief readily agreed, and seven years passed during which the couple were very happy, and had two children. Then one day, O'Quinn met Teigue O'Brien at the races, and brought him home, where they began drinking and gambling until O'Quinn had lost all his lands and property. He rushed to see his wife, as she was all that he now had left. To his horror, he found her in her swan dress with a cygnet under each wing. She gave him a look of sorrowful reproach, flew out over the misty lake and disappeared forever.

Various forms of this myth are found across Europe. One of the best known is the Swedish *Tale of Volund* (Weyland the Smith, in

England). In the tale, three sons of a king of the Finns – Volund, Slagfid and Egil – were out hunting when they came across three women spinning flax by a lakeshore. Near to them were their swan-dresses, for they were not mortal women but Valkyries, super-natural beings associated with warriors in battle. Their names were Olrun, Swan-white and All-wise. The brothers took them to their dwelling where they lived together for seven years, before the women flew off in their swan form in search of battles, never to return. In the saga *Helreid Brynhildar*, King Agnar steals the swan-dresses of the Valkyrie Brynhildr and her seven companions from the place where they had hidden them beneath an oak. They are then forced to give the king their service. A common German folktale with many variants involves a knight who sees a maiden bathing in a forest lake. He takes a gold chain which she had laid aside, and so she cannot fly away. The maiden marries the knight and bears him seven sons, each with a gold necklace, so that they can become swans in turn.

An Irish folktale also suggests that swan-maidens can be women under enchantment against their will.[5] One story concerns the tenth-century poet Mac Coise who was at the Boyne one day when he saw a flock of swans. He threw a stone at the flock, and struck one of the swans on the wing. Running to catch it, he saw that it had turned into a woman. The poet asked her why she was in this form and what had happened to her. The woman replied: 'In sickness I was, and it appeared to my friends that I had died, but really it was demons who had spirited me away.' The poet was able then to restore her to her own people.

However, it is not only females who take the form of swans. The strength and power of the swan can also suggest masculinity, so it is often athletic young heroes or princes who appear in folktales as swans.[6] A very common tale found across Europe concerns princes who are turned into swans by a curse, but are eventually returned to their human form with the help of their sister. An Irish version of the tale is entitled *The Twelve Swans*. In the story a king and queen had twelve sons, but the queen desired to have a daughter. One day the sons were out hunting and killed a raven. The queen saw the black raven bleeding on the snow and said to herself: 'How I would love a daughter like that, with black hair and white skin and red lips.' An old woman appeared beside her, and asked her if she would trade her twelve sons for a daughter. The queen replied that she would; and the hag said, 'It will be done,' and vanished. Soon after, the queen gave birth to a baby girl. But when the twelve sons came to see their new sister, they were all turned into swans and flew away. Although the queen realised why this had happened she was too afraid to say anything.

When the girl reached sixteen, she decided to go looking for her brothers, and after a search, found a castle with twelve swans swimming in a lake beside it. At nightfall the swans entered the castle and turned into twelve young men – they were her brothers under enchantment. The girl agreed to help them recover their human form, and a wise man told her that she must weave shirts out of bog cotton for the brothers and, as soon as they put them on, the spell would be broken. However, she could not say a word to anyone while she was weaving the shirts, or all her efforts would be in vain. The girl set about gathering the bog cotton and spinning it, and as she was doing this, a prince saw her and fell in love with her. Despite the fact that she would not speak, he asked her to marry him, and she nodded her agreement. They were married and soon the girl had a child, with the girl continuing to spin and weave the shirts all the time. However, the hag found out what the girl was doing, took the baby, and tricked the prince into believing that the girl had killed it. The girl was condemned to death, but carried on spinning all the while. Just as she was about to be burned at the stake, she finally had the twelve shirts ready. Her brothers appeared, still in the form of swans and she hurriedly threw the shirts over them. They all regained human form, except the youngest, who was left with one swan wing, because the last shirt was not finished. Now the girl could speak at last and so the hag's plot was revealed. The hag was killed, and the girl, the prince, their child, and the twelve brothers all lived happily ever after. A version of this tale called *The Wild Swans* appears in the works of Hans Christian Andersen, while another version called *The Six Swans* is found in Grimms' Fairy Tales.

The most famous Irish legend on the theme of enchanted swans is the *Children of Lir*.[7] Lir was a sea god who married Aobh, a foster daughter of Bodhbh Dearg, another god of the Tuatha Dé Danann (the Irish pantheon of gods). Lir and Aobh had two sets of twins. The first twins were a boy called Aodh and a girl called Fionnuala, and the second were the boys Fiachra and Conn. However, Aobh died while giving birth to Fiachra and Conn. Lir was so distraught at her death that Bodhbh Dearg took pity on him and gave him a second wife, Aoife, the sister of Aobh. While Aoife loved her stepchildren at first, over time she became jealous of Lir's love for them and began to plot their death. One day Aoife took the children with her to Lake Derravarragh in County Westmeath, with the intention of killing them. However, she could not bring herself to do that, and instead struck them with a magic wand and turned them into swans. Although they were in the form of swans, the four children retained their human wits and power of speech. Aoife told the four horrified children that they would remain in that shape for 900 years, until they heard a bell proclaim the voice of Christianity in Ireland, and until a prince from the north married a princess from the south. When the childrens' absence was realised, a search was made and the children were found at the lake. Bodhbh Dearg was horrified at what Aoife had done and, in a fit of rage, he changed her into a demon which had to wander through the air forever.

The four children stayed at Lake Derravarragh for 300 years, where they entertained visitors by singing beautiful music and conversing with them. After that, they flew away to the Sea of Moyle between Scotland and Ireland, where they spent another 300 years in cold and misery. Finally, they spent the last 300 years at Erris, County Mayo, where they endured even greater misery, tossed by storms and high seas. At the end of that time, they returned to their old home of Sídh Fionnachaidh in County Armagh, but found it empty and deserted. Mourning the death of everyone they had once known, they returned to Inishglory, an island in the bay of Erris, and while there a Christian missionary called Mochaomhóg came to the island and built a church. The swans therefore heard the bell of Christianity for the first time and attended the saint's services. Soon afterwards, the other part of the prophecy came true, when Deocha, the daughter of the king of Munster, wed Lairgnéan, the king of Connacht. As the curse was now over, the four swans regained their human form, but as they were 900 years old they were old and withered, and on the point of death. Mochaomhóg baptised them and they died at peace and were buried together. A version of this tale appears in European stories concerning the Knight of the Swan (see below).

A famous European story about a maiden forced into the form of a swan by enchantment is Tchaikovsky's ballet *Swan Lake*. The ballet derives from a German legend about a beautiful girl called Odette who is turned into a swan by a wicked magician, Von Rothbart. Odette has a human form only at night, and can only fully regain it through the power of eternal love from a man who will remain faithful to her. Odette and a young prince called Siegfried fall in love, and Odette begins to hope that the spell will be broken. However, Von Rothbart tricks Siegfried into being unfaithful by introducing him to his daughter Odile, who is virtually a double of Odette, and so Odette is doomed to remain a swan forever. When Siegfried realises what has happened he is full of remorse and begs Odette's forgiveness. She willingly grants it, and because their love can never be realised, she and Siegfried choose to die together rather than be parted, and throw themselves into a lake.

However, in some tales the humans turn into swans of their own free will.[8] In the tale *The Wooing of Étaín* Midhir sought to woo Étaín away from her husband Eochaid, but she would not go unless Eochaid agreed. Midhir came to Eochaid's hall and asked him for Étaín. Eochaid had no intention of letting her go, however, and he replied that all Midhir might do was put his arms around Étaín there in the hall before him. Midhir then put his arms around Étaín and the two of them immediately flew up through the skylight of the house. The lovers had turned into swans bound together by a gold chain, and so were able to make their escape. Another pair of lovers feature in the tale *The Dream of Óengus*. In the tale Óengus was in love with the beautiful maiden Caér Ibormeith, who took the form of a swan for one year and the form of a human for the following year. At Samhain Óengus went to see her at Loch Bél Dracon, where she was in the form of a swan surrounded by three fifties of swans with silver chains. Caér agreed to be with Óengus on condition that she could retain her swan shape and Óengus agreed. He put his arms around her, and they slept in the form of swans until they had encircled the lake three times. They then travelled to Brú na Bóinne where they sang so sweetly that the inhabitants fell asleep for three days and nights, and the lovers remained together from that time onwards. The story is an interesting variant on the swan-maiden motif, in that it suggests that the love can be successful if the man is willing to join with the woman in taking on the form of a swan. In the story *The Sons of Tuireann*, the three sons take some enchanted apples from an otherworld garden, and turn themselves into swans to escape over the sea from their pursuers. One legend about an Ulster prince of the seventh century, called Mongán, said he acquired secret lore by travelling to otherworld dwellings and by taking on the forms of a wolf, deer, salmon, seal and swan.

Swans also appear in legends in association with royalty.[9] A story about a Scottish exile in Ireland, Cano, son of Gartnán, includes an episode where he showed mercy to a flock of swans. As Cano travelled south through Ireland he and his men came upon a flock of swans. His men urged Cano to aim a shot at them. He aimed but missed, a thing that had never happened before. He then said: 'I have scared the swans of Cernae / it were better that I had not thrown / their sorrow at being disturbed / is like mine for my ill-cast stone.' He later refused to cast a stone at a flock of ducks, saying: 'I shall not harm a feather of the birds / of the Son of the Living God . . . That is not why I set out from Skye / to war on the swans of Cernae.' Whether it was due to his mercy to the swans or not, Cano later became king of Scotland. An early Irish text makes explicit the link between the swan and kingship: 'Truth in a ruler is as bright as the foam cast up by a mighty wave of the sea, as the sheen of a swan's covering in the sun, as the colour of snow on a mountain.'

The Ulster warrior Cúchulainn is associated with swans in several stories.[10] In one story, a girl called Derbforgaill fell in love with Cúchulainn, and she and her maidservant pursued him in the form of swans, joined together by a chain of gold. Cúchulainn aimed his sling at one of the birds and wounded it so badly that it fell to the ground. As the swan hit the ground, it returned to its human form, revealing Derbforgaill. Cúchulainn then sucked the stone out of her wound, but in doing so tasted her blood, and so was prevented by a taboo from marrying her. In another story *The Pursuit of Gruaidh Ghriansholus* he arrives on an enchanted island and sets up camp in a tent of fine white satin, thatched and covered with the down of a white-breasted swan. In the tale *The Cattle Raid of Cooley* Cúchulainn and his charioteer saw a flock of swans ahead. His charioteer told him that the bravest and most accomplished warriors do not kill swans, but take them back alive. Cúchulainn then threw a small stone and brought down eight of them. After that he threw a large stone and struck another twelve. He tied the stunned birds with strings and cords to the chariot and carried on to Emain Macha (Navan fort) with the flock of swans fluttering over it.

The episode of Cúchulainn with swans attached to his chariot echoes the figure in European legends of the Knight of the Swan or *schwannritter*. Various versions of the legend exist, but the central story concerns a mysterious knight who arrives in a boat pulled by a swan to help a noble lady in distress. He helps the lady and then marries her, but forbids her to reveal his true nature. She later forgets this promise and he leaves her, never to return. In the German versions of the legend the knight is usually Loherangin or Lohengrin, the son of Parzifal (Perceval), the Grail Hero. Lohengrin marries Elsa of Brabant, and at the end of the tale he returns to the Grail Castle. In the French version, the *chevalier au cygne* is called Helyas, who marries Beatrix of Bouillon. Sometimes the legend is also connected to stories of swan children, similar in form to the *Children of Lir*. In these stories, however, one of the children remains a swan, and later pulls along the Knight of the Swan's boat with a silver chain. The motif of swans pulling a chariot appears to be ancient.[11] In Greek myth, the sun god Apollo was said to travel north each winter in a chariot drawn by swans, to the Hyperborean lands of eternal summer. Adonis and Aphrodite have also been depicted in chariots drawn by swans. In Urnfield and Hallstatt in central Europe, model wagons have been found, drawn by long-necked water birds resembling swans. An example of this is the wheeled cauldron at Orastie in eastern Europe, which dates from the seventh to the sixth century BC.

The swan is associated with beauty in some Irish stories.[12] In the tale *Fate of the Children of Uisneach* the beautiful maiden Deirdre of the Sorrows was said to move like 'a swan upon the wave', while the handsome Sons of Uisneach were said to have skin 'like the swan upon the wave'. Similarly, the famous otherworld beauty, Niamh of the Golden Hair, was described as having skin 'whiter than the swan upon the wave'.

The swan also appears in some Celtic decoration.[13] A Bronze Age flesh hook (used for spearing meat boiling in a cauldron) decorated with swans was found in Dunaverney in County Antrim. A Bronze Age chariot fitting decorated with swans was found in Waldalgesheim in Germany. A Romano-Celtic sculpture from Alesia in Burgundy shows three mother goddesses with three children, alongside another child seated in a boat and accompanied by a swan.

Swans appear as singing beautifully in many tales, such the *Children of Lir* and *The Dream of Óengus* mentioned above.[14] In the seventh-century poem about his life in the woods, the hermit Marbán praises the swan's song. Similarly, in the *Life of Saint Colmán* when the saint and his monks were constructing a causeway, swans used to come every hour to sing to them. This is curious as in real life swans do not sing as such, even if the call of the whooper and Bewick swans could be described as melodic. Associated is the belief mentioned by many Classical writers, including Plato, Aristotle, Euripedes, Cicero, Seneca and Pliny, that swans sing just before they die.[15] Pliny believed the story to be untrue, but Aristotle says: 'These birds are wont to sing even when just about to die. They also fly afar over the main, and men ... who have been sailing on the African sea, have met with many singing mournfully and seen some of them die.' A work by the Greek writer Aeschylus includes the remark of a female character that 'she like the swan / expiring, dies in melody'. It may be that this idea of the 'swansong' arose because of a link between the swan and music in Classical myth. Orpheus the musician became a swan, and the swan was said by the Greeks to be a bird of Apollo, the god of music.

NOTABLE FACTS

The whooper and Bewick's swan are both native to Ireland, but only as winter visitors.[16] Bewick's swan is very similar in appearance to the whooper, and was only distinguished from it as a separate species in the nineteenth century. The mute swan is believed to have been introduced into Ireland some time after the Norman invasion.[17] One theory is that it was introduced by English landlords as an ornamental species to adorn their private lakes and ponds. In a 1589 work *A Briefe Description of Ireland* by Robert Payne it states that in Ireland 'there be great store of wild swans – much more plentiful than in England.' O'Sullivan Beare, writing in 1625, stated that Irish swans were very tame, and often had two yolks in their eggs. According to O'Sullivan Beare, Irish swans were also said to cover their nests until St Patrick's Day with blankets of feathers or grass.

In England the swan is a royal bird, which no subject can own as property when it is at large in a public river, except by grant from the Crown.[18] The reason for this is that swan was a prestige food of royalty and the aristocracy, with a full-grown bird providing about 9 kg (20 lb) of meat. In the reign of Edward IV it was further decreed that none but the King's son should have 'any mark of game of swans of his own, or to his use, except he have lands and tenements of freehold worth five marks per annum'. So esteemed was swan meat that the English monarchs formerly had swanneries not only on the Thames but in several other places, such as Clarendon in Wiltshire and on the Isle of Purbeck. An office existed in the Royal Household of 'Master of the King's Swans', sometimes called the swanship.

In bestowing the privilege of owning swans, the Crown granted a swan mark, and the king's swanherd kept a record of each swan mark in a book. This swan mark was cut in the beak of the swan with a sharp knife, and usually consisted of initials, chevrons, crescents, crosses and other devices, which often had a reference to the heraldic office of the swan owner. Along with various members of the aristocracy, swan holders included the Bishop of Norwich and Eton College.

The best time to kill a swan was early November before the summer weight was lost during the winter, and in former times swan was served up at every great feast. Not only was the flesh of the swan valuable, but its eggs too; in 1496, during the reign of Henry VII, it was ordered that stealing or taking a swan's egg would earn a year's imprisonment.

The use of swan as meat fell out of favour, both because its flesh came to be seen as too strong in flavour for modern tastes, and because of the rise in popularity of turkey, which was increasingly kept from the sixteenth century onwards.[19] Nowadays the practice of owning and marking swans and catching them for food has disappeared completely. However, the custom of catching swans has been continued along the Thames by two of London's oldest livery companies, the Dyers and the Vintners, still led by the Queen's Swan Marker. The purpose nowadays, however, is to monitor their numbers for conservation purposes. The numbers and health of swans and cygnets are checked, any harmful fishing tackle or hooks are removed, and the swans released back into the river, unharmed by the process. The tradition is also still maintained in Abbotsbury on the Fleet in Dorset.

The conservation status of the three species of swan in Ireland is fairly good, despite threats such as swans hitting overhead power lines, or dying from ingesting lead weights from discarded fishing lines. All three species tend to gather in flocks in winter on Ireland's lakes and rivers where they make a spectacular sight in the Irish landscape. W. B. Yeats immortalised this in his poem 'The Wild Swans at Coole', when he spoke of seeing 'nine-and-fifty swans' on the lake and hearing the 'bell-beat of their wings' overhead. As well as the swishing, humming sound of these massive birds in flight, each of the swans makes its own distinctive call. Despite its name, the mute swan produces loud hissing and explosive snorting sounds, especially when under threat. The whooper swan has a bugle-like note, like *whoop-a,* which gave it its name, while the Bewick's has a call like the whooper, but more high pitched and cackling. Although none of the species of swans can truly sing, even in death as the ancients believed, this does not detract from their extraordinary grace and beauty.

Goose — Gé — *Anser* spp. / *Branta* spp.

The goose is valued as a domestic bird for its flesh, eggs and feathers, but it is also noted for its aggression towards intruders. This made it a warlike bird in Celtic myth, symbolising watchfulness and bravery. In Ireland the wild goose was traditionally seen as more fish than fowl, from its habit of living by the seashore.

Domestic Goose – Gé tí – *Anser anser domesticus*

Brent Goose – Cadhan – *Branta bernicla hrota*

Barnacle Goose – Gé ghiúrainn – *Branta leucopsis*

Canada Goose – Gé Cheanadach – *Branta canadensis*

Greylag Goose – Gé ghlas – *Anser anser*

Greenland White-Fronted Goose – Gé bhánéadanach – *Anser albifrons flavirostris*

Pink-footed Goose – Gé ghobghearr – *Anser brachyrhynchus*

FOLK BELIEFS AND CUSTOMS

In Ireland the goose was associated with various weather lore.[1] For example, it was generally believed that the early arrival of wild geese meant that a prolonged and severe winter was in store. This is a very old belief, as the ninth-century Irish work *Cormac's Glossary* states that the brent goose usually arrived at the coasts of Erris and Umhall between 15 October and 15 November, and that when it appeared earlier, it brought storms and high winds. Similarly, in Counties Donegal and Galway, when the wild geese arrived, it was a sign that cold and frosty weather was on the way. In Donegal a sign of an approaching wind was when a goose stuck its neck up into the air, and beat its wings against its stomach. Fishermen would watch out for this, and if they saw it would not go out, believing that a storm was on the way. In County Mayo a sure sign of a coming storm was when wild geese were seen flying for a large distance. In County Mayo it was also said to be a sign of rain when wild geese flew low in the air; when they flew high it was said to be a sign of fine weather. In County Cork, the last week of September and the first week of October were called *Fómhair na nGéanna* (Autumn of the Geese). It was said this was when the seeds came on a long grass that grows in ditches and over fences, which geese were very fond of eating (probably goosegrass or cleavers, *Galium aparine*).

Other traditions surrounded the goose.[2] In Ireland domestic geese were called with the words 'Baddy, Baddy, Baddy'. In west Cork domestic geese were said to talk to each other in Irish as follows (in which the sound of the goose can be heard): Young goose – '*Ceoca coirce nú éorna é sea anso, 'nso, 'nso, 'nso?*' (which is 'this oats or barley here, 'ere, 'ere, 'ere?'); Old goose – '*Bíodh geall mara n-éiste tú anso, 'nso, 'nso, nso, | Go mbéarfear orainn anso, 'nso, 'nso, 'nso | is go gcasfar na sgrogaill orainn anso, 'nso, 'nso, 'nso!*' ('It's certain that if you don't whisht here, 'ere, 'ere, 'ere, / that they'll grab us 'ere, 'ere, 'ere / and wring our necks 'ere, 'ere, 'ere!'). In Britain and Ireland, a folk cure for many ailments was to place the open mouth of a goose into the mouth of the sick person, so that they could inhale the bird's breath. More specifically, an Irish folk cure for oral thrush was to put the beak of a fasting gander into the patient's mouth.

A story from County Galway concerns a hunter prevented from shooting at wild geese by a hare.[3] The hunter was out at night during a full moon, and each time he had the geese in the sights of his shotgun, a large hare got in the way, blocking his view. Not wanting to shoot the hare, he went home in a rage, frustrated at his lack of success. The following day he told a priest what had happened, and the priest told him that the geese were the souls of people who had promised to return to their own country, but were unable to do so before they died. Their souls took the form of geese to fly back to their own country and the hare was a good soul trying to help them. If the hunter had succeeded in shooting them, they would never have been able to fulfil their promise. The priest told the hunter that he should hunt only during the day, and leave the night to the spirit world.

In England the sound of wild geese flying overhead was said to be a pack of ghostly hounds in the air, called Gabriel's Hounds or the Seven Whistlers.[4] They were generally regarded as an omen of death, and miners in particular if they heard them would not venture underground. Gabriel was said to be a hunter doomed to chase a flying hart forever through the sky, due to his impiety. In Wales it was said that the witch's 'familiar' or helper spirit often took the form of a goose or gosling.

Some Irish sayings about the goose include 'Don't send the goose with a message into the fox's den', 'Don't put the fox minding the goose', and 'when the fox is the preacher let the goose not listen to his sermon.'[5] A riddle from County Galway runs as follows: '*Ní fuil is ní feoil is ní cnámh é / Ach is as fuil agus feoil a d'fhás sé. / Bain an ceann de agus gléas deoch dhó / agus beidh sé ag scéalaíocht go maidin dhuit*' – 'It's not blood, or flesh or bone / but it grows out of flesh and blood. / Take the top off it and give it a drink / and it will tell stories until morning.' The answer to the riddle is *Cleite gé*, or a goose's feather used as a quill. The saying 'Don't kill the goose that lays the golden egg' comes from a story in Aesop's Fables about a man who is lucky enough to own a goose that lays a golden egg every day. Although the man was rich as a result, he became impatient and greedy. Thinking that all the golden eggs must be inside the goose, he killed it so that he could gain all the riches at once. However, to his surprise and disappointment he found that the goose was just like every other goose inside, and so that was the end of his golden eggs.

MYTHS AND LEGENDS

The domestic goose features in some Irish legends.[6] For example, the goose appears in a tale involving St Kevin of Glendalough. According to the tale, Kevin was looking for a site for his monastery and asked the chieftain of the local noble family, the O'Tooles, for some land. The chieftain mocked him for his request, pointing to a goose with a broken wing and promising him as much land as the goose could encircle in its flight. Immediately upon his words, the injured goose rose into the air and encircled all the valley of Glendalough. Another version of the tale relates that the goose was a pet of the chieftain O'Toole which had grown old and sick, and that Kevin asked the chieftain for all the lands that the bird flew over on its first flight, if the saint restored it to health. The chieftain agreed and Kevin blessed the goose, whereupon it flew over a great sweep of land in the valley, returning to land at the chieftain's feet.

The eggs of the domestic goose are larger than those of the chicken, and so were considered of greater value.[7] A story from *The Cycle of the Kings* centres around this fact, and concerns the bad luck that befalls a king who took goose eggs belonging to a saint. The *Feast of Dún na nGéd* relates how the High King of Ireland Domhnall, son of Aed, arranged a feast for his inauguration, and ordered his men to go out and get all the goose eggs they could find. His men could not find any until they came to a hut occupied by a holy woman, who had a basket full of goose eggs. Despite her protestations, they took them from her. The eggs were for a saint, whose practice was to stand all day in the River Boyne up to his armpits reciting the psalms, and in the evening to have one egg and a half with four sprigs of cress. When the saint returned from his prayers, he was angry to discover that his eggs were gone, and laid his heaviest curse upon the feast. Later at the feast, the goose eggs were placed before each provincial king on a silver platter, except for Domhnall's foster son Congal, the King of Ulster, who received only a hen's egg on a wooden platter. This insult enraged Congal so much that he left, vowing revenge. He later fought Domhnall in a great fight at Magh Rátha and was killed amid much slaughter. Thus Domhnall lost his foster son and the curse was fulfilled.

Wild geese are also sometimes mentioned in Irish tales and legends.[8] An Irish folktale, *The Twelve Wild Geese,* relates how twelve brothers, who are changed into wild geese by enchantment, are returned to their human form with the help of their sister. The tale is a version of another Irish tale entitled *The Twelve Swans* (see Swan). Two main species of wild goose are mentioned in early Irish literature; *cadhain*, assumed on the basis of modern usage to be the brent goose, and *giugrand*, the barnacle goose. However, a certain amount of confusion reigns, as sometimes *cadhain* has also been translated as the barnacle goose. Nevertheless, the two species are separately distinguished in the seventh-century poem about the hermit Marbán and his life in the woods, which mentions the 'dark' calls of both barnacle and brent geese. Similarly in the tale *The Intoxication of the Ulaid*, the men of Ulster are compared, among other birds, both to brent geese (*cadan*), and 'to a flock of shrill barnacle geese' (*giugrand gúr*).

Two incidents in the tale *The Cattle Raid of Cooley* provide evidence that brent geese were eaten in early Ireland.[9] In one incident Cúchulainn welcomes a warrior called Lugaid, saying to him that 'if birds fly over Mag Murthemne you shall have a brent goose [*caud*] and a half' as a token of his hospitality. He also offers Lugaid a salmon and a half, and three kinds of herb. Shortly afterwards, Cúchulainn makes a similar offer to another warrior, Fergus. In the tale of *Suibhne Geilt* or Mad Sweeney, about a hermit living as an outcast in the woods, Sweeney speaks of 'when the brent goose [*cadhain*] comes / at Samhain, up to May Day.' The ninth-century Irish work *Cormac's Glossary* gives the origin of the Irish name for brent goose *cadan* as *cad a faind*, 'pure its feathers'.

The barnacle goose is also mentioned in some early Irish texts.[10] The hermit Sweeney says: 'I have heard the cry of the barnacle goose [*gioghruinn*] / over bare Imleach Iobhair.' A ninth-century poem about the end of summer relates how the call of the barnacle goose (*giugrand*) heralds the arrival of winter. An old belief existed in Ireland that the barnacle goose did not reproduce like other birds, but instead grew out of the barnacle shellfish *Lepas anatifera,* which bears a certain resemblance in its colouring and shape to the head of the barnacle goose.[11] Gerald of Wales in his twelfth-century work, *The History and Topography of Ireland,* was the first to recount this belief. Gerald relates how the geese first appeared as excrescences on fir logs along the seashore, hanging by their beaks while their bodies were enclosed in shells. As the geese grew, according to Gerald, they developed their feathers, and then finally slipped into the waters, or flew off. Thus barnacle geese were not egg-laying creatures of flesh like other birds, but a kind of fish, and so in Ireland, bishops and other religious men could eat them without sin during a fast. Throughout the Middle Ages, this belief that the barnacle geese of Ireland and Scotland sprang from shellfish or trees continued to be mentioned by writers like William Caxton in his work *Mirrour of the World* in 1481, and Bartholomaeus Chassanaeus in his *Catalogus Gloriae Mundi* in 1671. This led to the widespread practice in Ireland of eating barnacle or brent geese during fast days such as Lent (see below).

The domestic goose is famous for its territorial attitude and aggressive behaviour towards those it perceives to be interlopers, and this made it a symbol of watchfulness and aggression to the Celts of Britain and the continent.[12] Geese were sometimes buried with warriors in Iron Age Czechoslovakia, as if the birds were tokens of bravery and protection. At the pre-Roman Celtic shrine of Roquepertuse in Provence a huge stone goose stood, guarding the sanctuary from invaders. A bronze figurine of a warrior-goddess found at Dinéalt in Brittany depicts her wearing a helmet with a crest in the form of a goose thrusting forth its neck in a threatening manner. The Celtic Mars was also associated with geese, and is depicted accompanied by them in several locations, such as Risingham, Caerwent and Housesteads in Britain. In his work *De Bello Gallico,* Julius Caesar states that there was a taboo among the Celts of Britain against eating geese. However, geese have been found as funerary offerings in graves in Gaul, such as at Tartigny and Mirabeau. For some reason, the goose does not seem to appear with the same symbolism of aggression and watchfulness in Gaelic Ireland.

Geese were similarly valued in ancient Rome for their abilities as watchbirds, and were sacred to the goddess Juno.[13] A famous story recounted how geese saved the Capitol in Rome from invading Gauls in 390 BC. The Gauls had captured all of Rome except for the Capitol where a Roman general officer Marcius Manlius held out. However, the Capitol was saved from being overrun by a party of Gauls when the cackling of the geese kept near the Temple of Juno alerted Manlius. The event was commemorated long after by an annual procession with a golden goose. In ancient Greece and Rome, the goose was also sacred to the goddess Aphrodite, and goose fat was considered an aphrodisiac. In Norse mythology, the ancient Germans sacrificed geese to Odin at the autumnal equinox, and the goddess Freya was depicted as goose- or swan-footed.[14]

NOTABLE FACTS
All breeds of domestic goose in Europe come from the Greylag goose, which is a native of northern Europe.[15] The domesticated goose appears in lists of livestock in the early Irish Brehon Laws, where it was claimed that the grazing on grass of two geese was equivalent to one sheep.[16] One third of a goose's value was in its flesh, one third for its brood, and one third for its 'potential' (presumably its value as a breeding bird). From medieval times onwards, the feast of Michaelmas on 29 September was known in Ireland as *Fomhar na nGéan*, or the Goose Harvest, when geese hatched in spring were ready for the market.[17] A popular Michaelmas custom was the eating of a goose for dinner on this day. The raising of fowl was traditionally women's business, and farmer's wives who had large flocks made presents of geese to friends and donated them to the poor. Michaelmas was also the traditional time to eat goose in Britain. Indeed, when the Gregorian calendar was introduced into Britain in 1752, one of the arguments against the change was that the geese would not be fattened properly by the

new date for Michaelmas, eleven days earlier. On the continent, by contrast, the usual custom is to eat goose on Martinmas, 11 November. Goose is still a popular domestic bird across the world today, both for its eggs and meat.[18] Modern breeds of domestic goose valued for their eggs include the Buff, the Buff Back, the Embden, the Grey Back or Pomeranian, the Pilgrim, the Roman and the West of England. Breeds of domestic goose valued for their meat include the Poitou and the Toulouse. The feathers of domestic geese provided quills used for writing, until the advent of the steel nib in the nineteenth century.[19] Indeed the word 'pen' derives from Latin *penna* meaning feather.

Due to the above-mentioned belief that barnacle geese grew from shellfish and so were not really fowl, there was a widespread tradition in Ireland of eating barnacle or brent geese during Lent, when Roman Catholics were meant to abstain from eating meat. In 1891 it was reported that the Roman Catholic Bishop of Ferns gave permission to people in his diocese to eat geese on Fridays, while in the west of Ireland the tradition of eating barnacle or brent goose during Lent continued right up to the middle of the twentieth century.[20] This was not so much because of a belief in the myth of their origin as shellfish as from the notion that as sea birds they had acquired fishy characteristics.

Of the species of wild goose in Ireland the brent goose is the most common, with about 30,000 birds arriving from Greenland each winter.[21] The light-bellied race of brent goose is the variety that winters in Ireland, and Ireland hosts the vast majority of them worldwide. This gives Ireland a special responsibility for their conservation and protection. The Irish brent geese perform the longest migration of any goose at 7,000 km from their summer grounds in Arctic Canada.[22] This is thought to involve non-stop journeys of more than 3,000 km, including a heroic crossing of the Greenland icecap. Ireland provides an important habitat for another species, the Greenland white-fronted goose, with about half the world's population of about 27,000 overwintering here.[23] Barnacle geese also spend their summers in Greenland, with about 7,000 arriving in Ireland each winter.[24] They can mostly be seen in the north-west, in Counties Mayo, Sligo and Donegal.

Magpie — Snag Breac — *Pica pica*

The chattering, raucous magpie is widely disliked for its noise and swaggering attitude, but it is also grudgingly respected for its cleverness. The magpie's distinctive black-and-white 'pie' feathers gave it a duality in folk belief, as a bird that could be both good and bad, and usually also mischievous.

FOLK BELIEFS AND CUSTOMS

The magpie is associated above all else in Irish and British folklore with the idea that encountering it foretells the future in various ways, depending on the number of birds that are seen.[1] In both Britain and Ireland, seeing a single magpie was considered unlucky. In Ireland generally, the bad luck could be averted if you immediately raised your hat to the magpie in greeting, while in County Clare you could also salute it or even bow. In Ireland to see a lone magpie in the morning when setting out on a journey was considered a particularly bad omen, while to see four magpies in a row was a certain sign that some relative had died. In County Donegal, to see a lone magpie was considered very unlucky by fishermen when going out fishing. In Britain it was generally also bad luck to see a lone magpie. Misfortune could only be averted by bowing, making the sign of the cross on the ground, taking off your hat, spitting twice over your left shoulder, and/or wishing the magpie good morning. However, in Scotland one magpie was said to foretell a birth, two a sorrow, three a wedding and four a death. In west Cork the belief was that it was unlucky to see one, happiness to see two, three meant you would wed, four meant someone would die.

Famously these ideas were expressed in various well-known rhymes, which counted the number of magpies up to seven, eight, ten or twelve. Today the most common version of the rhyme runs like this:

Corncrake – Traonach
Crex crex

Crane – Corr Léana

Grus grus

Heron – Corr Réisc

Ardea cinerea

Mute Swan – Eala Bhalbh
Cygnus olor

Brent Goose – Cadhan
Branta bernicla hrota

Magpie – Snag Breac
Pica pica

Barn Owl – Scréachóg Reilige
Tyto alba

Hooded Crow – Feannóg
Corvus corone cornix

Raven – Fiach Dubh
Corvus corax

One for sorrow
Two for joy
Three for a girl
Four for a boy
Five for silver
Six for gold
Seven for a secret
That has never been told

In County Wicklow the version ran slightly differently with 'Three for a wedding, Four for a boy'. In County Mayo also, it was 'Three for a letter, Four for a boy', but 'Seven for the tale that never was told.' A Yorkshire version of the rhyme counts as far as ten: 'One for sorrow, Two for joy, Three for a letter, Four for a boy, Five for silver, Six for gold, Seven for a secret that has never been told, Eight for a wish, Nine for a kiss, Ten for a marriage never to be old.'

Another version widely found in Britain and Ireland was quite different:

One for anger
Two for mirth
Three for a wedding
Four for a birth
Five for rich
Six for poor
Seven for a witch
I can tell you no more

In the north of England several versions of this are the same for numbers one to four, but vary from five upwards. One version continues: 'Five for heaven, Six for Hell, Seven the deil's ain sel'; while a longer version went: 'five for a fiddle, six for a dance, Seven for England, Eight for France'. In Lancashire a rather rude version counts as far as twelve. It is the same as the standard version for numbers one to six, but continues: 'Seven for a bitch, Eight for a whore, Nine for a burying, Ten for a dance, Eleven for England, Twelve for France'. The contrasting fortunes of each number reflect the duality of the magpie. In many parts of Europe it was believed that the magpie was the offspring of the dove and the raven, taking positive aspects of its personality from the white dove, and negative aspects from the black raven.

A lot of magpie folklore concerns the fact that it is continually chattering loudly.[2] In County Donegal the sight of magpies gathering together and chattering noisily was a sign of storm and rain; while in County Mayo, simply seeing a crowd of magpies was enough to say that rain was coming. In Britain it was widely believed that magpies chattering upon a roof meant bad luck was on the way, or that strangers or guests were about to call (not that the two options are mutually exclusive!). In Scotland a person who was garrulous, lying and interfering was called a magpie, and the magpie was also called the messenger of the Campbells. It was said to a meddling chatterbox 'what a messenger of the Campbells you have become!' The magpie was therefore said to be lucky for that clan, and unlucky for everone else (perhaps the link comes from the fact that the name Campbell means 'crooked mouth' (*cam beul*) in Scots Gaelic). In Scotland the magpie was also called the Devil's Bird and was believed to have a drop of the devil's blood upon its tongue. It was said that it could receive the gift of speech if its tongue was scratched and a drop of blood from a human tongue inserted into the wound. The magpie was in fact widely believed in Britain to be a very good mimic of other birds and even people, and was said to be able to repeat words like a parrot.

The magpie is known for its large, completely domed nest, and a popular tale concerns this fact.[3] According to the tale, the magpie alone knew the secret of making the perfect nest, and as a result, many other birds came to it for guidance. The magpie agreed and began its demonstration by laying two sticks across each other, and then covering them with moss and feathers. At each further stage of construction, however, it was constantly interrupted by other birds saying that they already knew how to do that stage. Eventually, the magpie flew off in frustration, leaving the other birds to their own devices. As a result, no other bird can make a nest as well as the magpie. In England and France it was believed that the magpie had knowledge of a herb that could open any bond. The magpie was believed to tie up the entrance to its nest and use the herb to open it again.

Various other lore existed in Ireland, Britain and Europe about the magpie.[4] The magpie was the answer to an Irish riddle, which went as follows: 'It is black; it is white; it hops on the road like hailstones.' Among Irish Travellers, to see a magpie among a flock of crows meant that you would meet another Traveller that day. In Scotland the magpie was also said to be the only bird that did not go into the ark with Noah, as it preferred to sit on the roof. Also, in Scotland eating the leg of a magpie was said to be a cure for one who is bewitched. In Germany and Sweden it was believed that witches and wizards transformed themselves into magpies. In Brittany it was said that the magpie was once as beautiful as the peacock, but it mocked and insulted Jesus on the cross. As a result, Christ cursed the magpie, stripping it of its colourful plumage, and saying that it would always live a hard life.

MYTHS AND LEGENDS

The magpie appears in some Irish folktales, usually connected with the notion that it can have the power of speech.[5] One tale concerns a man called Donald O'Nery, who used a magpie to take revenge on two neighbours. The neighbours in question wished to have Donald's land for themselves and killed his only cow so that he would be destitute and forced to sell. Donald skinned the cow and set off for the town to sell it. As he walked along, a magpie landed on the cowhide and began to chatter. The magpie had been taught to imitate human speech, and so Donald caught it and brought it with him. He stopped at an inn, where the landlady was surprised to hear the magpie apparently speaking like a person. Donald told the landlady that the magpie told him everything and knew a great deal. For instance, he said that the magpie had told him that the landlady had far better liquor than she had given Donald. The landlady was amazed at the truth of this statement, and offered to buy the magpie off Donald. Donald agreed and sold the bird for a hatful of silver. He then returned to his two neighbours and showed them the hat full of silver, saying that there was huge demand for cowhide at the moment. Hearing this, the greedy neighbours killed

their own livestock and took the hides to market, but they just got the usual very low price for them. Donald therefore had his revenge on them, as they were very much out of pocket.

In another tale, the magpie also plays a useful role to a man who has been wronged. The tale concerns a Donegal man called Proinsias Mac Lochlainn who was attacked, robbed and badly beaten. A magpie nearby saw what was happening and cried out 'Íocfaidh, íocfaidh' ('You will pay, you will pay'). The robber paid no attention and carried on with his beating, so the magpie flew over and pecked him between the eyes. The robber was now alarmed and asked the magpie, 'Who will pay?' The magpie replied, 'Your son's son after you.' The robber then fled, leaving Proinsias for dead. However, Proinsias was discovered by a man passing by, and brought to safety, where he made a full recovery in time. He recounted to the neighbours all that had happened, and soon the whole neighbourhood was waiting to see what would happen to the robber's family. The robber himself later died, and his grandson went to America. In time, word reached the community that the grandson had been similarly attacked and robbed in America, and had died from his wounds. It is interesting to note that in this tale the magpie is trying to prevent a thief from carrying out his work, given that the magpie has traditionally had the reputation of being a thief itself.

The magpie is well known for its fondness for bright objects, such as coins and rings, which is what provided the inspiration for Rossini's opera *La Gazza Ladra* or 'The Thieving Magpie'.

The magpie also features in a version of the well-known tale of Labhraidh Loingseach, the Leinster king who had horse's ears. According to the tale, Labhraidh kept his hair long so that no one knew his secret, except his barber. The barber was sworn to secrecy on pain of death, but the burden of the secret became so great that he told his secret to a willow tree. In the usual version of the tale, the willow was cut down to make a harp, which would play nothing except the refrain, 'Labhraidh Loingseach has horse's ears', revealing the secret. In this version, some magpies in the tree overheard the barber, and went and told the secret to all the other magpies in the area. The magpies then gathered at Labhraidh's court, calling out all night '*Dá chluas chapuill ar Labhraidh Loingseach*' ('two horse's ears on Labhraidh Loingseach'). Labhraidh heard them as he was lying in bed and, realising his secret was out, he was so shocked that his soul left him and he died.

In Classical mythology the magpie was associated with the god of wine, Bacchus or Dionysus. In Greek myth, the Pierides, the daughters of Pierus, a king of Macedonia, challenged the Muses to sing, and were turned into magpies.[6]

NOTABLE FACTS

The evidence points to the magpie being a relatively recent arrival in Ireland, as earlier authors all state that it was not found here.[7] The magpie is first mentioned in the twelfth-century work *The History and Topography of Ireland* by Gerald of Wales, who stated that there were no magpies in Ireland. In the *Polycronicum* of Ranulph Hydin, written around 1360, the magpie was also named among various animals not found in Ireland. Later, in Derrick's *Image of Ireland*, written in 1581, it stated that 'no pies to pluck the thatch from house / Are breed in Irishe grounde.' A few years later in 1589, Robert Payne wrote in his work *A Brief Description of Ireland* that: 'There is not that place in Ireland where any venomous things will live. There is neither mol [mole], pye, nor carren crow.' Later in 1617 Fynes Moryson wrote: 'Ireland hath neither singing nightingale, not chattering pye, nor undermining moule.' However, O'Sullivan Beare, writing in 1625 in his work *The Natural History of Ireland*, stated that he knew the magpie from his youth in Ireland in County Cork in the 1590s. Despite this, he gives a rather confused account of it. While accurately describing its chattering nature, he says the magpie is 'black and dotted with white spots ('*nigra est albis punctis variegata*'), which is surely not how anyone who knew the magpie well would describe it. This does, however, fit the description of the common starling *sturnus vulgaris,* another bird noted for its chattering and mimicry. It may be that O'Sullivan Beare assumed that Irish starlings were like another species which he must have seen during his exile in Spain, the spotless starling or *Sturnus unicolor*. This suggests that the magpie was indeed missing from Ireland in the late sixteenth century, or O'Sullivan Beare would surely have remembered it more accurately.

It seems that the magpie arrived into Ireland as a breeding bird sometime in the latter half of the seventeenth century. According to contemporary writers, it arrived first, as might be expected, in the extreme south-east of the country, in Wexford. In 1682 a colonel in Cromwell's army, Solomon Richards, commented that under a dozen magpies had recently arrived in Wexford on a black easterly wind, none having been seen in Ireland before. He reported that they had spread so that they were in every wood and village in the county and were much detested by the native Irish, who believed that they 'shall never be rid of the English while these magpies remain'. This is echoed by Jonathon Swift, who wrote in 1711 to his muse Stella about Wexford, saying that its inhabitants are Old English, and citing as proof that: 'magpies have always been there, and nowhere else in Ireland, til of late years.' Rutty in his *Natural History of Dublin*, published in 1772, gives a similar explanation for the magpie's arrival, saying that magpies had been naturalised in Ireland since the latter end of King James II's reign (the 1680s), having been driven hither by a strong wind.

Though nowadays usually regarded solely as a pest, the magpie traditionally had some uses for humans.[8] In falconry the magpie was the usual prey of the male falcon, which was smaller in size and called the tiercel, while the larger female falcon was usually flown at herons. Also, in the Middle Ages in Britain, magpies were often housed with the poultry to give alarm at the approach of predators or thieves. In the late twentieth century the population of magpies increased dramatically in Britain and Ireland, as they took advantage of suburban gardens and open spaces, so much so that they are now more common in urban areas than in the countryside, with 320,000 breeding pairs recorded in 2004 throughout Ireland. This has led to the magpie being demonised as the scourge of songbirds, blamed for their decline and destruction everywhere. In fact, a fifteen-year study carried out in Britain found that magpies had little or no effect on songbird numbers.[9] Indeed, whatever amount of depredation is carried out on songbirds by magpies is far surpassed by that of the domestic cat. Perhaps it is time that we grew a little fonder of the chattering, swaggering magpie, or at least ceased to demonise it as a pest.

Owl — Ulchabhán — *Strigiformes*

The owl's habit of flying at night, and its skill as a silent predator, has made it a bird of ill omen and death throughout Europe since Roman times. However, to the ancient Greeks it was seen as a bird associated with wisdom and victory in battle. In a further contrast, the owl was sometimes portrayed in folklore as a rather foolish and bumbling kind of bird.

Barn Owl – Scréachóg reilige – *Tyto alba*

Long-eared Owl – Ceann cait – *Asio otus*

Short-eared Owl – Ulchabhán réisc – *Asio flammeus*

FOLK BELIEFS AND CUSTOMS

Irish folklore is curiously lacking in folklore about the owl, and what folklore does appear usually depicts it as an object of humour rather than fear.[1] For example, in Donegal a person who thought they had a great voice for singing, but was actually not very good, was called a *scréachóg reilige* or barn owl (literally a 'churchyard screecher'), especially a woman with a high, screeching voice. A lazy person who slept all day, and only went out at night, was also called a barn owl in Donegal. One of the names of the owl in Irish is *Pilib an Chleite* (Feathery Philip), and in west Cork *Lá Pilib an Chleite* (Feathery Philip's Day) was a day that never came (such a day was also known as Tibb's Eve). Hence a saying about delay or procrastination was *Dá bhfanainn go Lá Philib a' Chleite ní thiocfadh sé chúm* – 'If I waited until Feathery Philip's Day (Tibb's Eve), it would never come to me.' In Donegal the barn owl was also said to spit exactly like a cat at a person who annoyed them. The lack of folklore about the owl can be at least partly attributed to the fact that the best-known species of owl in Britain, the tawny owl *Strix aluco*, is missing from Ireland, along with its famous characteristic hooting call.

It is widely assumed that the screeches and wails of the barn owl gave rise to legends of the banshee, but this not really supported by the folklore. In fact, in many parts of Ireland, especially in the south-east, the banshee is known by the name *badhbh* or 'bow', which is another name for the scaldcrow or hooded crow, reflecting the banshee's mythic origins as a corpse-hungry war goddess (see Hooded Crow).[2] The raven is also associated with the banshee in some stories (see Raven). The lack of an association with the cries of the barn owl is all the more unusual when it is considered that it fulfils much the same function as the banshee in Britain and Europe as an omen of death. In fact, rather than the owl giving rise to the legend of the banshee, the reverse appears to be true, namely that in Irish folk beliefs the powerful legend of the banshee displaced the barn owl from its usual place as the omen of death. Of course, that is not to deny that the shrieks and cries of the barn owl were no doubt sometimes attributed to the banshee, along with the night-time cries of other creatures like the fox. In an exception to this, in County Clare the Anglo-Irish Westropp family were said to receive a warning of a death in the family by the appearance of a white owl, or a headless coachman.

The barn owl or screech owl was generally believed throughout Europe to be a bird of ill omen, a belief that stretches back to Roman times.[3] In Britain its calls generally meant that someone would die, and it was believed to attend the windows of dying persons. Shakespeare refers to the barn owl's bad reputation in *A Midsummer Night's Dream*: 'Whil'st the scritch-owle, scritching loud, puts the wretch that lies in woe, in remembrance of a shroud.' In Wales the cries of a barn or screech owl near a house with a sick person was believed to an omen of death, and in Monmouthshire it was called *Aderyn y corph* – 'death bird'. Furthermore, in England it was believed that if an owl appeared at a birth it foreboded ill luck to the infant. In Sweden it was believed by country people to be bad luck to talk about owls, for fear of angering them.

Various other lore surrounded the owl, for example, the idea that it could foretell or influence the weather.[4] In Scotland the barn owl was said to foretell rain by a particularly weird hooting – hence the saying: 'when the owl is sad, the floods are on us.' In England the owl's calling heralded hailstones, and in Glamorgan in Wales, it foretold snow. In Britain and many other parts of Europe, owls were nailed to barn doors and walls to avert hail and lightning, a belief that can be traced as far back as the Roman writer Columella, writing in the first century AD. The owl was also associated with some folk cures.[5] For example, the ancient Greeks believed that any child who ate an owl's egg would never become an alcoholic; while a 1643 work by John Swan stated that eating an owl's egg broken into a cup would cure a drunkard of his drunkenness. In England it was also believed that eating powdered owl's eggs improved bad eyesight, and in Yorkshire a broth made out of owl was said to be good for whooping cough. In Wales the owl was one of the birds associated with the King of the Fairies, Gwynn ap Nudd.[6]

The owl is connected in some stories with the wren, explaining why the owl is forever persecuted by the other birds.[7] A Welsh tale relates how, after the wren had beaten the eagle to be king of the birds, the other birds were so upset that they decided to drown the wren in a pan full of their tears. However, the plan was foiled by the owl, which clumsily overturned the pan and spilled the tears. The other birds swore vengeance and have persecuted the owl ever since. The brothers Grimm recount another version, where the birds were angry with the wren for attaining his status as king through trickery, and so set another test of kingship, namely who could descend deepest into the earth. The wren promptly slipped down into a mousehole and declared himself king again. They decided to starve him out and posted the owl as sentry, but the owl fell asleep and the wren escaped. A similar old European legend relates that the wren had lost all its feathers, and so each of the other birds gave it one of their own feathers to keep it warm. However, the owl refused, saying that winter was coming and it feared the cold. Hearing this, Jesus Christ then told the owl that from that day on it would be the most wretched of birds, always shivering with cold and never leaving its abode except by night. From that day onwards if the owl appears by day, the other birds pursue it and persecute it unsparingly, and the owl says 'Hou! Hou!', as if it were nearly dead from cold. The stories are interesting in that they present the owl in a rather foolish light, as a bumbling, selfish creature. It is likely that these stories refer to the tawny owl *Strix aluco*, rather than the barn owl, as the tawny owl is often known to be mobbed by smaller birds when they discover it roosting in the daytime.

MYTHS AND LEGENDS

The owl does not seem to feature in early Irish myths and legends; however, it makes an appearance in those of Wales, again probably the tawny owl being the bird concerned.[8] For example, the owl appears in the Welsh legend of *Math Son of Mathonwy*. As punishment for her adultery, Blodeuedd, wife of Lleu Skilful Hand, was turned into an owl. Thus, like the owl, she could never show her face in the daylight, and lived in fear of other birds, which attacked and molested her wherever they found her. In the legend,

Blodeuedd's husband Leu Skilful Hand takes the form of an eagle for a while, and it may be that the owl of Blodeuedd, representing darkness and negativity, is contrasted with the eagle of Lleu Skilful Hand, representing light and goodness. The owl appears in a more positive light as a source of wisdom in the Welsh legend *How Culhwch won Olwen*, when the hero Culhwch and his men approach the Owl of Cwm Cawlwyd for advice. The owl is one of the oldest creatures in the world, and has seen the forest in the valley where it lives cut down and grow back three times. The owl also appears in some ancient Celtic art.[9] A third-century BC bronze cauldron-mount found in Jutland in Denmark is in the form of an owl; while a first-century BC linchpin found in Manching in Germany is decorated with the image of an owl with cruel, jutting beak and staring eyes.

In ancient Rome owls were greatly feared as messengers of death, and it was thought that three Roman emperors, Augustus, Valentinian and Commodus Antonius, died after an owl had alighted on the roof of their villas.[10] For this reason, any owl seen in the Capitol was treated very severely, being caught and burnt, and its ashes thrown into the Tiber. Shakespeare refers to this in *Julius Caesar* when an owl appears as an omen of Caesar's death: 'Yesterday, the Bird of Night did sit, Even at Noone-day, upon the market place, howting and shreeking.' The Roman author Pliny stated that it was a dire omen to see an owl in daytime. The Romans believed that the owl was sacred to Hecate, the goddess of the underworld, and so was linked to witchcraft. The Roman poets Horace and Ovid both mention that owl's feathers were used in witch's charms. For example, Horace's witch Canidia used the plumage of the owl in her incantation.

However, in ancient Greece the owl was sacred to Pallas Athene, goddess of wisdom and victory, because it could see in the dark.[11] If the inhabitants of Athens saw the owl out flying at night, it was believed to be a sign that the goddess was protecting their city. The owl was depicted on Greek coins, and to see an owl was actually a good omen, especially of victory in battle. In Greek mythology the owl's sorrowful cry was believed to be owing to its continually lamenting its fall from better days. The species of owl meant was probably the little owl, *Athene noctua*.

NOTABLE FACTS

The barn owl used to be a common species throughout Ireland until modern times.[12] Indeed, barn owls were to be seen in the centre of Dublin in the mid-nineteenth century, nesting in St Stephen's Green and roosting in the tower of St Patrick's Cathedral. However, the intensification of agriculture and the use of pesticides against rodents have seen its numbers plummet to the point where it is now under threat. Another reason for the barn owl's decline is the loss of many of its favourite nesting sites in old structures, such as barns and other agricultural buildings, as they have been modernised. The concern about their numbers is so great that Birdwatch Ireland have been running the Barn Owl Project for a number of years, carrying out research into barn owl numbers and behaviours. The Project also provides a nest-box scheme, through which artificial nest boxes are provided at suitable habitats. The other two species of owl found in Ireland are the long-eared and short-eared owls.[13] The long-eared owl is Ireland's most common species of owl, but is a difficult bird to see as it spends the day roosting close to tree trunks, emerging only at night to hunt its favourite prey, wood mice and brown rats. The short-eared owl is a winter visitor of open countryside and coastal areas and sand dunes, mostly along the east and south coasts. It reverses the usual habits of owls by being largely out and about in the daytime.

Hooded Crow — Feannóg — *Corvus corone cornix*

The hooded crow, with its black-and-grey feathers and habit of feeding on carrion, was a symbol of death, war and bloodshed in Celtic myth, and was associated with the goddess of war in various forms. In folklore, the hooded crow was also an omen of death and was linked to the banshee, the fairy woman who was heard keening at the death of members of certain Irish families. The hooded crow was also seen in folklore as a clever and wily bird.

FOLK BELIEFS AND CUSTOMS

In Ireland the hooded crow (also known as the scaldcrow, grey crow or Royston crow) was generally considered unlucky.[1] To hear a hooded crow or raven squawking near the house usually betokened the death of a relative. Similarly in Ireland to see a hooded crow fly over the house was an omen of death. A belief among Irish Travellers is that scaldcrows were said to be old Traveller wives who were so fond of fighting that they went neither to heaven nor to hell, and the grey Galway shawl can still be seen on their backs. They were said to be old friends and always to bring good luck.[2] The O'Tooles of County Wicklow chose the hooded crow as their emblem, and are recorded as going into battle with the cry: 'Fennockabo!' (*feannóg abú*).[3] In County Clare the scaldcrow was considered unlucky and much feared as an incarnation of the war goddess, the Badhbh or banshee (see below). In Ireland generally the banshee or *badhbh* was said to appear in the form of a scaldcrow or hooded crow, at the death of members of certain families. In Ireland the raven and the hooded crow were said to 'tell the truth' with their croaks, and an Irish saying was, 'The raven told it, the grey crow told it.'[4]

Some Irish folklore merely mentions the word 'crow', which could also refer to the rook, jackdaw or raven. In Ireland, it was also thought to be very unlucky for a person going on a journey to meet a crow in the doorway, and for the crow to call out.[5] The journey should then be called off. The croaking of crows to each other is humourously depicted in this exchange in Irish from County Cork:[6] *'Bhác, bhác, fuair an capaill bás'. 'Bhác, bhác, cá bhfuair sé bás?'; 'Bhác, bhác, i gcúntae an Chláir'; 'Bhác, bhác, a' bhfuil sé méith?'; 'Bhác, bhác, saill go leor'; 'Bhác, bhác, a' leogfá mise leat?'; ' Bhác, bhác, níl ann ach dorainnín cnámh!'* This translates as: 'Bawk, bawk, the horse died'. 'Bawk, bawk, where did it die?'; 'Bawk, bawk, in County Clare'; 'Bawk, bawk, and is it fat?'; 'Bawk, bawk, juicy enough'; 'Bawk, bawk, will you let me go with you?' 'Bawk, bawk, sure there's nothing but a handful of bones!' The fact that the crows are discussing eating carrion suggests they are hooded crows, even though they are only described as *preácháin* ('crows'). In County Donegal some weather lore concerns the 'crow'.[7] If the crows fly low, caw loudly and look quite bewildered, it is a sign that a storm is coming. If they are seen flying low with one wing pointing towards the ground or flying in groups, then heavy rain is pending. Also, to see a crow diving is a sign of wind.

The scaldcrow or hooded crow is seen as a very clever creature, and some Irish folktales recount how it gets the better of various other creatures.[8] For example, one folktale tells of how it outwitted a hawk. According to the tale, a hawk stayed with a crow for a year to learn all its tricks, and things went very well. The hawk learnt many tricks, and at the end of the year said that it was ready to go. However, the crow persuaded him to wait another year, because there was one more trick to learn which was better than the rest. So the hawk stayed, but at the end of the year he said that he had learned nothing more than what he had previously known. The hooded crow then finally told him about the trick: 'When you are out with another bird, fly out in front of it, turn around beneath it with your belly facing up, and attack the other bird from below.' Then the two birds flew out together, and before the hawk realised what was happening, the crow played the very same trick and killed him.

Another Irish tale explains how the Old Crow of Achill outwitted the eagle. According to the tale, the Crow survived a very cold night by hiding in the eagle's nest and killing her fledgling to take its place. The Crow escaped detection by pretending to be the fledgling, and sending the eagle on a mission to discover if there had ever been a colder night. By the time the eagle had discovered the deception and returned to the nest in a rage, the Old Crow had safely gone (see Eagle).

However, another tale relates how the scaldcrow was itself bested by the fox. According to the tale, a scaldcrow and a fox met and decided to steal the fish from a man called Darby O'Drive. As Darby came home one evening in a cart, with the fish he had caught in a basket behind him, the fox lay across on the road in front of him and pretended to be dead. Darby was delighted at the chance to get a fox skin, and picked up the fox and threw him into the car. As soon as he had his chance without being seen, the fox put his head into the basket and threw the fish out one by one. The scaldcrow picked them up quickly and put them in the fork of an oak tree. However, Darby turned around and saw the fox taking the fish, so the fox had to jump out of the car at once and run. He ran quickly to where the scaldcrow had the fish in the tree, but when he got there, the scheming crow told him he was not getting any of them. The wily fox then thought of a plan to outwit the crow. He asked the scaldcrow if he could at least have the herring at the bottom of the pile of fish and the crow foolishly consented. When she pulled the herring from the bottom of the pile, they all fell down and the fox began laughing. The scaldcrow was so mad she flew at the fox, but he quickly devoured her, saying, 'I'd rather a fowl than a fish!'

In Europe, England, Wales and the Scottish Lowlands, the carrion crow *Corvus corone corone* exists in place of the hooded crow; while in the Scottish Highlands the hooded crow exists as in Ireland.[9] A saying from the Scottish Highlands concerns how the hooded crow cannot be made ashamed for stealing other birds' eggs. According to the saying, the lapwing traditionally says to the hooded crow: 'I never saw your like for stealing eggs.' The crow brazenly replies: 'Nor did we ourselves, tho' 'tis we who are older.' In Scotland the Cailleach, or hag, could appear in the guise of a raven or hooded crow. She was said to be a terrible being that feasted on the bodies of men. In England in Sussex, hearing a carrion crow croak three times meant that someone would die. In Shropshire a crow flying in front to a person setting out on a journey was a sign of bad luck, and meant the person should turn back; while in Devon to see a crow croaking on the bough of a tree foretold death, and whichever way it flew off indicated the direction the funeral would follow. In Wales to see crows landing in a yard on a moonlit night was an omen of death. The Cornish St Neotus was said to have impounded carrion crows in an enclosure, to stop them attacking people. In Wales to find a crow feather stuck in the ground before your feet was a sign of good luck. In Europe generally, a common belief was that if a crow landed to the right of a person it was lucky, and to the left unlucky.

MYTHS AND LEGENDS

The hooded crow appears in some stories of Irish saints, usually as a malign adversary.[10] A story from Donegal relates how the hooded crow had everything on Tory Island under enchantment, especially the birds, until St Colmcille arrived. The hooded crow tried to bring him under her spell as well, but the saint broke it with the words: '*A éin léith an bhrollaigh bháin / Guidhimsa Dia agus Aon-Mhac Muire / agus do cheann héin go rabh á dhealgadh!*' (O grey bird with the white breast / I pray to God and to Mary's only son / that your own head be severed!). One version of the legend of St Patrick on Croagh Patrick states that he was assailed by demons in the shape of crows. After his prayers did not get rid of them, the saint threw his bell at them, which succeeded in overcoming them. The bell fell into a hole called *Log na nDeamhan* (Hollow of the Demons), which can be seen to this day. The life of St Cellach of Killala recounts how he was ordered to be killed by King Guaire. As he was led out to be killed, scaldcrows, ravens and kites gathered around, anticipating his death. St Cellach addresses each of them in turn, saying to the hooded crow: 'O scaldcrow, and O scaldcrow, grey-coated, sharp-beaked, paltry fowl! The intent of thy desire is apparent to me, no friend thou art to Cellach.' After the saint is killed, all the birds, including the scaldcrow, have their fill.

The hooded crow's habit of feeding on the bodies of the dead, and thus appearing to exult in blood and warfare, linked it to Irish war goddesses like the Morrigan, Macha and Badhbh.[11] These war goddesses appear frequently in Irish myth, helping and protecting their warriors in battle by instilling fear in their enemies with their fearsome appearance and cries, and often taking on the appearance of a crow or raven. For example, in the *Book of Invasions* the Morrigan is described as the 'crow of battle' or Battle-Crow, and was said to sometimes fight her battles in the shape of a crow. The Morrigan most famously appears to the hero Cúchulainn in the legend *The Cattle Raid of Cooley* to offer her help in battle. However, after he scorned the help of a woman, she warned him that she would oppose him in every way possible, and changed her appearance from a woman in a red dress into a black crow before disappearing. Another war goddess who appears is the Badhbh, whose name simply means 'scaldcrow'. In contrast to the Morrigan, the Badhbh helps Cúchulainn on a number of occasions, but also appears at his death, alighting on his shoulder. The fact that the great warrior does not strike out at her is proof that he is indeed dead (in some traditions it is the Morrigan who lands on

Cúchulainn's shoulder). The Badhbh also appears in the tale *Da Derga's Hostel* as an ugly, black, crow-like hag, a harbinger of the deaths that are to follow. The goddess Macha, associated with Emain Macha or Navan Fort, the seat of the Royal Court of Ulster, was also described as a crow in the ninth-century work *Cormac's Glossary*. This image of the war goddess became that of the banshee in Irish folklore, a fairy woman whose cries are heard when a death in a particular family is imminent, and who sometimes is also seen in the form of a crow.

The war goddess is in fact an aspect of the land goddess in her role as protector, and the goddess Ériu, who gave her name to Ireland, was said to appear sometimes as a wide-eyed, most beautiful queen, and sometimes as a sharp-beaked grey-white crow. The scaldcrow also appears as an omen of death in Irish legends.[12] For example, a tale of the Fianna relates how Queen Ailne, on hearing of the death of her husband Meargach and her two sons in battle, keened a lament which included the line: 'I knew by the voice of the battle-crow over your *dún* [fort] every evening, since you went from me comely and terrible, that misfortune and grief were at hand.' The hooded crow also appears in some folktales, usually connected with some malign female. In one Irish folktale, a princess marries a prince who is under enchantment, so that he can only appear in the daytime in the form of a white dog. After they are married, the princess has each of her three children stolen by a grey crow when they are a week old. The grey crow turns out to be an evil fairy queen, who is responsible for placing the princess's husband under enchantment. Needless to say, after various adventures, the children are returned and the evil queen is killed.

The hooded crow is not always associated with female deities, but is sometimes simply an emblem of battle.[13] A ninth-century poem regarding Fionntan's conversation with the Hawk of Achill relates that the god Lugh fought so bravely at the battle of Maigh Tuireadh that: 'After the son of Eithne of the armies / went ravens and scaldcrows / the cause of gnawing on bones / beside Lugh of the heroic hand.' In the tale *The Martial Career of Conghal Cláiringhneach*, when Conghal and his rival Lughaidh muster to do battle at Tara: 'Royston (hooded) crows and ravens and seagulls came around Tara at the noise, mindful of the enmity of one to the other.'

There is no Classical lore about the hooded crow, as it is not native to either Greece or Rome, and the carrion crow seems to have been regarded there as much the same as the raven. It may be that the hooded crow's black-and-grey appearance was sufficiently different from the raven and other crows to explain why in Ireland and Scotland it developed its own distinctive identity in folklore and legend.

NOTABLE FACTS

The carrion crow *Corvus corone corone* and the hooded crow *Corvus corone corvix* are generally regarded as subspecies of the same bird. The carrion crow is identical to the hooded crow except that it is all black, in contrast to the hooded crow's grey breast and back. The hooded crow is found all over Ireland and in the Highlands of Scotland, while the carrion crow is found in England, Wales and the Scottish Lowlands.[14] This difference was noted as long ago as the twelfth century by Geoffrey of Wales who wrote about Ireland: 'There are no black crows in this country, or there are very few. What there are, are of different colours.' However, the picture is not static, and the evidence is that the hooded crow is steadily retreating northwards in Britain, under pressure from the carrion crow. Even in the Scottish Highlands, the carrion crow has reached as far as Caithness and the Orkneys to the east. Historically, the hooded crow was also present in many parts of England, and one of the names – Royston crow – refers to a town in Hertfordshire. Indeed, the hooded crow was once a winter visitor as far south as Kent and other southern counties.

All of the crow species make amusing pets if they are reared from hatching, and the hooded crow is no exception. This has been known since ancient times, and seems to have been a common habit in early Ireland. Indeed, the Brehon Laws mention offences that may be committed by pet crows, which were expected to be kept on a string.[15] Nevertheless, carrion and hooded crows have long been detested by gamekeepers and farmers for their habit of eating chicks and eggs, and for their harassment of ewes and newborn lambs, pecking out eyes or even tongues. Historically, of course, crows have been most hated and feared for their habit of eating carrion, including human flesh, even if this thankfully hardly ever happens nowadays. All of this has meant their relentless persecution by shooting and trapping, which does not seem to affect their numbers much. Perhaps that is because the hooded crow will take whatever it can get, using clever means if necessary. For example, it is noted in coastal areas for picking up mussels and other shellfish and dropping them from a height to get at their contents. The hooded crow is so adaptable and successful that it is in no danger from humans whatsoever, and is set to be part of our landscape for the foreseeable future.

Similar birds

> Rook – Rúcach – *Corvus frugilegus*
>
> Jackdaw – Cág – *Corvus monedula*
>
> Chough – Cág cosdearg – *Pyrrhocorax pyrrhocorax*

Various lore surrounded the rook in Ireland and Britain.[16] A very old tradition in Ireland held that the rook had three drops of the devil's blood in it; at the same time, however, it was considered very bad luck to hunt the rooks out of a rookery. In Ireland it was believed that if a person saw rooks looking down a chimney it meant that someone in the house would die in the near future. The rook is associated with St Brendan, according to one story. The story goes that St Brendan's Cathedral in Ardfert was originally to be built in a field called the Gallan Field. Construction began, but on the very first night a large flock of rooks removed the stones and mortar to the west of Ardfert village, where the church was then built. In Britain a colony of rooks near the house was said to be lucky, but the sudden desertion of a rookery was a warning of impending evil. The jackdaw is known as a bird that loves to collect bright and shiny things and so in Ireland those who hoarded patently useless things were said to be as bad as the jackdaws.[17] The Brehon Laws mention that jackdaws were kept as pets in early Ireland.[18] The chough is Ireland's rarest crow, occurring mainly in the west and south of Ireland along coastal cliffs and grassland.[19] The chough is Cornwall's national bird, and an old Cornish legend states that King Arthur was turned into a chough. The Latin name *pyrrhocorax* means 'fire raven', from an old Classical belief that the chough had a tendency to start fires by carrying lighted sticks onto the roofs of houses. This reputation may have arisen from the chough's bright red bill and legs, as needless to say it has no basis in fact.

Raven — Fiach Dubh — *Corvus corax*

The raven, with its black feathers, harsh croaking calls and habit of feeding on carrion, was a symbol of death, war, and bloodshed in Celtic and European myth. However, its distinguished appearance and obvious intelligence also made it a symbol of wisdom and nobility. The raven is also noted for its complex range of calls which appear to mimic human speech. This made it a bird deemed to have oracular powers, and an ability to carry messages.

Folk Beliefs and Customs

In Ireland the raven was generally seen as an omen of death.[1] For example, to hear a hooded crow or raven squawking near the house usually betokened the death of a relative. Similarly in Ireland to see a raven fly over the house was also an omen of death. In Donegal it was enough to see a raven coming towards the house to be a sign that death would follow. In west Cork it was said that when a person was dying, the raven would be up on the roof of the house, hopping and screeching. Then when the person had died, the saying was that 'The raven has his eyes!' However, the raven was not always seen as unlucky.[2] In Dublin it was believed that to see a raven with white on its wing flying on the right hand of any person, while croaking at the same time, was an infallible sign of good luck. In Donegal it was said that the raven was only heard calling on the hottest days in summer, and an old saying was that a summer's day was so hot that the raven had his tongue out!

Some other lore surrounded the raven in Ireland.[3] A very old tradition in Ireland held that the raven had three drops of the devil's blood in it. In Ireland it was also believed that the raven could be used to make oneself invisible, by invoking the devil's aid. This involved getting a raven's heart, splitting it open with a black-handled knife, making three cuts and putting a blackbean in each cut, and then planting it. As the beans sprouted, one was put in the mouth while saying: 'By virtue of satan's heart, and by strength of my great art, I desire to be invisible.' This was said to work as long as the bean was kept in the mouth. The raven was not always a cursed bird, however. An old Irish tradition relates that when Christ was born in Bethlehem, the raven was the first bird to fly low across the heavens, bringing the good news of the nativity to mankind.

The raven was also associated with the banshee, along with the hooded crow. A tale from County Clare concerns the Ross Lewin family, who were supposed to have a banshee.[4] According to the tale, one night in about 1776 the family saw a little old woman with long, white hair and a black cloak, running about a nearby church ruin, clapping her hands and wailing. When they approached the church, the apparition vanished. The family returned home to find their mother in terror. She had been sitting at the window when a great raven flapped three times at the glass. Later they found out that the head of the household had died suddenly that very evening.

An old Irish saying was, 'The Raven thinks her own brood is white', which is another way of saying that 'love is blind'. A folktale illustrates how the raven lost out as a result.[5] According to the tale, a raven came across a fox out hunting, and promised the fox that he would catch plenty of food for him, if the fox promised in return to leave his chicks alone. 'All right, but how will I know them?' replied the fox. 'They are the fairest chicks in the forest', said the raven. The raven went away to do some hunting, and returned to his nest sometime later. To his horror, he found the nest broken apart and the chicks gone. The raven searched angrily for the fox, and when he found him demanded: 'Why didn't you leave my chicks alone as you promised?' The fox replied: 'I spared all the chicks with white feathers, and ate only the ones with dark feathers – you told me your chicks were fair.' The raven replied; 'Don't you know that to the raven his chicks are fair? You should have known that.' 'I see your point,' said the fox, and went on his way, leaving the poor raven still convinced that his chicks were the fairest. Despite this, the raven's glossy black feathers are often used as an image of dark-haired beauty (see below). This may explain an Irish folk cure for baldness that involved burning a raven, and boiling the ashes with mutton fat. The mixture was then rubbed on the scalp when cooled.

In Britain ravens had a similarly negative association as birds of death.[6] It was said that ravens appearing about the bedchamber of an ill person was an omen of their demise, apparently out of a belief that the raven could 'smell' approaching death. Superstitions about the raven appear to be particularly strong in Scotland. In Shakespeare's *Macbeth*, Lady Macbeth welcomes the arrival of Duncan – the man she wants her husband to kill – with the words: 'The raven himself is hoarse / That croaks the fatal entrance of Duncan / Under my battlements.' In the Highlands of Scotland the raven was said to live thirty times the age of man, or 2,000 years, and no Highlander would willingly kill a raven. In the Highlands it was also taken as an extremely encouraging sign to hear a raven croak when setting out deer-stalking. The spirits of the departed were supposed to take the form of ravens; when St Columba was at sea one time, he saw a vast number of them of extraordinary size chasing one another.

Some lore surrounded the raven in Scotland.[7] In Scotland the raven was said to be the first bird to build a nest in the spring, followed by the mallard and then the rook. The raven began to build its nest on St Brigid's Day, 1 February, and by tradition the first day of spring: 'A nest on St Brigid's Day / an egg at Shrove-tide / and a bird at Easter / if the raven have not these / Then it dies.' A traditional charm was said on St Brigid's Day to ask for the saint's protection of the livestock: 'From the blue peregrine of Creag Duilion / From the brindled eagle of Ben-Ard / From the swift hawk of Tordun / From the surly raven of Bard's Creag.' Similarly on the quarter days of Bridget's Day, May Day, Lammas and Halloween, special cakes called bannocks were eaten, and a piece thrown over each shoulder alternatively as a gift to the wolf, fox, eagle, raven, marten and harrier to spare livestock. In Scotland the Cailleach, or hag, could appear in the guise of a raven or hooded crow. She was a terrible being who feasted on the bodies of men.

In England the most famous ravens are those inhabiting the Tower of London.[8] According to legend, there have always been ravens in the Tower of London and, should they ever leave, the monarchy will fall. Despite the legend, it seems that the tradition of keeping ravens in the Tower dates back only to Victorian times, when pet ravens began to be kept by yeomen or other staff. There is also a suggestion that some of the ravens may have been a punning gift in the late nineteenth century by the Earl of Dunraven, who was interested in Celtic mythology and raven myths. The post of Raven Master to take care of the Tower's ravens officially was established in 1968, and in 2004 there was an unkindness of seven ravens in residence: Hardey, Cedric, Gwylum, Munin II, Hugin II, Odin and Thor. The ravens are still a very popular tourist attraction, even if they are known to steal food from visitors.

Various European lore concerned the raven.[9] In Germany it was said that ravens were inhabitated by the souls of the damned, or even the devil himself, while in the Languedoc in France it was the souls of wicked priests that dwelled within them. In many parts of Europe it was believed that ravens had knowledge of magical stones that could act as a talisman in the treatment of assorted human ailments. The stone had to be obtained on St Vitus' Day (15 June); the beaks of nestlings in the raven's nest had to be muzzled, and when the henbird discovered what had happened, she would fly away to collect the magic stone that would set her chicks free.

The stone could then be stolen before the raven flew away again. This stone was said to be a valuable aid in childbirth. Other stones could also be obtained that would grant invisibility to the bearer, and even prolong life and restore it to the dead, but these stones could only be got through more elaborate preparations. By contrast, the Roman naturalist Pliny believed that bringing a raven's egg into a house would result in a very difficult labour for any woman of the house giving birth.

MYTHS AND LEGENDS

The raven is linked to Irish saints in some Irish legends.[10] The life of St Cellach of Killala recounts how he was ordered to be killed by King Guaire. As he was led out to be executed, scaldcrows, ravens and kites gathered around, anticipating his death. St Cellach addressed each of them in turn, saying to the raven: 'O raven, thou that makest croaking! If hungry thou be, O bird! From this rath depart not until thou have a surfeit of my flesh.' After the saint was killed, all the birds, including the raven, had their fill. However, a saint gets the better of ravens in a story recounted by Gerald of Wales in his twelfth-century work *The History and Topography of Ireland*. The story recounts how St Kevin cursed the ravens of Glendalough because they spilled the milk of a sick student of his, so that on the saint's feast day they are prevented from alighting on the earth or from taking food. In Europe, St Benedict was said to have a tame raven which, at his command, carried away and disposed of a poisoned loaf of bread.[11]

The raven had the reputation in Ireland of being a bird that foretold death and bloodshed.[12] For example, the ninth-century *Cormac's Glossary* mentions the raven in this way. The *Glossary* explains the word *nat* or buttock with a little story which ends with the following rhyme: 'The barebeaked raven will say *grác* / gnawing foremen's buttocks tonight.' The *Glossary* also defines the old Irish word for raven, *brandubh*, as deriving from *brandae* – blackness and destructiveness. In the tale *The Cattle Raid of Cooley*, the two enchanted bulls that were the cause of the battle were originally two fighting swineherds. So quarrelsome were they that they turned into two ravens, which were continually scolding one another and making a great noise. When the ravens were approached by curious bystanders, they turned back into human form, and said: 'It is not right that you should welcome us, for there will be many dead bodies of friends, and much crying on account of us two.' They then turned into water beasts, and continued their quarrelling in that form. In the tale *The Destruction of Da Derga's Hostel*, three otherworldly men foretold the coming bloodshed by saying: 'Great omens! Cutting off of lives, satisfaction of crows, sustenance of ravens, din of slaughter.'

The legendary warrior band of early Ireland, the Fianna, are linked to the raven in several tales.[13] In the tale *The Battle of Gabhra*, the warrior Oscar encountered a fairy woman washing bloody clothes in a stream on the way to the battle. The woman informed him that: 'It is not long before the ravens will be croaking over your own head after the battle.' Naturally, Oscar was later killed at the battle and buried at the battle site by the grieving Fianna. A tale from *The Colloquy of the Ancients* concerns three ravens that came every year to each snatch a youth of the Tuatha Dé Danann. The ravens came each year while the youths were playing hurling, and the elders were playing chess and other games. The Tuatha Dé Danann sought the help of Caoilte of the Fianna, who promised that he and his men would kill the ravens when they next arrived (which, as it happened, was the next day). The following morning three ravens came out of the north from the deep sea and, landing on a sacred tree that stood on the green, emitted three 'lugubrious ill-omened screeches'. The warrior Cascorach killed one of the ravens by firing a chessman down its throat, while Fermaise killed the second, and the wounded Caoilte the third. As reward for killing the ravens, the Tuatha Dé Danann cured Caoilte of the poison from a spear that had sickened him, and so restored him to full health. The reference to a chesspiece is a play on the old word for raven *bran*, and the name of an old form of chess, *brandubh*.

In the Welsh tale *The Dream of Rhonabwy* similar elements occur when King Arthur and Lord Owein played a game of gwyddbwyll (a form of chess), while Arthur's young pages and servants attacked Owein's ravens.[14] The two played on, despite being told that the pages were killing and stabbing the ravens, and continued even when the tables turned and the ravens miraculously rallied, killing Arthur's men by carrying them up into the air and pulling them to pieces. The fighting only finished when the ravens had killed all of Arthur's retinue and the sons of the nobles of Britain. Then Rhonabwy woke up and realised that the whole episode had been a dream. The tale is meant to be humorous, but is interesting because it links raven with nobility, along with the usual themes of bloodshed and death. It is likely also to reflect the fact that young boys have always liked to throw stones at birds.

The legendary warrior Cúchulainn is associated with the raven in several tales, especially *The Cattle Raid of Cooley*.[15] In one incident involving a humorous play on words, Cúchulainn gave a warrior called Glas, son of Derga, a great blow. Glas staggered as far as King Ailell's tent, saying *Fiacha! Fiacha!*, or 'Ravens! Ravens!', before he dropped dead. While this was no doubt to signify that he was dying, Ailell and the warrior Fergus misunderstood him and thought he was saying the word 'debts', which is also *fiacha* in Irish. Fergus then remarked: 'By my word . . . all his debts are paid now.' Later, when the warrior Ferdia agreed to meet Cúchulainn at a ford to fight him, he remarked that it was 'a ford the ravens will be croaking over', indicating that it would be a fight to the death. During the battle, the war goddess Morrigan perched in the form of a bird on the pillar stone at Temuir Cuailgne saying: 'Fierce is the raven, men are dead, a sorrowful saying.'

Cuchulainn is also linked to the raven in other stories. In the tale *The Only Son of Aoife*, Cúchulainn killed his own son Conlaoch in combat without realising who he was. When he discovered the truth, he was almost driven mad with grief and cried out the lament: 'I am a raven that has no home . . . I am a ship that has lost its rudder . . . grief and sorrow will be with me from this time.' In the story *The Wasting Sickness of Cúchulainn*, the armies awaiting the arrival of Cúchulainn saw two black ravens croaking. They laughed, and said: 'it is likely that the ravens are telling of the arrival of the angry man from Muirthemne.' In the legend *The Intoxication of the Ulaid*, the advancing army of the Ulaid is described as 'a flock of ravens yonder in the east'. In a story from the place-name lore or *dindshenchus* about a place called *Srub Brain* ('Raven's Point'),

Cúchulainn is depicted as slaying demonic otherworld ravens. According to the tale, Cúchulainn was on the ramparts of Dún Dealgan (Dundalk) when he saw a flock of 'thrice three fifties' of the birds on the sea in front of him. Their hoarse calling and cries brought grief to any who heard them, and they were huge in size, with sail-like wings and a loathsome appearance. Cúchulainn pursued them in a frenzy, killing them one by one with his sling until there was only one left. He killed the last one by cutting off its head, and then he bathed his hands in its blood and put the severed head on a rock. This rock Cúchulainn named *Srub Brain* or 'Raven's Point'. The story is curious in that the ravens appear to be seabirds, swimming in the sea with strong feet. The likelihood is that the birds are an exaggerated version of the cormorant or *fiach mara* – 'sea raven' – as it is also known.

The god Lugh is connected to the raven in several stories.[16] At the second battle of Maigh Tuireadh, Lugh is warned by ravens of the approach of the Fomorians. The ninth-century poem regarding the Hawk of Achill further relates that Lugh fought so bravely at the battle of Maigh Tuireadh that: 'After the son of Eithne of the armies / went ravens and scaldcrows / the cause of gnawing on bones / beside Lugh of the heroic hand.' In the tale *The Martial Career of Conghal Cláiringhneach*, when Conghal and his rival Lughaidh muster to do battle at Tara: 'Royston (hooded) crows and ravens and seagulls came around Tara at the noise, mindful of the enmity of one to the other.' The word *lugos* is said to mean raven, and at the Gaulish town Lugdunum, associated with Lugh, coins were found which depict ravens. It is interesting to note that Lugh appears as Cúchulainn's patron in some stories, and there is evidence of a connection between the two. While the raven is undoubtedly linked to Lugh because of his prowess as a warrior, its role as an intelligent creature with oracular powers must also be a factor, in a similar manner to its association with the Norse god Odin (see below). The raven is also associated with other Celtic gods.[17] At several locations in Britain, such as Felmingham Hall in Norfolk, and Willingham Fen in Cambridgeshire, the Celtic sky god is depicted accompanied by ravens. At Moux in Burgundy, France, a sculpture was found which depicts a peaceful, bearded god, with a raven on each shoulder in the same manner as Odin. In the Welsh tale *Branwen Daughter of Llyr*, the king Bran, whose name means 'raven', was killed and his head buried in London. According to the tale, as long as the head remained buried there, it protected Britain from plague.

The raven or carrion crow appears in many examples of Iron Age Celtic art.[18] A spectacular example is a raven-crested helmet dating from the third century BC which was found in Romania. The iron helmet is surmounted by a bronze raven, with red-enamelled eyes and articulated wings, that would have flapped up and down in a very lifelike manner when its wearer charged towards the enemy. Ravens frequently appear on both British and Gaulish coinage, normally on the back of a horse, digging in with their claws while while holding a small cake or pellet in their beaks. The meaning of the imagery is not clear, but it is worth noting that ravens are known to jump onto the backs of sheep, and probe their wool for parasites. Romano-Celtic statuettes of ravens with pellets in their beaks have also been found at Felmingham Hall in Norfolk and Milber Downs in Dorset. A Gaulish goddess called Nanosuelta is depicted in several stone reliefs accompanied by a raven, and other objects such as beehives, pots and fruit. The goddess was probably a deity of the hearth and home, and the raven may have represented an additional role of the goddess as the protector of the dead in the otherworld. Similar goddesses, such as Epona, were also depicted with ravens.

Ravens have also been found in ritual burials in Celtic Britain.[19] At Winklebury in Hampshire, an Iron Age pit contained a spreadeagled raven at the bottom, along with a pig burial. At Danebury, also in Hampshire, pits contained so many ravens that they must have been a special focus of ritual. At Jordan Hill in Dorset a Romano-Celtic temple contained a dry well, which was filled with pairs of tiles, inside each of which was a coin and the skeleton of a raven. Given its association with death, the raven was probably fulfilling some role as a messenger to the underworld in these ritual burials. Finally, the raven is depicted at a shrine at Mavilly in Burgundy, France, associated with a healing spring believed to cure eye ailments. It may be that the raven's sharp eyesight, and ironically its known habit of pecking out eyes, made it an appropriate bird for sufferers to propitiate with offerings. To the Romans, the crow and raven were known for their sharp eyesight and ability to miss nothing; 'To pierce a crow's eye' was a Roman adage for something impossible. The Norse god Odin who had two ravens as companions (see below), was generally depicted as one-eyed.

The dark colour of the raven was often used in legends to signify beautiful black hair, and even today the term 'raven-haired' is a description of beauty.[20] Often this is part of a threefold description, where the person's dark hair, red cheeks and white skin are all praised for the impression they made together. For example, in the tale *The Exile of the Sons of Uisliu* Deirdre sees a raven in the snow drinking the blood of a flayed calf, and remarks: 'I could love a man with those colours: hair like a raven, cheeks like blood and body like snow.' A similar episode occurs in the Welsh tale *Peredur Son of Evrawg* when the knight Peredur sees a raven feeding on a duck in the snow and thinks of how the colours remind him of his love: 'her hair was black as jet, her skin was white as snow, and the two red spots on her cheeks like the blood on the snow.' In a story of the Fianna, one of the warriors called Caireall was described as having three colours: 'the colours of a calf's blood on his cheeks, the colour of the raven on his dark hair, his body's colour as a lamb from the river.' Perhaps for similar reasons, it was believed in ancient Greece that a raven's egg could restore black colour to grey hair. However, the person applying the eggs to their hair had to be careful to keep their mouth full of oil at the same time, or else it could turn their teeth black as well! It was not only the Greeks, however, who were vain about their hair colour. The Roman writer Martial joked about his friend Lentinus who was dyeing his hair black: '*Mentiris iuvenem tinctis Lentine capillis / Tam subito corvus, qui modo Cygnus eras*' – 'You pretend to be a young man with dyed hair, Lentines / so suddenly a crow where recently a swan.'

The raven is noted for the variety of its calls, and also for its ability to mimic human speech; this made it a bird whose cries were used as oracles to predict the future.[21] A medieval Irish text, *Fiachaireacht* or 'Raven Lore', sets out in great detail the meaning of each call of the raven in terms of future events. The text is also interesting in that it assumes the raven would be domesticated, as it gives significance to the raven calling from different parts of the interior of a house. For example, it begins:

> If the raven calls from above an enclosed bed in the midst of the house, it is a distinguished grey-haired guest or clerics that are coming to thee . . . if it be a lay cleric the raven says *bacach*; if it be a man in orders it calls *gradh gradh*, and twice in the day it calls. If it be warrior guests or satirists that are coming it is *gracc gracc* it calls, or *grob grob*, and it calls in the quarter behind thee, and it is thence that the guests are coming.

The text then goes on to list the other kinds of visitors the raven could predict from its calls, including women, robbers, strangers, relatives and so on. As would be expected from the raven's reputation, a good many of the events predicted involve death. So if the raven called with a small voice *err err* or *úr úr*, it denotes sickness in the house or livestock; if it called *carna carna* ('flesh, flesh') from the sheep fold, it indicated that there were wolves among the sheep. The position from which the raven called is also significant. If from a high tree it denoted the death of a young lord, if from a stone the death of a peasant, and so on. By no means all the events predicted are evil, however: 'If it go with thee on a journey or in front of thee, and if it be joyful, thy journey will prosper and fresh meat will be given to thee.' The text is fascinating as it indicates a belief not only in the raven's ability to predict the future, but also its intelligence. That it indicates ravens were domesticated is not surprising, as keeping crows as pets is mentioned in the Brehon Laws, and there are many examples in Britain up to the present day (see below).

The raven appears as an important bird in Norse myth.[22] Odin, the father of the gods, had two ravens, Huginn and Muninn – Thought and Memory. Every day they were loosed to fly over Midgard and Odin said of them: 'I always fear that Thought may fail to wing his way home, but my fear for Memory is greater.' The two ravens often perched on Odin's shoulders when he sat in his hall in Asgard. The followers of Odin carried an image of a raven on their shields and banners; and the *Landeyda* or Land Ravager, a famous war banner that bore the emblem of a raven, was reputed to have been woven in one day by the granddaughter of Sigurd, a hero of Norse mythology who had the power to understand the speech of birds. According to legend, when Brian Boru defeated the Vikings at the Battle of Clontarf, he captured their standard which featured a raven. The raven became a symbol of County Dublin ever after, and still features on the Fingal County Council coat of arms.

The raven was traditionally used as a guide to mariners seeking land.[23] The Vikings used ravens on their voyages in this way; and are said to have found Iceland by this method. Similarly, the *Lebor Gabála Érenn* or *Book of Invasions of Ireland* contains a version of the Biblical story of Noah and the flood, where Noah sent out the raven to seek land and it did not return. In the Irish version the raven was once white, and the dove black. At the end of forty days in the ark Noah released the raven to look for land, but it did not come back. Then he released the dove. The first time it came back because it could find nowhere to land, but the second time it came back with an olive twig in its beak. Then Noah blessed the dove and cursed the raven, so God gave the colour of the dove to the raven, and the sheen of the raven to the dove, on account of the raven's insubordination. Interestingly, in the early Irish tale *The Wooing of Étaín*, when the *sídh* or otherworld fort of Midir of the Tuatha Dé Danann is dug up, two white ravens come out of it.

The Romans also considered the crow or raven to be an omen of death, and also a bird with oracular powers.[24] The Roman naturalist Pliny believed that the croaking of a crow was an omen of very bad luck. Pliny also said that to hear ravens swallowing their voices as if choked was the very worst omen of all. The Roman statesman Cicero was said to have been warned of his own death by fluttering ravens, and then awakened by a raven pulling at his bedclothes on the day he was murdered. However, a Roman general called Valerius adopted the nickname *Corvus*, or 'Crow', when a crow or raven attacked one of his adversaries and pecked out his eyes during a battle. The Romans dedicated the raven to Apollo, the god of divination. Roman augurs depended greatly upon the notes of the raven, and were said to be able to distinguish sixty-five different calls. A raven came to tell Apollo that his lover Koronis had been unfaithful; incensed, Apollo sent his sister Artemis to kill the girl.

NOTABLE FACTS

Ravens are found widely throughout Ireland, settling mostly on coastal cliffs, upland cliffs and in old quarries, and in 2004 there were about 3,500 breeding pairs.[25] The raven is most famous for its love of dead animals or carrion (including human), but in fact the raven will also catch and kill live prey such as rabbits, rats and stoats.[26] Nevertheless, the major part of the raven's diet is, in fact, insects and other invertebrates which it digs out of the soil with its large bill. Ravens have long been detested by livestock farmers, especially sheep farmers, for their habit of attacking lambs, especially in picking out their eyes. More pleasantly, ravens are known for their acrobatic flight, particularly during courtship, when they tumble, roll over and even fly upside down for short periods.[27] Although we associate ravens with remote upland areas nowadays, they were once widespread throughout Britain and Ireland, even in large urban areas, where they were actually valued for their role in refuse disposal.[28] In fact, the raven was breeding in every British county at the beginning of the nineteenth century, and in London as late as 1830. The major reason for the decline was the campaign of relentless persecution that has been raged since the arrival of the shotgun. Another reason in Britain, strangely, was that there was a large trade in taking raven nestlings as pets, as they make amusing companions. Charles Dickens, for example, had two pet ravens, and the trade continued until the twentieth century in Britain. Given the raven's intelligence and adaptability, it would be no wonder if the raven joined the fox in making a return to urban areas, something that would certainly make life more interesting for us all.

Birds and the Ogham Alphabet

One of the best ways for birds to provide inspiration for us today is through the rich symbolism that has developed around them over the centuries. As we have seen, the use of birds as powerful symbols in myth and legend is an ancient one, and it still compels many people today. Symbols provide an excellent way for us to remember the essence of the mythology surrounding each bird, and so can provide a focus in these times when so many kinds of information are clamouring for our attention. As an imaginative exercise, then, it is worthwhile arranging some of our Irish birds in terms of their symbolism, using a convenient method which will help us to remember them. Such a method is provided by the old Irish ogham alphabet.

The ogham alphabet has a form called *Enogam* or 'bird-ogham' that contains a list of birds for each of the ogham letters. This is one of many different varieties of ogham that evolved over time, and which can be found in the medieval work *Auraicept na n-Éces* or 'The Scholar's Primer'. Most of these varieties are scholarly exercises rather than having any practical uses, but some may have been used to help students memorise useful lists of everyday objects. *Enogam* was probably one of these. The list as it appears in *Auraicept na n-Éces* is as follows: B *besan* (pheasant?), L *lachu* (duck), F *faelinn* (seagull), S *seg* (hawk), N *naescu* (snipe), H *hadaig* (night raven?), D *droen* (wren), T *truith* (starling), C – , Q *querc* (hen), M *mintan* (titmouse or tomtit), G *géis* (swan), NG *ngéigh* (goose), ST *stmólach* (thrush), R *rócnat* (small rook?), A *aidhircleóg* (lapwing), O *odoroscrach* (scrat?), U *uiseóg* (lark), E *ela* (swan), I *illait* (eaglet). Bird ogham today can provide us with a useful framework for exploring the symbolism surrounding our most important birds. One of its advantages is that it includes some familiar garden birds, like thrush and starling, that otherwise do not have much folklore.

However, there are some problems with the list as its stands. Some of the birds are very obscure, so much so that it is not clear what birds are being referred to: *besan*, *hadaig* and *odoroscrach* in particular are not found anywhere else. Also, the swan is repeated in the letters G (*géis*) and E (*ela*), and lastly there is no bird mentioned for the letter C. Considering that some very important birds in myth and folklore are also excluded from the list, a justification can be made for an amended list more relevant to our purposes. An amended list follows below, which replaces the obscure names, provides a name for the letter C, and changes the name for the letter G to remove repetition.

Some of the other ogham alphabet lists are appropriate sources to use along with bird-ogham to create a picture for each bird. These include *dathogam* 'colour-ogham', *ogam tirda* 'agricultural-ogham' and *danogam* 'art-ogham'. Along with myths, legends and folklore, another important source of modern bird symbolism is heraldry, which since early Medieval times has used many different birds as symbols to portray various qualities and virtues. Often heraldry has in effect provided a distilled image of the lore surrounding each bird since ancient times, and is an important source for exploring how birds have been depicted over the centuries. It has been in use in Ireland since Anglo-Norman times and was adopted by the Gaelic chieftains, who developed their own forms of it. It is hardly surprising then that birds appear on the coats of arms of many Irish families. Any examination of the symbolism of Irish birds, therefore, has to include heraldry, and this is incorporated into what follows.

┬ B *Brundederg* ROBIN

According to folklore, the robin got its red breast from plucking the thorns from Christ's head at his crucifixion. In folktales the robin helped heroes carry out their deeds, and by tradition the robin watched over the dead. The robin is also associated with the Christmas season, bringing cheer to the heart of winter. In heraldry it was the symbol of the O'Sullivan clan. The robin therefore symbolises courage, compassion and help to those in need.

ᚂ L *Lachu* DUCK

Ducks are said in heraldry to be a symbol of a person of many resources, as the duck can elude its enemies in many ways, by flying, running, swimming, or diving for cover. Drakes, mallards, teal, eider-duck and sheldrake are all ducks that appear in heraldry. In art-ogham the letter L stands for *luamnacht* or pilotage, meaning to navigate a boat through currents and tides. The duck is a therefore a symbol of adaptability, guidance and resourcefulness.

ᚃ F *Faelinn* SEAGULL

The seagull in heraldry sometimes appears on the coat of arms of European ports, symbolising its link to the sea. To many people, the loud, raucous cry of the seagull represents the sound of the sea in all its moods, both calm and rough. The souls of sailors were traditionally said to appear in the form of seagulls, and to watch over seafarers on their journeys. The seagull symbolises independence, adventure and travel to other lands.

ᚄ S *Seg* HAWK

The falcon or hawk is said in heraldry to depict a person who does not rest until their objective is achieved, and is hot and eager in pursuit of their goal. It frequently appeared in the arms of nobility, due to the popularity of the sport of falconry. The falcon is found as an emblem as early as the thirteenth century, along with the hawk, goshawk and kite. It is often shown with the accessories of falconry such as bells and lure. The hawk therefore is a symbol of single-mindedness, speed and sporting prowess.

ᚅ N *Naescu* SNIPE

The flight of the snipe is so speedy and changeable that the name 'sniper' was given to those hunters with the skill to shoot it. The male snipe during courtship dives quickly through the air, so that the wind through his feathers makes a sound like a goat bleating. This gave it the alternative names in English of 'heather-bleat', and in Irish *gabhairín reo* – 'little goat of the frost'. The mountain goat is also famously nimble on its feet, scaling rocks to evade capture. In colour-ogham the letter N stands for *necht*, meaning clear or pure. The snipe therefore symbolises nimbleness, precision and sensitivity.

⌐ H *H-áinle* SWALLOW

The swallow is said to depict in heraldry a person who is elegant, prompt and ready in doing business, and also a bringer of good news. The martlett or martin appears very frequently in heraldry. It is said to signify a person who has to subsist by their own virtue and merit, rather than any inherited wealth. Traditionally this was the fourth son of the family who could not expect to inherit any land. The martlett is usually also depicted without any feet, because of an old idea that martins and swallows had no feet, and therefore could never land, having to stay in the air perpetually on the move. The swallow is also, of course, a traditional herald of summer. The swallow therefore is a symbol of restlessness, change and new beginnings.

⌐ D *Droen* WREN

According to ancient myth, the wren became the king of the birds by tricking the eagle out of the title. Despite its small size, the wren is known for its bold, confident manner and loud song. Therefore in heraldry it is said to depict rebellion, independence of spirit and freedom. In art-ogham the letter D stands for *draidheacht* or druidry, reflecting the old Irish belief in the power of the wren to predict the future through its calls. The wren therefore is a symbol of boldness, freedom and speaking up for truth.

⳾ T *Truith* STARLING

The starling has the power to imitate the calls of other birds, and even of human speech. In the Welsh tale *Branwen Daughter of Llyr*, the Welsh princess Branwen taught a starling words, and used it to send a message to her father Llyr, telling him that she was being kept prisoner. Starlings are also famous for their huge flocks, called murmurations, in which the birds somehow communicate with their fellows when to wheel and turn together. The starling therefore symbolises communication, messages and cooperation.

⳾ C *Colm* DOVE

The dove appears very frequently in heraldry, usually the turtle dove or ringed dove, as an emblem of purity, loving constancy and peace. It is often depicted as signifying the soul, and the Holy Spirit with an olive branch in its mouth. It frequently appears in the coats of arms of bishops, and was used in the arms of the English king Edward the Confessor. In art-ogham the letter C stands for *cruitireacht* or harping, and the harp is an ancient symbol of heavenly music. The dove is therefore a symbol of purity, devotion and peace.

⳾ Q *Querc* HEN

As a herald of the dawn, the cock or rooster usually appears in heraldry to symbolise the sun, and it is an image of the Christian resurrection. The cock is also said to signify an able man in politics. Due to the link with cockfighting, the cock also signifies in heraldry a hero who fought with courage and perseverance. The cock is therefore a symbol of resurrection, courage and perseverance.

╋ M *Mintan* TOMTIT

The tomtits or tits are well loved for their cheerful nature, bright colours and agile acrobatics at the bird table. In colour ogham the letter M stands for *mbracht,* meaning speckled or multicoloured. This suggests the playful, comical harlequin of many colours. In trade ogham the letter M stands for *milaideacht* or soldiering, and the bright plumage of the tit suggests the dashing smartness of military uniforms. The tomtit therefore symbolises playfulness, joyfulness and youthful high spirits.

╫ G *Gcorr* CRANE

The crane is often depicted in heraldry, usually holding a stone to signify vigilance. This derives from an old belief that cranes lived in communities where each crane took turns to stand sentry. If the crane standing on guard fell asleep, it would drop the stone from its foot and thus wake itself up, remaining vigilant. Cranes, herons and storks were emblems of filial duty and a close parental bond. The stork is often depicted holding a snake, while the heron is often shown holding an eel. The crane therefore symbolises vigilance, close family bonds and protectiveness.

╫ NG *Ngéigh* GOOSE

The goose is not very common in heraldry, but is said to signify resourcefulness. The species that is most often depicted is the Barnacle goose, which was thought to grow out of the barnacle shellfish that clings steadfastly to rocks. The domestic goose was traditionally used to guard the farmhouse as it is aggressive towards outsiders, and it was therefore an emblem of a warlike, defending spirit. The goose therefore symbolises resourcefulness, steadfastness and bravery.

╫ ST *Stmólach* THRUSH

The thrush is noted for its complex and beautiful song, as is its cousin the blackbird, which is also a member of the thrush family. Their songs are among the most uplifting of all birdsongs. The mistle thrush or 'storm cock' is famous for singing even in stormy winter weather. In colour-ogham the letter S stands for *sorcha* or bright. The thrush therefore symbolises musical ability, especially song, beauty and optimism.

⑂ R *Rócnat* CROW

In heraldry there is no distinction made between the raven, rook and crow. The crow and raven signify divine providence. They are said to symbolise someone who is a strategist in battle, and watchful and vigilant for friends. The raven was said to have been first used in heraldry by the Danes as a battle standard. The raven was also traditionally believed to collect bright objects and was therefore a symbol of knowledge. In colour-ogham the letter R stands for *ruadh* or red, suggesting battle. The crow or raven therefore symbolises fate, shrewdness and skill in battle.

✛ A *Aidhircleóg* LAPWING

In heraldry the lapwing is symbolic of strategy because it outwits its enemies by leading them away from the nest. It does this by flying off in a way that suggests it is injured. It is therefore said to signify a person who is a shrewd strategist, and who achieves their goals with wile and cunning rather than confrontation. In colour-ogham the letter A stands for *alad* meaning piebald. This reflects the lapwing's light and dark plumage, and suggests its ability for duplicity. The lapwing therefore symbolises strategy, cunning and covert action.

✛ O *Caillech Oidhche* OWL

The owl frequently appears in heraldry and is said to signify a person who is vigilant and of acute wit. The owl is traditionally always depicted full faced. Its acute eyesight allows the owl to see far into the darkness. The owl was sacred to the Greek goddess of wisdom, Pallas Athene, who watched over the city of Athens to protect it from harm. The cries and hoots of the owl were traditionally thought to foretell misfortune. The owl therefore symbolises wisdom, foresight and vigilance.

╫ U *Uiseóg* Lark

The lark is seen as a bird of cheerfulness and high spirits, but also as rather unreliable. The sweet song of the lark as it soars in the sky is an uplifting token of early summer. In colour-ogham the letter U stands for *usgdha* or resinous, while in agricultural-ogham the letter U stands for *usca* or heather-brush. The colour of resin is similar to honey, which is reminiscent of the sweetness of the skylark's song, while the heather-brush calls to mind the freedom of the heathlands where it lives. The skylark therefore symbolises a carefree attitude, optimism and a good nature.

╫ E *Ela* Swan

The swan is a favourite bird to appear in heraldry because of its gracefulness. It is said to signify a lover of poetic harmony, music and learning, and of grace, sincerity and perfection. It is occasionally depicted swimming. Sometimes a cygnet rather than a swan is depicted, with a ducal coronet and chain to denote dignity. In Celtic myth the swan was associated with heroes and maidens, while in England it is a bird of royalty. The swan is therefore a symbol of grace, beauty, dignity and nobility.

╫ I *Illait* Eagle

In heraldry the eagle is said to depict a person of noble nature, who is strong, brave and alert. It is also said to signify a person who is magnanimous and judicious. The eagle is the king of the birds, whose wings indicate protection and whose gripping talons symbolise ruin to evildoers. The eagle was adopted by the Romans as their ensign, as a symbol of courage and power. It appears very frequently in early coats of arms. The eagle is usually shown with its wings 'displayed' (spread out), unlike other birds. The Roman link meant that it was adopted as an emblem by the Holy Roman Empire, by German emperors (Kaisers) and Russian czars, as a symbol of their claim to succession to Rome. As a Christian symbol, the eagle represents salvation, redemption and resurrection. The eagle therefore symbolises nobility, justice, courage and power.

Postscript: The Universal Beauty of Birds

As we have seen throughout this book, birds have always been a central part of our lives and culture. Somehow, with their colourful feathers, power of flight and ability to sing, they mirror our souls. This is still as true as ever, because although most of us now live in urban areas, birds are still all around us in streets and gardens, where they enrich our lives with their beautiful songs and colourful plumage. Birds have provided inspiration for countless works of art and music, and been woven into the beliefs and practices of many religions and cultures across the world. The fact that they have also provided us with the practical benefits of their flesh, eggs and feathers has only added to their importance. It is no exaggeration to say that even without these material uses, birds would still be dear to humankind. It is no surprise, then, to find that the themes which have been explored in this book can also be found throughout the world.

One universal theme to emerge is that the beauty of birds is appreciated everywhere.[1] For example, the peacock is admired for its impressive display of feathers wherever it is found. In China, the peacock symbolised dignity and beauty and had the power to drive evil away. It was said to dance at the sight of beautiful women, and peacock feathers were used as insignia denoting rank by Chinese officials. Feathers were graded as 'one-eyed', 'two-eyed', 'three-eyed', 'flower' and 'green', depending on rank. Native Americans were also noted for the important part feathers played in their customs. For example, war chiefs of the Plains Indians wore the eagle-feather headdress or war bonnet to show their prowess in battle, which has become one of the most famous images of the Native American. The Aztecs also decorated their clothes with feathers of the colourful quetzal bird, to honour their god Quetzacoatl, the plumed serpent of the wind and knowledge.

Another widespread theme is the notion that souls or spirits can take on the form of birds, a motif that appears in countless folk tales.[2] For example, a tale about the Tartar hero Kartaga relates how he was unable to kill an evil swan-woman. Despite all his efforts she remained alive, because her soul was safely locked in a golden casket in the form of seven little birds. It was only when Kartaga was able to find the casket and kill the birds inside that he was successful. Similarly, a tale from Nigeria relates how a king kept his soul in a little brown bird, which perched on a tall tree beside the gate to the palace. Whoever killed the bird would not only kill the king but inherit his kingdom. The king was betrayed by his queen who informed her lover of the whereabouts of the king's soul. The lover then shot the bird with an arrow, and duly inherited the kingdom. Souls can also take the form of birds in rituals. The Native American Acagchemem tribe in California worshipped the buzzard, which they ritually killed each year to ensure success in hunting. The Acagchemem believed the buzzard contained the soul of a woman who had fled to the mountains, and there been changed into a bird by one of the gods.

Another theme found throughout the world is the idea that birds can foretell future events, either by their behaviour or their calls.[3] In China, for example, the magpie is a symbol of good luck – its call heralds good news or the arrival of a guest. Indeed, very often the good news concerned involves marriage, and for this reason the magpie is a Chinese symbol of marital bliss. Also in China, as in the west, the croaking of ravens was deemed significant. If heard between eight and ten o'clock it was a good sign, but between ten and midnight it was a harbinger of death. To the Nguni people of southern Africa swallows were *intaka zanzi* or 'birds of the home', and their arrival at a home was thought to bestow the promise of future riches.

The beautiful songs of birds have always been an inspiration to poets and artists.[4] The nightingale with its unworldly, melodic, haunting song was a favourite, being the subject of countless poems. To Persian poets in particular, the nightingale was a central symbol of love, and it was said by them that it sang with its breast pierced by a thorn, to dull the pain of unrequited longing. More cheerfully, the call of the lark has long been a symbol of the joys of spring and the morning, and provided inspiration, among others, to

Shakespeare: 'Lo! Here the gentle lark, weary of rest, / From his moist cabinet mounts up on high, / and wakes the morning, from whose silver breast / The sun ariseth in his majesty.'

But we do not have to be poets or artists to appreciate the importance of birds. There is a special quality about them that makes us feel connected to the wider whole of nature. Without the sight of birds soaring above us in flight, or the sound of them singing from a nearby tree, our lives would truely be missing something of great value, some element of hope or uplift of the spirit. In addition, the obvious intelligence and bright-eyed alertness of many birds makes us feel as if they can communicate with us, and understand humans concerns. Even though their beautiful songs and feathers may be really meant to impress each other and not us, nevertheless it is for these reasons that birds will always be loved and treasured by humankind.

References

ASPECTS OF BIRD FOLKLORE

1. Green, M. (1996): *Celtic Art*, London, pp. 126, 129.
2. Gantz, J. (1981): *Early Irish Myths and Sagas*, Penguin Books, pp. 62, 240–1; Gregory, Lady A. (1902, 1904): *Complete Irish Mythology*, The Slaney Press (1994), p. 363.
3. Gregory, *op. cit.*, pp, 88, 148, 211, 365, 375–6; Stokes, W. (1868): *Cormac's Glossary*, Calcutta, p. 160.
4. Gregory, *op. cit.*, pp. 66, 95, 168; Jackson, K. (1971): *A Celtic Miscellany* London, p. 176.
5. Gregory, *op. cit.*, pp. 143, 424; Keating, G. (1902, 1908–14): *The History of Ireland*, (Trans. Comyn, D., Dinneen, P.), vol. 3, p. 221; Smyth, D. (1988): *A Guide to Irish Mythology*, Dublin, p. 131.
6. Gregory, *op. cit.*, pp. 339–40, Gantz, *op. cit.*, pp. 64–6.
7. Stokes, W. (1893): 'The Voyage of the Hui Corra', *Revue Celtique*, vol. 14, Paris, p. 45.
8. Gwynn, E. (1913, 1924, 1935): *The Metrical Dindshenchus*, vols. 3, 4, 5, Dublin, vol. 3, p. 370; O'Donoghue, D. (1893): *Voyage of St Brendan the Abbot*, Brendaniana, pxi; Yeats, W. B. (1888, 1892): *The Book of Fairy and Folktales of Ireland*, Dublin (1994), London, pp. 221–2.
9. O'Grady, S. (1892): *Silva Gadelica*, London, pp. 394–5; Macsweeney, P. (1904): *Martial Career of Conghal Cláiringhneach*, London, p. 135; Gantz, J. (1976): *The Mabinogion*, London, pp. 80, 156; Gwynn, E. (1924): *op. cit.*, vol. 4, pp. 213–5, 351.
10. Ingersoll, E. (1923): *Birds in Legend, Fable and Folklore*, London, p. 214; Kendrick, T. D. (1927): *The Druids*, London, p. 82; Keating, *op. cit.*, vol. 2, p. 349.
11. Kelly, F. (1997): *Early Irish Farming*, Dublin, pp. 104–5, 107, 189, 576, 302.
12. www.logaimn.ie
13. McKinnon, D. (1904–8): *The Glenmasan Manuscript*, Edinburgh, p. 111; Mac Neill, E. (1908): *Duanaire Finn*, vol. I, Irish Texts Society, pp. 84, 372–3; Gregory, *op. cit.*, p. 306; Jackson, *op. cit.*, p. 67; O'Keeffe, J. G. (1913): *Buile Suibhne*, Dublin, p. 75; Meyer, K. (1901): *King and Hermit*, London, pp. 16–17.

ROBIN

1. O'Sullivan, P. (1991): *Irish Superstitions and Legends of Animals and Birds*, Cork, p. 30; Ó Dochartaigh, L. (1977/79): 'An Spideog i Seanchas na hÉireann' *Béaloideas*, Iml. 45/47, p. 176; Hastings, C. (2009): *Ag Bun na Cruaiche: Folklore & Folklife from the Foot of Croagh Patrick*, Dublin, p. 79.

2. Ó hÓgáin, D. (1991): *Myth, Legend and Romance: An Encyclopaedia of the Irish Folk Tradition*, New York, p. 35.

3. Swainson, C. (1885): *Provincial Names and Folk Lore of British Birds*, London, p. 15.

4. Tate, P. (2007): *Flights of Fancy: Birds in Myth, Legend and Superstition*, London, p. 121.

5. O'Sullivan, P. (1991), *op. cit.*, p. 31; Tate, *op. cit.*, p. 124.

6. Swainson, *op. cit.*, pp. 17–8; Loyd, L. (1882): *Bird Facts and Fallacies*, London, p. 76; Tate, *op. cit.*, pp. 122–3; O'Sullivan, D.C. (2009): *The Natural History of Ireland by Philip O'Sullivan Beare*, Cork, p. 137.

7. Swainson, *op. cit.*, p. 18.

8. Tate, *op. cit.*, p. 123.

9. Ó hÓgáin, *op. cit.*, p. 35.

10. O'Sullivan, P. (1991), *op. cit.*, pp. 30–1; Ó Dochartaigh (1977/79), *op. cit.*, pp. 181, 194–5; Swainson, *op. cit.*, p. 14; Opie, I. & Tatum, M. (eds) (1989): *A Dictionary of Superstitions*, Oxford, pp. 328–30.

11. O'Sullivan, P. (1991), *op. cit.*, p. 35; Westropp, P. J. (2000): *Folklore of Clare*, Ennis, p. 46; Ó Dochartaigh (1977/79), *op. cit.*, pp. 182–4; Ó Cróinín, S. (1980): *Seanachas Amhlaoibh Í Luínse*, Dublin, p. 152; Gwynn Jones, T. (1930): *Welsh Folklore and Folk Custom*, London, p. 205; Opie & Tatum, *op. cit.*, pp. 328–9.

12. O'Sullivan, P. (1991), *op. cit.*, p. 29; Ó Dochartaigh (1977/79), *op. cit.*, pp. 173–4; Gallagher, M. (2009): *Tuar na h-Aimsire Traditional Weather Signs*, Letterkenny, p. 6.

13. Ó Dochartaigh (1977/79), *op. cit.*, p. 191; O'Farrell, P. (2004): *Irish Folk Cures*, Dublin, p. 81.

14. O'Sullivan, P. (2008): *The Magic of Irish Nature*, Dublin, p. 41; O'Sullivan, D. C. (2009), *op. cit.*, p. 139.

15. Ó hEochaidh, S. (1969/70): 'Seanchas Éanlaith Iar-Uladh', *Béaloideas*, Iml. 37/38, p. 283; Ó Dochartaigh (1977/79), *op. cit.*, pp. 171–2.

16. Ó Dochairtaigh (1977/79), *op. cit.*, p. 171.

17. www.logainm.ie; Ó Dochartaigh (1977/79), *op. cit.*, p. 171.

18. Cocker, M; Mabey, R. (2005): *Birds Britannica*, London, p. 339.

19. Ó Dochartaigh, L. (1982): 'An Spideog i Scéalaíocht na hÉireann', *Béaloideas*, Iml. 50, pp. 96, 115; Hyde, D. (1890): *Beside the Fire: a Collection of Irish Gaelic Folk Stories*, London, p. 165.

20. O' Sullivan, P. (1991), *op. cit.*, pp. 34–5; Curtin, J. (1894) *Hero Tales of Ireland*, pp. 391–2, London; Ó Dochartaigh (1982), *op. cit.*, p. 102.

21. O' Sullivan, P. (1991), *op. cit.*, p. 31; Swainson, *op. cit.*, pp. 15–6; Tate, *op. cit.*, p. 121–2.

22. Cocker & Mabey, *op. cit.*, pp. 335–6.

23. Cabot, D. (1995): *Irish Birds*, (2004), London, p. 27.

24. Cocker & Mabey, *op. cit.*, p. 336.

WREN

1. O'Sullivan, P. (1991), *op. cit.*, p. 31; Westropp, *op. cit.*, p. 47; O'Sullivan, P. (2008), *op. cit.*, p. 42.

2. Wood Martin, W.G. (1902): *Traces of the Elder Faiths of Ireland*, London, pp. 148–9; O'Sullivan, P. (1991), *op. cit.*, p. 32; O'Sullivan, D. C. (2009), *op. cit.*, pp. 139–41.

3. Ó hÓgáin, *op. cit.*, p. 28; Muller, S. (1996 / 1997): 'The Irish Wren Tales and Ritual. To Pay or Not to Pay the Debt of Nature', *Béaloideas* Iml. 64/65, p. 156.

4. Danaher, K. (1972): *The Year in Ireland – Irish Calendar Customs*, Cork, pp. 243–50; Lucas, A. T. (1960): 'Furze: A Survey of its History and Uses in Ireland', *Béaloideas*, Iml. 26, p. 184.

5. O'Hegarty, P. S. (1943): 'The Wren Boys', *Béaloideas*, Iml. 13, pp. 275–76.

6. Armstrong, E. (1958): *The Folklore of Birds* (1970), New York, p. 156.

7. Danaher, *op. cit.* pp. 250–6

8. Ó Duilearga, S (1948): *Leabhar Sheáin Uí Chonaill*, Dublin, p. 355.

9. Breathnach, P. (1986): *Maigh Cuilin: A Táisc agus a Tuairisc*, Connemara, p. 74.

10. Armstrong, *op. cit.*, pp. 142–3, 149; Northall, G. F. (1892): *English Folk-Rhymes*, London, pp. 229 –31.

11. Owen, T. (1959): *Welsh Folk Customs*, Cardiff , pp. 63–6; Sikes, W. (1880): *British Goblins: Welsh Folkore, Fairy Mythology Legends & Traditions*, London, p. 258.

12. Armstrong, *op. cit.*, p. 152; Frazer, J. G. (1922): *The Golden Bough*, London (1987), p. 537; Opie & Tatum, *op. cit.*, p. 451.

13. Frazer, *op. cit.*, pp. 537–8; Armstrong, *op. cit.*, pp. 144–6.

14. Forbes, A. R. (1905): *Gaelic Names of Beasts*, Edinburgh, p. 349.

15. Ó hÓgáin, *op. cit.*, p. 28; Ó Coigligh, C.: *Seanchas Inis Meáin*, Coisceim Press, p. 70; Ó Cuiv, B. (1980): 'Some Gaelic Traditions about the Wren', *Éigse* vol. 18 / 1, p. 63; Breathnach, *op. cit.*, p. 112.

16. Ó hÓgáin, *op. cit.*, p. 28; Muller, *op. cit.*, pp. 158–9, 162–3.

17. O'Sullivan, P. (1991), *op. cit.*, p. 33; Ó Coigligh, *op. cit.*, p. 69; Ó Cuiv, *op. cit.*, p. 62; Sébillot, P. (1906): *Le Folklore de France*, vol. 3, Paris, pp. 180–1.

18. Opie & Tatum, *op. cit.*, p. 330; Atwood Lawrence, E. (1997): *Hunting the Wren: Transformation of Bird to Symbol*, Knoxville, TE, p. 39.

19. Ó Cróinín, S. (1980), *op. cit.*, p. 152; Ó hEochaidh, *op. cit.*, pp. 289–90.

20. Gallagher, M., *op. cit.*, p. 8; Hastings, C., *op. cit.*, p. 80.

21. www.logainm.ie

22. Stokes (1868), *op. cit.*, p. 60; Best, R. I. (1916): 'Prognostications from the Raven and the Wren', *Ériu* vol. 8, Dublin, pp. 125–6.

23. O'Grady (1892), *op. cit.*, p. 59; Stokes, W. (1907): *The Birth and Life of St Moling*, London, p. 57; Stokes (1868), *op. cit.*, p. 60); Ó Cuiv, *op. cit.*, p. 49.

24. Jackson, *op. cit.*, pp. 65, 70; O'Keeffe, *op. cit.*, p. 135.

25. Gantz (1976), *op. cit.*, pp. 108–9, 147.

26. Opie & Tatum, *op. cit.*, p. 451.

27. Green, M. (1992): *Animals in Celtic Life and Myth*, London, p. 161.

28. Muller, *op. cit.*, p. 131.

29. Ó Cuiv, *op. cit.*, pp. 57–8.

30. *Ibid.*, p. 59.

31. Armstrong, *op. cit.*, p. 143.

32. Ó Danachair, C. (1957): 'Some Distribution Patterns in Irish Folk Life', *Béaloideas*, Iml. 25, pp. 108–123.

33. Chambers, E. K. (1903): *The Medieval Stage*, vol. I, Oxford, p. 236.

34. *Ibid.*, pp. 275, 294.

35. *Ibid.*, pp. 282, 305.

36. *Ibid.*, p. 345.

37. www.Catholicculture.org/culture , retrieved 29.12.2014.

38. Armstrong, *op. cit.*, pp. 145–7.

39. Cocker & Mabey, *op. cit.*, pp. 329, 332; Watters, J. (1853), *The Natural History of the Birds of Ireland*, Dublin, pp. 99–100; Armstrong, E. (1955): *The Wren*, London, p. 134; Cabot, *op. cit.*, p. 29

40. Armstrong (1955), *op. cit.*, p. 7.

KINGFISHER

1. Opie & Tatum, *op. cit.*, pp. 216–7; Tate, *op. cit.*, pp. 71; Loyd, *op. cit.*, p. 114; O'Sullivan, P. (1991), *op. cit.*, p. 48.

2. Tate, *op. cit.*, p. 72.

3. Swainson, *op. cit.*, p. 106.

4. O'Meara, J. (1982): *Gerald Of Wales: The History and Topography of Ireland*, London, p. 44.

5. O'Sullivan, D. C. *op. cit.*, pp. 143–5; Tate, *op. cit.*, p. 69.

6. Bulfinch, T. (1993): *The Golden Age of Myth and Legend*, Hertfordshire, pp. 85–92.

7. Cocker & Mabey, *op. cit.*, p. 300.

8. *Ibid.*, p. 300.

SEAGULL

1. Gallagher, *op. cit.*, p. 7; Hastings, *op. cit.*, p. 80; Swainson, *op. cit.*, p. 205.

2. Ó hEochaidh, *op. cit.*, p. 298; Opie & Tatum, *op. cit.*, pp. 345–6; Armstrong (1958), *op. cit.*, p. 213.

3. Ó Duilearga, S. (1981): *Leabhair Stiofán Uí Ealaoire*, Dublin, p. 317.

4. Ó Cróinin, S. (1985): *Seanachas ó Chairbre*, Dublin, pp. 318–9; Ó hEochaidh, pp. 271, 314–5.

5. Gregorson Campbell, J. (1902): *Witchcraft and Second Sight in the Highlands and Islands of Scotland*, Glasgow, pp. 23, 42–3.

6. Ingersoll, *op. cit.*, p. 261.
7. Dillon, M. (1962): *Lebor na Cert*, Dublin, p. 85; Anderson, G. (2008): *Birds of Ireland: Facts, Folklore and History*, Cork, p. 163; MacSweeney, *op. cit.*, p. 185; Mac Neill, *op. cit.*, pp. 32–3.
8. Cocker & Mabey, *op. cit.*, p. 231.
9. Cabot, *op. cit.*, p. 166.
10. Watters, *op. cit.*, p. 252; Cocker & Mabey, *op. cit.*, p. 234.

OYSTERCATCHER
1. Anderson, *op. cit.*, p. 132.
2. Danaher (1972), *op. cit.*, p. 37; Carmichael, A. (1900, 1928, 1941), *Carmina Gadelica*, vols 1, 2, 4, Edinburgh, vol. 1, p. 171; Forbes, *op. cit.*, p. 318; Anderson, *op. cit.*, p. 132.
3. Anderson, *op. cit.*, p. 132.
4. Ó Cróinin (1985), *op. cit.*, pp. 318–9; Ó hEochaidh, *op. cit.*, pp. 314–5; Carmichael, *op. cit.*, p. 171.
5. www.logainm.ie
6. Cabot, *op. cit.*, p. 193.
7. Cocker & Mabey, *op. cit.*, p. 190.
8. Watters, *op. cit.*, p. 169.

PLOVER
1. O'Sullivan, P. (1991), *op. cit.*, p. 48; Forbes, *op. cit.*, p. 321; Gwynn Jones, T. (1930): *Welsh Folklore and Folk Custom*, London, p. 205.
2. Tate, *op. cit.*, pp. 73–4.
3. Ó Duilearga (1948), pp. 219–21.
4. Ó hÓgáin, *op. cit.*, p. 57; Curtin, J. (1894) *Hero Tales of Ireland*, London, p. 66; O'Keeffe, *op. cit.*, pp. 103–5.
5. Watters, *op. cit.*, p. 176; Yarrell, W. (1885): *A History of British Birds*, vols 1–4, London, vol. 3, pp. 272–3, 284; Cocker & Mabey, *op. cit.*, pp. 204–5.

DUCK
1. Ó hÓgáin, *op. cit.*, p. 420; Hastings, *op. cit.*, p. 82; Ó Coigligh, *op. cit.*, p. 17; Gallagher, *op. cit.*, p. 6.
2. Ó Duilearga (1948), *op. cit.*, p. 4; Ó hEochaidh, *op. cit.*, p. 271.
3. Hastings, *op. cit.*, pp. 79–80; Carmicheal (1928), *op. cit.*, vol. 2, p. 189; Forbes, *op. cit.*, p. 268
4. Gregory, Lady, A. (1920): *Visions & Beliefs in the West of Ireland*, Colin Smythe (1970), p. 198; Carmichael, *op. cit.* vol. 1, pp. 172–3, 310–1, vol. 4, pp. 180–1; Forbes, *op. cit.*, p. 268.
5. Curtin (1894), *op. cit.*, pp. 400–1; Curtin, J. (1890): *Myths and Folktales of Ireland* (1975) New York, pp. 24–5.

6. Gregory (1994), *op. cit.*, pp. 117, 301; Kelly (1997), *op. cit.*, p. 107; Raynor, L. J. (1988): *Legends of the Kings of Ireland*, Cork, pp. 74, 79; Stokes (1868), *op. cit.*, pp. 103, 160; Macalister, R. A. S. (1938–9, 1956): *Lebor Gabála Érenn* Parts 1–2, 5, Irish Texts Society, Pt 1, pp. 112–3.

7. Stokes (1868), p. 160.

8. O'Meara (1982), *op. cit.* p. 79.

9. Kelly, *op. cit.*, p. 107.

10. *Ibid.*, p. 298.

11. Green (1992), *op. cit.*, pp. 24, 52.

12. *Ibid.*, pp. 212–3; Green, M. (1992a): *Dictionary of Celtic Myth and Legend*, London, p. 88.

13. Hobson, J. C. (2009): *Backyard Ducks and Geese*, Wiltshire, pp. 12, 29–32, 38–41.

14. Cocker & Mabey, *op. cit.*, p. 91.

15. Collins, R. (2007) 'Why did the Duck Cross the Road?' *Irish Examiner*, www.irishexaminer.com, retrieved 1.9.2014.

DOMESTIC CHICKEN

1. Danaher (1970), *op. cit.*, p. 230; Breathnach, *op. cit.*, p. 92; Gregory (1970), *op. cit.*, p. 150; O'Farrell, *op. cit.*, p. 32.

2. Hastings, *op. cit.*, pp. 82, 88–90; Ó hÓgáin, *op. cit.*, p. 31; Ó hEochaidh, *op. cit.*, pp. 212, 315; O'Sullivan, P. (1991). *op. cit.*, pp. 50, 52; Ó Súilleabháin, S. (1967): *Irish Folk Custom and Belief*, Dublin, p. 30.

3. O'Sullivan, P. (1991), *op. cit.*, p. 51; Ó hÓgáin, *op. cit.*, p. 31; Ó Duilearga (1981), *op. cit.*, p. 317.

4. Hastings, *op. cit.*, p. 87; Minihane, P. (2003): *Beara Woman Talking: The Lore of Peig Minihane*, Cork, p. 28 Ó hEochaidh, *op. cit.*, pp. 218–9, 225; O'Sullivan, P. (1991) *op. cit.*, pp. 50, 53; Danaher (1972, *op. cit.*, p. 239; Ó hÓgáin, *op. cit.*, p. 85; Ó Duilearga (1981), *op. cit.*, p. 216.

5. Gregory (1970), *op. cit.*, pp. 116, 133, 150; Curtin (1894), *op. cit.*, p. 101; O'Sullivan, P. (1991), *op. cit.*, p. 52.

6. O'Sullivan, P. (1991), *op. cit.*, p. 31; Ó hÓgáin, *op. cit.*, p. 31; Gregory (1970), *op. cit.*, pp. 235, 279; O'Sullivan, S. (1977): *Legends from Ireland*, London, pp. 29–31; Ó Súilleabháin (1967), pp. 191–2; Hastings, *op. cit.*, p. 79.

7. Westropp, *op. cit.*, p. 37; Crofton Croker, T. (1824): *Researches in the South of Ireland* (1969), Shannon, p. 92; O'Sullivan, P. (1991), *op. cit.*, p. 50.

8. Ó hÓgáin, *op. cit.*, p. 31; O'Sullivan, P. (1991), *op. cit.*, p. 51; Ó hEochaidh, *op. cit.*, pp. 229, 236; Opie & Tatum, *op. cit.*, pp. 133, 135–6; Minihane, *op. cit.*, p. 27; Ó Cróinín (140), *op. cit.*, p. 140; Roe, H. (1939): 'Tales, Customs and Beliefs from Laoighis', *Béaloideas*, Iml. 9 Uimh. 1, p. 32.

9. Opie & Tatum, *op. cit.*, p. 134.

10. *Ibid.*, p. 133.

11. Danaher (1972), *op. cit.*, pp. 75–6.

12. Opie & Tatum, *op. cit.*, p. 133.

13. Ó hEochaidh, *op. cit.*, pp. 211–2.

14. O'Sullivan, S. (1977), *op. cit.*, pp. 106–7; Ó hEochaidh, *op. cit.*, p. 225; Keating, *op. cit.*, vol. 3, p. 73.

15. O'Meara, *op. cit.*, pp. 76–7.

16. Kelly, *op. cit.*, pp. 102, 571.

17. Green (1992), *op. cit.*, pp. 34, 125.

18. *Ibid.*, pp. 23, 34, 142; Green (1992a): *Dictionary of Celtic Myth and Legend*, London, pp. 62–3.

19. Ingersoll, *op. cit.*, pp. 41, 45.

20. Crossley Holland, K. (1980): *The Penguin Book of Norse Myths*, pp. 123, 173; Tate, *op. cit.*, p. 5.

21. Kelly, *op. cit.*, p. 102.

22. Scrivener, D. (2008): *Poultry: Breeds and Management*, Wiltshire, p. 13.

23. Anderson, *op. cit.*, p. 291.

24. Danaher (1972), *op. cit.*, pp. 128, 187, 250.

SKYLARK

1. Danaher (1972), *op. cit.*, p. 37; O'Sullivan, P. (1991), *op. cit.*, pp. 29, 50; Gregorson Campbell (1902), *op. cit.*, p. 249; Ó hEochaidh, *op. cit.*, pp. 283, 316.

2. Ó Duilearga (1948), *op. cit.*, p. 344.

3. O'Sullivan, S. (1977), *op. cit.*, pp. 41–2; Swainson, *op. cit.*, p. 94; Loyd, *op. cit.*, p. 53.

4. O'Sullivan, P. (1991), *op. cit.*, p. 50.

5. Forbes, *op. cit.*, p. 301; Opie & Tatum, *op. cit.*, p. 227.

6. Ó Baoill, D. (1992): *Amach as Ucht na Sliabh*, Ballyshannon, pp. 8–9.

7. O'Sullivan, P., *op. cit.*, p. 50; Ó hEochaidh, *op. cit.*, p. 283.

8. Ó hÓgain, *op. cit.*, p. 75.

9. Gregory (1994), *op. cit.*, p. 120; O'Rahilly, C. (1967): *Táin Bó Cuailnge*, p. 235.

10. Swainson, *op. cit.*, p. 94; Loyd, *op. cit.*, pp. 56, 156.

11. Loyd, *op. cit.*, p. 57; Yarrell, *op. cit.*, vol. 1, p. 621; Cocker & Mabey, *op. cit.*, p. 309.

12. Cocker & Mabey, *op. cit.*, p. 310.

13. Watters, *op. cit.*, p. 93.

SWALLOW

1. Hastings, *op. cit.*, pp. 78–9; Gallagher, *op. cit.*, p. 7; Ó Coigligh, *op. cit.*, pp. 82, 115; Ó hÓgáin, *op. cit.*, p. 420; Ó hEochaidh, *op. cit.*, p. 291; Westropp, *op. cit.*, p. 39.

2. O'Sullivan, P. (1991), *op. cit.*, p. 39; Wood Martin, *op. cit.*, p. 144; Danaher, K. (1967): *Folk Tales from the Irish Countryside*, Cork, pp. 114–5; Ó hEochaidh, *op. cit.*, p. 291; Ó hÓgáin, *op. cit.*, p. 35; Ó Cléirigh, T. (1928): 'Gleanings in Wicklow', *Béaloideas*, Iml. Uimh. 3, p. 250.

3. Opie & Tatum, *op. cit.*, pp. 25, 387; Swainson, *op. cit.*, pp. 53–4.

4. Swainson, pp. 50, 53; Loyd, *op. cit.*, p. 92; Tate, *op. cit.*, pp. 135–6.

5. Swainson, *op. cit.*, p. 51; Tate, *op. cit.*, p. 141.

6. Gregory (1994), *op. cit.*, pp. 164, 244, 475; O'Rahilly (1967), *op. cit.*, pp. 146, 188; Curtin (1894), *op. cit.*, pp. 95–6; Jackson, *op. cit.*, p. 63.

7. Grigson, G. (1958): *The Englishman's Flora* (1996), Oxford, p. 71; Tate, *op. cit.*, p. 141.

8. Cocker & Mabey, *op. cit.*, p. 316.

9. *Ibid.*, p. 317.

10. White, G. (1788–9): *The Natural History of Selborne* (1977), pp. xxi, 31.

11. Cabot, *op. cit.*, p. 34.

12. *Ibid.*, p. 36; Opie & Tatum, *op. cit.*, p. 388.

13. Cocker & Mabey, *op. cit.*, p. 298.

14. Watters, *op. cit.*, p. 118.

15. Opie & Tatum, *op. cit.*, pp. 330, 387

CUCKOO

1. Swainson, *op. cit.*, p. 118; Opie & Tatum, *op. cit.*, pp. 112–4; Wood Martin, *op. cit.*, p. 142; O'Sullivan, P. (1991), *op. cit.*, p. 38; Danaher (1972), *op. cit.*, p. 125; Tate, *op. cit.*, pp. 26–7; Ó hEochaidh, *op. cit.*, p. 276; Ó Cróinín (1985), *op. cit.* p. 496; Westropp, *op. cit.*, p. 39.

2. O'Sullivan, D. C., *op. cit.*, p. 105; Gregorson Campbell (1902), *op. cit.*, p. 271; Danaher (1972), *op. cit.*, p. 125; Opie & Tatum, *op. cit.*, pp. 112–3; Tate, *op. cit.*, pp. 24–5.

3. O'Sullivan, P. (1991), *op. cit.*, p. 38; Danaher (1972), *op. cit.*, p. 150; O'Sullivan, D. C., *op. cit.*, p. 105; Gregorson Campbell (1900), *op. cit.*, p. 276; Tate, *op. cit.*, p. 28.

4. Watters, *op. cit.*, p. 101; O'Sullivan, P. (1991), *op. cit.*, p. 38; Wood Martin, *op. cit.*, p. 142; Danaher (1972), *op. cit.*, p. 125; Breathnach, P. (1986): *Maigh Cuilin: A Táisc agus a Tuairisc*, Connemara, p. 84.

5. O'Sullivan, P. (1991), *op. cit.*, p. 38; Ó Cróinín (1985), *op. cit.* p. 153; Gallagher, *op. cit.*, p. 6.

6. Opie & Tatum, *op. cit.*, p. 112; Smith, C. E. & Kelman, J. H.: *Trees Shown to the Children*, London, p. 103; Grigson, G. (1959): *The Cherry Tree*, London, p. 127.

7. Ó hEochaidh, *op. cit.*, pp. 276, 283; Forbes, *op. cit.*, p. 263.

8. Ó hEochaidh, *op. cit.*, pp. 276; Forbes, *op. cit.*, p. 263; Gregorson Campbell (1902), *op. cit.*, p. 272.

9. www.logainm.ie

10. Jackson, *op. cit.*, p. 63; O'Keeffe, *op. cit.*, p. 33; Gregory (1994), *op. cit.*, p. 212; Gwynn, *op. cit.*, vol. 3, p. 97; McKinnon, *op. cit.*, p. 111.

11. MacNeill, M. (1962): *The Festival of Lughnasa*, Oxford, pp. 556–7; O'Grady. (1892): 'Agallamh na Senorach', *Silva Gadelica* (1999) Ontario, p. 23; Jackson, *op. cit.*, p. 102.

12. Swainson, *op. cit.*, p. 113.

13. O'Sullivan, D. C., *op. cit.*, p. 105.

14. Cocker & Mabey, *op. cit.* pp. 278–9; Cabot, *op. cit.*, p. 52.

15. Cabot, *op. cit.*, p. 52.

DOVE

1. Ó hÓgáin, *op. cit.*, p. 35; O'Sullivan, P. (1991), *op. cit.*, p. 48; Ó hEochaidh, *op. cit.*, pp. 278, 283.

2. Swainson, *op. cit.*, p. 168; Carmicheal, *op. cit.*, vol. 2, pp. 184–5; Opie & Tatum, *op. cit.*, p. 127; Watters, *op. cit.*, p. 121.

3. Swainson, *op. cit.*, p. 168; Opie & Tatum, *op. cit.*, pp. 308–9; Loyd, *op. cit.*, p. 199.

4. Cabot, *op. cit.*, pp. 17, 44.

5. *Ibid.*, p. 179.

6. Kelly (1997), *op. cit.*, p. 107.

7. www.birdwatch.ie

8. Curtin (1890), *op. cit.*, p. 90; Curtin (1894), *op. cit.*, p. 178.

9. Hyde, *op. cit.*, p. 89.

10. Keating, *op. cit.*, vol. 3, pp. 41, 101; Ó Cuinn, C. (1990): *Scian a Caitheadh le Toinn – Scéalta Inis Eoghain*, Dublin, p. 73; MacNeill, M., *op. cit.*, pp. 562–3.

11. Anderson, *op. cit.*, p. 183; O'Keeffe, *op. cit.*, p. 153; McNeill, E., *op. cit.*, pp. 372–3; Meyer, K. (1901), *op. cit.*, pp. 16–7; Meyer, K. (1902): *Comrac Liadaine ocus Cuirithir*, or *Liadain and Cuirithir*, London, p. 15.

12. Green (1992), *op. cit.*, p. 216; Green (1992a), *op. cit.*, p. 85.

13. Ingersoll, *op. cit.*, p. 130; Tate, *op. cit.*, pp. 36–7; Bulfinch, *op. cit.*, p. 325; Swainson, *op. cit.*, p. 170; O'Sullivan, D. C., *op. cit.*, p. 123.

14. Tate, *op. cit.*, p. 37; Macalister, *op. cit.*, Pt. 1, pp. 121–3.

15. Swainson, *op. cit.*, p. 170; Tate, *op. cit.*, pp. 37–8.

16. Cocker & Mabey, *op. cit.*, pp. 261–2.

17. Yarrell, *op. cit.*, vol. 3, p. 18; Blume, M. (2004): 'The hallowed history of the carrier pigeon', *The New York Times*, retrieved 30.9.2014; Cocker & Mabey, *op. cit.*, p. 264; Allen, K. (2007): 'Reuters: a brief history', *The Guardian*, www.theguardian.com, retrieved 30.9.14.

18. www.pigeoncontrolresourcecentre.org, retrieved 30.9.14.

19. Cabot, *op. cit.*, p. 45; Cocker & Mabey, *op. cit.*, p. 270.

BLACKBIRD

1. O'Sullivan, P. (2008), *op. cit.*, p. 46; Swainson, *op. cit.* p. 7; Opie & Tatum, *op. cit.*, p. 26; Forbes, *op. cit.*, p. 246; Gallagher, *op. cit.*, p. 5; Hastings, *op. cit.*, pp. 79–80.

2. Danaher (1972), *op. cit.*, p. 85; Forbes, *op. cit.*, p. 246.

3. O'Sullivan, P. (1991), *op. cit.*, p. 40; Ó hEochaidh, *op. cit.*, p. 280; Breathnach, *op. cit.*, pp. 121–2; O'Sullivan, D. C., *op. cit.*, p. 131; Tate, *op. cit.*, p. 1; www.bto.org, retrieved 6.10.14.

4. Swainson, *op. cit.*, p. 7; Tate, *op. cit.*, p. 1; Forbes, *op. cit.*, p. 246.

5. Ó hEochaidh, *op. cit.*, p. 280; Gwynn Jones, *op. cit.*, p. 155; Loyd, *op. cit.*, p. 65.

6. Curtin (1890), *op. cit.*, pp. 159, 166–7, 183; Curtin (1894), *op. cit.*, p. 383; Gregory (1994), *op. cit.*, p. 197.

7. O'Sullivan, S. (1966): *Folktales of Ireland*, London, pp. 15–8; Gantz (1976), *op. cit.*, p. 164; Green (1992a), *op. cit.*, p. 73; Forbes, *op. cit.*, p. 305.

8. Ó hÓgáin, *op. cit.*, p. 75; O'Meara, *op. cit.*, p. 78.

9. O'Sullivan, P. *op. cit.*, p. 40; Gregory (1994), *op. cit.*, pp. 296–8; O'Rahilly (1967), *op. cit.*, p. 169.

10. Meyer, K. (1904): 'Finn and the Man in the Tree', *Revue Celtique*, vol. 25, Paris, pp. 347–9; McNeill, E, *op. cit.*, p. 198; Meyer, K. (1910): 'Reicne Fothaid Canainne', *Fianaigecht*, Dublin, p. 17.

11. Stokes (1868), *op. cit.*, p. 7; Murphy, G. (1933), *Duanaire Finn*, vol. 2, Irish Texts Society, pp. 204–5; Gregory (1994), *op. cit.*, p. 306; Jackson, *op. cit.*, pp. 63, 69, 74, 125; Murphy, G. (1956): *Early Irish Lyrics*, Dublin.

12. Cocker & Mabey, *op. cit.*, p. 352; Cabot, *op. cit.*, p. 19.

13. Cocker & Mabey, *op. cit.*, p. 352.

14. Anderson, *op. cit.*, p. 203.

15. Gregory (1994), *op. cit.*, p. 171; Murphy, G. (1933), *op. cit.*, pp. 204–5, 372–3; O'Sullivan, D. C. *op. cit.*, p. 131; Swainson, *op. cit.*, p. 4; Anderson, *op. cit.*, p. 209; Watters, *op. cit.*, p. 31.

EAGLE

1. Ó Duilearga (1948), *op. cit.*, p. 371; Yarrell, *op. cit.*, vol. 1, p. 14; Swainson, *op. cit.*, p. 135.

2. Yeats, *op. cit.*, pp. 104–7; O'Sullivan, P. (1991), *op. cit.*, p. 45.

3. O'Sullivan, P. (1991), *op. cit.*, pp. 45–6.

4. Forbes, *op. cit.*, p. 269; Carmichael, *op. cit.*, vol. 1, pp. 172–3, vol. 2, pp. 34–5; Armstrong (1958), *op. cit.*, pp. 132–3.

5. Tate, *op. cit.*, p. 49; Anderson, *op. cit.*, pp. 310–1.

6. Pauli, R. (1889): *The Life of Alfred the Great*, Trans. by B. Thorpe, London, p. 164; Cocker & Mabey, *op. cit.*, pp. 123–4; Brennan, J. (2013): *Donegal Folk Tales*, Dublin, pp. 48–52.

7. O'Sullivan, S. (1996), *op. cit.*, pp. 15–8.

8. O'Rahilly, *op. cit.*, p. 260; Gregory (1994), *op. cit.*, pp. 164, 272, 306; Murphy, G. (1933), *op. cit.*, pp. 372–3; Jackson, *op. cit.*, p. 65.

9. Ó hÓgáin, *op. cit.*, pp. 219, 224; Thorpe, L. (1966): *Geoffrey of Monmouth: The History of the Kings of Britain*, London, pp. 80, 219, 283.

10. Gantz (1976), *op. cit.*, pp. 165, 172–3; Green (1992a), *op. cit.*, p. 89; Green (1992), *op. cit.*, p. 170; Gwynn Jones, *op. cit.*, p. 21; Jackson, *op. cit.*, p. 252.

11. Green (1992a), *op. cit.*, p. 88.

12. Green (1992), *op. cit.*, pp. 142, 149, 159, 222; Green (1992a), *op. cit.*, p. 88.

13. Crossley Holland, *op. cit.*, pp. 15, 31–2, 61, 77.

14. Tate, *op. cit.*, p. 43.

15. Swainson, *op. cit.*, p. 134; Opie & Tatum, *op. cit.*, pp. 129, 451.

16. Cocker & Mabey, *op. cit.*, p. 133; Ingersoll, *op. cit.*, p. 32.

17. D'Arcy, G. (1999): *Ireland's Lost Birds*, Dublin, p. 65; Anderson, *op. cit.*, pp. 310, 313; Yarrell, *op. cit.*, vol. 1, p. 14; Cabot, *op. cit.*, p. 94.

18. Cocker & Mabey, *op. cit.*, p. 120.

19. www.goldeneagletrust.org, retrieved 8.12.2014.

HAWK

1. Yeats, *op. cit.*, pp. 289–90; Ó Duilearga (1948), *op. cit.*, pp. 4–5.

2. www.logainm.ie

3. Carmichael, *op. cit.*, vol. 1, pp. 156–7, 172–3, vol. 2. pp. 34–5.

4. Stokes, W. (1890): *Lives of the Saints from the Book of Lismore*, Oxford, pp. 224–5; O'Meara, J. (1982), *op. cit.*, p. 83.

5. Gregory (1994), *op. cit.*, pp. 38, 306, 416, 437; O'Rahilly, *op. cit.*, p. 190; O'Grady (1892), *op. cit.*, pp. 424–5.

6. Gregory (1994), *op. cit.*, pp. 264, 416; Stokes, W. (1892): *The Bodleian Dinnshenchus*, London, p. 491.

7. Gantz (1976), *op. cit.*, pp. 152, 265.

8. O'Rahilly, *op. cit.*, p. 269; Gregory (1994), *op. cit.*, pp. 228, 475; O'Rahilly, C. (1924): *The Pursuit of Gruaidhe Griansholus*, Irish Texts Society, pp. 34–5; Curtin (1894), *op. cit.*, pp. 383, 417.

9. Gregory (1994), *op. cit.*, p. 243, 469; Curtin (1894), *op. cit.*, p. 401; Macalister (1956), *op. cit.*, Pt 5, pp. 111–3.

10. Ó hÓgáin, *op. cit.*, p. 224; Meyer, K. (1907): 'The Colloquy between Fintan and the Hawk of Achill', *Anecdota* I, Halle/Seele, pp. 24–39.

11. Crossley Holland, *op. cit.*, pp. 15, 42–3, 70–1.

12. Loyd, *op. cit.*, p. 143; Green (1992), *op. cit.*, pp. 56, 58.

13. Kelly, *op. cit.*, pp. 302–3.

14. Yarrell, *op. cit.*, vol. 1, pp. 53, 55; Kelly, *op. cit.*, p. 303; Cocker & Mabey, *op. cit.*, pp. 128, 142–3; Anderson, *op. cit.*, p. 112.

15. Ball, F. E. (1920): *A History of the County Dublin*, vol. 6, RSAI, Dublin, p. 13; Watters, *op. cit.*, p. 4; Yarrell, *op. cit.*, pp. 54–5; Anderson, *op. cit.*, p. 111.

CURLEW

1. Ó hÓgáin, *op. cit.*, p. 420; O'Sullivan, D. C., *op. cit.*, p. 145; O'Sullivan, P. (1991), *op. cit.*, p. 49; Ó hEochaidh, *op. cit.*, pp. 267–8; Gallagher, *op. cit.*, p. 6; Hastings, *op. cit.*, pp. 80, 82.

2. O'Sullivan, P. (1991), *op. cit.*, p. 29.

3. *Ibid*, p. 49; Ó Duilearga (1981), *op. cit.*, p. 214; Ó hEochaidh, *op. cit.*, pp. 267–8; Anderson, *op. cit.*, p. 144.

4. Forbes, *op. cit.*, p. 265; Yarrell, *op. cit.*, p. 501.

5. Swainson, *op. cit.*, pp. 200–1.

6. Yarrell, *op. cit.*, vol. 3, p. 504; Watters, *op. cit.*, p. 144.

7. Watters, *op. cit.*, p. 144.

8. Cocker & Mabey, *op. cit.* p. 222.

9. Anderson, *op. cit.*, p. 143.

10. Cabot, *op. cit.*, p. 132; Ó Murchadha, G. (1932): 'Eachtraí, Véursaí, agus Paidreacha ó Iarthar Chorcaighe', *Béaloideas* Iml. 3, Uimh. 4, 464.

11. Stokes, W. (1868), *op. cit.*, p. 126.

12. Carmichael, *op. cit.*, vol. 4, pp. 178–81; Forbes, *op. cit.*, p. 337; Swainson, *op. cit.*, p. 192.

13. Anderson, *op. cit.*, p. 150; Kelly, *op. cit.*, p. 298; O'Grady (1999), *op. cit.*, p. 20; O'Sullivan, D. C., *op. cit.*, p. 125; Cocker & Mabey, *op. cit.*, pp. 215–6; O'Keeffe, *op. cit.*, p. 75.

14. Cabot, *op. cit.*, p. 68.

15. Cocker & Mabey, *op. cit.*, pp. 216–7.

CORNCRAKE

1. O'Sullivan, P. (1991), *op. cit.*, p. 39; Ó Murchadha, *op. cit.*, p. 463; Forbes, *op. cit.*, p. 253.

2. O'Sullivan, P. (1991), *op. cit.*, p. 39; Forbes, *op. cit.*, pp. 240, 254; Loyd, *op. cit.*, p. 228.

3. O'Sullivan, P. (1991), *op. cit.*, p. 39.

4. *Ibid.*, p. 39.

5. Forbes, *op. cit.*, p. 254.

6. Loyd, *op. cit.*, pp. 227–8; Tate, *op. cit.*, p. 108.

7. www.logainm.ie

8. Meyer, K. (1906): 'The Triads of Ireland', *Todd Lecture Series*, No. 13, London, p. 19.

9. Jackson, *op. cit.*, p. 63.

10. O'Meara, *op. cit.*, p. 41.

11. Watters, *op. cit.*, p. 141; Cocker & Mabey, *op. cit.*, p. 178.

12. Cocker & Mabey, *op. cit.*, p. 179; Cabot, *op. cit.*, p. 49.

CRANE

1. O'Toole L. & O'Flaherty, R. (2011): 'Out of Sight, Out of Mind? On the Trail of a Forgotten Irish Bird', *Archaeology Ireland*, 13–16, Dublin, p. 14; Kelly, *op. cit.*, p. 125; De Bhaldraithe, P. (2012): 'True or False? The Crane Revisited', *Archaeology Ireland*, 22–24.

2. Cocker & Mabey, *op. cit.*, p. 185.

3. Gregory (1994), *op. cit.*, p. 170; D'Arcy, *op. cit.*, p. 92.

4. O'Grady (1892), *op. cit.*, p. 5.

5. Stokes (1890), *op. cit.*, p. 270; O'Toole & O'Flaherty, *op. cit.*, p. 16; O'Rahilly (1967), *op. cit.*, p. 187.

6. McNeill, E. (1908), *op. cit.*, pp. 118–9.

7. Green (1992a), *op. cit.*, p. 68; Gregory (1994), *op. cit.*, p. 365.

8. Meyer (1906), *op. cit.*, p. 33; Forbes, *op. cit.*, p. 255.

9. Green (1992), *op. cit.*, p. 214; Green (1992a), *op. cit.*, p. 208.

10. O'Toole & O'Flaherty, *op. cit.*, p. 14.

11. Green (1992a), *op. cit.*, p. 68; Green (1992), *op. cit.*, pp. 159–60; O'Toole & O'Flaherty, *op. cit.*, p. 16.

12. Tate, *op. cit.*, pp. 14–5, 18; Cocker & Mabey, *op. cit.*, p. 184; O'Meara, *op. cit.*, p. 41.

13. Kelly, *op. cit.*, pp. 126–7, 236; O'Meara, *op. cit.*, p. 40; O'Sullivan, D. C., *op. cit.*, p. 115; Yarrell, *op. cit.*, vol. 3, pp. 181–2; Thompson, W. (1849, 1850, 1852): *Natural History of Ireland*, vols 1–3, London, vol. 2, p. 132; Cocker & Mabey, *op. cit.*, p. 184.

14. Cocker & Mabey, *op. cit.*, p. 184.

15. *Ibid.*, p. 184; Tate, *op. cit.*, p. 18.

16. Kelly, *op. cit.*, p. 127; Watters, *op. cit.*, p. 132.

17. Kelly, *op. cit.*, pp. 125–7; Yarrell, *op. cit.*, vol. 3, p. 189.

18. Cocker & Mabey, *op. cit.*, p. 186; www.thegreatcraneproject.org.uk retrieved 8.12.2014;

www.goldeneagletrust.org, retrieved 8.12.2014.

19. Loyd, *op. cit.*, pp. 166–7

HERON

1. O'Sullivan, P. (2008), *op. cit.*, p. 43; Ó hÓgáin, *op. cit.*, p. 420; Gallagher, *op. cit.*, p. 7; Ó Cróinín (1980), *op. cit.*, p. 347.

2. O'Sullivan, P. (1991), *op. cit.*, p. 50; Thompson *op. cit.*, vol. 2, p. 137.

3. Ó Súilleabháin, *op. cit.*, p. 26; Mac Gréine, P. (1932): 'Further Notes on Tinkers' Cant', *Béaloideas*, Iml. 3, Uimh. 3, p. 302; Opie & Tatum, *op. cit.*, p. 198; Carmichael, *op. cit.*, vol. 2, pp. 132–3.

4. O'Meara, *op. cit.*, p. 91; Reeves, W. (1874): *Adamnán's Life of St Columba*, Edinburgh, chp 35; Ó hEochaidh, *op. cit.*, p. 275; D'Arcy, *op. cit.*, p.92.

5. Meyer (1906), *op. cit.*, p. 33; Forbes, *op. cit.*, p. 255.

6. Green (1992), *op. cit.*, p. 176; O'Keeffe, *op. cit.*, p. 97.

7. Kelly, *op. cit.*, p. 128; Gantz (1981), *op. cit.*, p. 255.

8. O'Keeffe, *op. cit.*, pp. 39, 75, 87, 103; Murphy (1933), *op. cit.*, pp. 372–3; Jackson, *op. cit.*, pp. 67, 126.

9. Yarrell, *op. cit.*, vol. 1, pp. 53, 55.

10. Thompson, *op. cit.*, vol. 2, p. 141; Yarrell, *op. cit.*, vol. 4, p. 169; Loyd, *op. cit.*, p. 171.

11. Kelly, *op. cit.*, p. 127; Watters, *op. cit.*, p. 132.

12. Cocker & Mabey, *op. cit.*, p. 55.
13. O'Sullivan, D. C., *op. cit.*, p. 119.
14. Cabot, *op. cit.*, p. 113.

SWAN

1. O'Sullivan, P. (1991), *op. cit.*, p. 41; Ó hÓgáin, *op. cit.*, p. 35; Watters, *op. cit.*, pp. 194–5; Ó hEochaidh, *op. cit.*, p. 264.
2. Carmichael, *op. cit.*, vol. 1, pp. 52, 310–1, 262–3, vol. 2, pp. 182–3, 194–5, vol. 4, pp. 180–1.
3. Cocker & Mabey, *op. cit.*, pp. 64–5; Yarrell, *op. cit.*, vol. 4, p. 329.
4. Westropp, *op. cit.*, p. 108; McCullough, J. A. (1930): *The Mythology of All Races*, vol. 2, Boston, pp. 259–60.
5. Wilde, W. (1853): *Irish Popular Superstitions* (1979) Dublin, p. 126.
6. Danaher (1967), *op. cit.*, pp. 100–4.
7. Ó hÓgáin, *op. cit.*, p. 272; Green (1992), *op. cit.*, pp. 175–6.
8. Gregory (1994), *op. cit.*, pp. 38, 77, 422; Gantz (1981), *op. cit.*, p. 57, 110–12; Ó hÓgáin, *op. cit.*, p. 301.
9. Raynor, *op. cit.*, pp. 74, 79; Ó hÓgáin, *op. cit.*, p. 263.
10. Green (1992), *op. cit.*, p. 174; O'Rahilly (1924), *op. cit.*, pp. 30–1; O'Rahilly (1967), *op. cit.*, p. 147.
11. Armstrong (1958), *op. cit.*, pp. 45, 61; Green (1992a), *op. cit.*, p. 203.
12. Gregory (1994), *op. cit.*, pp. 289, 399, 400.
13. Green (1992), *op. cit.*, pp. 40–1, 129; Green (1992a), *op. cit.*, p. 203.
14. Jackson, *op. cit.*, p. 70; Kelly, *op. cit.*, p. 299.
15. Swainson, *op. cit.*, p. 151; Loyd, *op. cit.*, p. 177; Watters, *op. cit.*, p. 195.
16. Cabot, *op. cit.*, pp. 115–6.
17. Kelly, *op. cit.*, p. 299; Cabot, *op. cit.*, p. 114; Thompson, *op. cit.*, vol. 3, p. 7; O'Sullivan, D. C. *op. cit.*, p. 95.
18. Yarrell, *op. cit.*, vol. 4, pp. 329–31, 336; Cocker & Mabey, *op. cit.*, p. 61; Loyd, *op. cit.*, p. 180.
19. Cocker & Mabey, *op. cit.*, pp. 62–3.

GOOSE

1. Ó hÓgáin, *op. cit.*, p. 420; Stokes (1868), *op. cit.*, p. 43; Gallagher, *op. cit.*, p. 8; Ó Coigligh, *op. cit.*, p. 17; Ó hEochaidh, *op. cit.*, p. 244; Hastings, *op. cit.*, p. 82; Ó Cróinín (1980), *op. cit.*, p. 155.
2. O'Sullivan, P. (1991), *op. cit.*, p. 42; Ó Murchadha, *op. cit.*, p. 463; Opie & Tatum, *op. cit.*, p. 127; O'Farrell, *op. cit.*, p. 122.
3. Breathnach, *op. cit.*, p. 341–3.
4. Opie & Tatum, *op. cit.*, p. 172; Gwynn Jones, *op. cit.*, p. 43.
5. O'Sullivan, P. (1991), *op. cit.*, p. 43; Breathnach, *op. cit.*, p. 104.
6. Ó hÓgáin, *op. cit.*, p. 75; O'Sullivan, P. (1991), *op. cit.*, pp. 42–3.

7. Dillon, M. (1946): *The Cycle of the Kings*, Oxford, pp. 59–64.

8. Yeats, *op. cit.*, pp. 227–81; Kelly, *op. cit.*, pp. 299–300; Dinneen, P. S. (1927): *Foclóir Gaedhilge agus Béarla*, Irish Texts Society, p. 144; Jackson, *op. cit.*, p. 70; Gantz (1981), *op. cit.*, p. 202.

9. O'Rahilly (1967), *op. cit.* pp. 158–61; O'Keeffe, *op. cit.*, p. 109; Stokes (1868), *op. cit.*, p. 43.

10. O'Keeffe, *op. cit.*, p. 87; Murphy (1956), *op. cit.*, pp. 160–1.

11. Kelly, *op. cit.*, p. 300; O'Meara, *op. cit.*, pp. 41–2; Danaher (1972), *op. cit.*, p. 56.

12. Green (1992), *op. cit.*, pp. 125–6, 214; Green (1992a), *op. cit.*, p. 107.

13. Tate, *op. cit.*, p. 50; Ingersoll, *op. cit.*, p. 253; Cocker & Mabey, *op. cit.*, p. 74.

14. Armstrong (1958), *op. cit.*, pp. 30–1.

15. Hobson, *op. cit.*, p. 12.

16. Kelly, *op. cit.*, p. 105.

17. Danaher (1972), *op. cit.*, p. 188; Armstrong (1958), *op. cit.*, pp. 25, 28.

18. Hobson, *op. cit.*, pp. 32–7, 41–2.

19. Cocker & Mabey, *op. cit.*, p. 75.

20. Danaher (1972), *op. cit.*, p. 57.

21. www.birdwatchireland.ie; Cocker & Mabey, *op. cit.*, p. 80.

22. Cocker & Mabey, *op. cit.*, p. 80.

23. Cabot, op. cit., p. 117.

24. www.birdwatchireland.ie

MAGPIE

1. 1 Ó hÓgáin, *op. cit.*, p. 35; Westropp, *op. cit.*, pp. 15, 45; O'Sullivan, P. (1991), *op. cit.*, pp. 36–7; Ó hEochaidh, *op. cit.*, p. 260; Opie & Tatum, *op. cit.*, p. 236; Forbes, *op. cit.*, p. 303; Ó Cróinín (1985), *op. cit.*, p. 497; Ó Cléirigh, *op. cit.*, p. 250; Hastings, *op. cit.*, p. 86; Wood Martin, *op. cit.*, p. 147; Swainson, *op. cit.*, p. 76; Tate, *op. cit.*, p. 79.

2. Gallagher, *op. cit.*, p. 6; Hastings, *op. cit.*, p. 80; Opie & Tatum, *op. cit.*, p. 235; Gregorson Campbell (1900), *op. cit.*, p. 227; Forbes, *op. cit.*, p. 303; Swainson, *op. cit.*, p. 76; Thompson, *op. cit.*, vol. 1, p. 333.

3. Tate, *op. cit.*, p. 80; Loyd, *op. cit.*, p. 31.

4. O'Sullivan, P. (1991), *op. cit.*, pp. 36–7; Mac Gréine, *op. cit.*, p. 302; Forbes, *op. cit.*, p. 303; Swainson, *op. cit.*, p. 76.

5. Yeats, *op. cit.*, pp. 294–5; Ó hEochaidh, *op. cit.*, pp. 260–3; Ó Duilearga (1948), *op. cit.*, pp. 183–4.

6. Ellis, E. (1899): *1,000 Mythical Characters Briefly Described*, New York, p. 113.

7. O'Meara, *op. cit.*, p. 47; Yarrell, *op. cit.*, vol. 2, pp. 318–9; Swainson, *op. cit.*, p. 80; Thompson, *op. cit.*, vol. 1, pp. 307, 328; O'Sullivan, D. C. *op. cit.*, pp. 111–3; Anderson, *op. cit.*, p. 238.

8. Yarrell, *op. cit.*, vol. 1, p. 55; Cocker & Mabey, *op. cit.*, p. 403.

9. Cocker & Mabey, *op. cit.*, p. 404.

OWL

1. Ó hEochaidh, *op. cit.*, p. 255; Ó Cróinín (1980), *op. cit.*, p. 165.

2. Ó hÓgáin, *op. cit.*, p. 45; Westropp, *op. cit.*, p. 9.

3. Swainson, *op. cit.*, pp. 126–7; Opie & Tatum, *op. cit.*, pp. 295–6; Gwynn Jones, *op. cit.*, p. 205; Tate, *op. cit.*, p. 95.

4. Forbes, *op. cit.*, p. 317; Armstrong (1958), *op. cit.*, p. 119; Tate, *op. cit.*, p. 98; Loyd, *op. cit.*, p. 139

5. Tate, *op. cit.*, p. 98; Armstrong (1958), *op. cit.*, p. 117.

6. Gwynn Jones, *op. cit.*, pp. 51–2.

7. Atwood Lawrence, *op. cit.*, pp. 28–9; Loyd, *op. cit.*, p. 141.

8. Gantz (1976), *op. cit.*, pp. 116, 164–5; Green (1992), *op. cit.*, p. 173.

9. Green (1996), *op. cit.*, p. 109.

10. Tate, *op. cit.*, pp. 93, 95; Opie & Tatum, *op. cit.*, pp. 295–6; Swainson, *op. cit.*, p. 127; Watters, *op. cit.*, p. 22.

11. Swainson, *op. cit.*, p. 127; Tate, *op. cit.*, p. 97; Forbes, *op. cit.*, p. 306; Cocker & Mabey, *op. cit.*, p. 287.

12. Watters, *op. cit.*, p. 22; www.birdwatchireland.ie

13. Cabot, *op. cit.*, p. 69.

HOODED CROW

1. Ó hÓgáin, *op. cit.*, p. 35; Ó Súilleabháin, *op. cit.*, p. 47.

2. Mac Gréine, *op. cit.*, p. 302.

3. Kelly, *op. cit.*, p. 192.

4. Westropp, *op. cit.*, p. 64; Dinneen, *op. cit.*, p. 68; Armstrong (1958), *op. cit.*, p. 78.

5. Opie & Tatum, *op. cit.*, p. 90.

6. Ó Cróinín (1980), *op. cit.*, p. 151.

7. Gallagher, *op. cit.*, p. 5.

8. Ó Duilearga (1948), *op. cit.*, pp. 4–5; O'Sullivan, S. (1966), *op. cit.*, pp. 15–8; O'Sullivan, P. (1991), *op. cit.*, p. 37.

9. Forbes, *op. cit.*, p. 258; Armstrong (1958), *op. cit.*, p. 83; Opie & Tatum, *op. cit.*, pp. 111, 147; Gwynn Jones, *op. cit.*, p. 205; Loyd, *op. cit.*, p. 23.

10. Ó hEochaidh, *op. cit.*, p. 256; MacNeill, M., *op. cit.*, p. 509; O'Grady (1892), *op. cit.*, p. 59.

11. Gregory (1994), *op. cit.*, pp. 17, 47, 57, 69, 460; Ó hÓgáin, *op. cit.*, p. 45; Green (1992a), *op. cit.*, pp. 38, 72, 138.

12. Gregory (1994), *op. cit.*, p. 272; Curtin (1890), *op. cit.*, pp. 16–7.

13. Meyer (1907), *op. cit.*, p. 31; MacSweeney, *op. cit.*, p. 185.

14. O'Meara, *op. cit.*, p. 46; Cocker & Mabey, *op. cit.*, p. 419.

15. Kelly, *op. cit.*, p. 130.
16. O'Sullivan, P. (1991), *op. cit.*, pp. 35–6; Opie & Tatum, *op. cit.*, p. 331.
17. O'Sullivan, P. (1991), *op. cit.*, p. 36.
18. Kelly, *op. cit.*, p. 130.
19. Cocker & Mabey, *op. cit.*, pp. 407–8.

RAVEN

1. Ó hÓgáin, *op. cit.*, p. 35; Ó Súilleabháin, *op. cit.*, p. 47; Ó hEochaidh, *op. cit.*, p. 256; Ó Cróinín (1985), *op. cit.*, p. 438.
2. Wood Martin, *op. cit.*, p. 142; Ó hEochaidh, *op. cit.*, p. 256.
3. O'Sullivan, P. (1991), *op. cit.*, p. 36; Loyd, *op. cit.*, p. 15.
4. Westropp, *op. cit.*, pp. 8–9.
5. O'Sullivan, P. (1991), *op. cit.*, p. 35; Ó Murchú, P. (1996): *Gort Broc: Scéalta agus Seanchas ó Bhéarra*, Dublin, pp. 15–6; O'Farrell, *op. cit.*, p. 64.
6. Opie & Tatum, *op. cit.*, p. 324; Tate, *op. cit.*, p. 112; Forbes, *op. cit.*, p. 324.
7. Carmichael, *op. cit.*, vol. 2, pp. 34–5, 172–3; Armstrong (1958), *op. cit.*, p. 83.
8. Kennedy, M. (2004): 'Tower's raven mythology may be a Victorian flight of fancy.' *The Guardian*, www.guardian.co.uk, retrieved 21.12.2012; Cocker & Mabey, *op. cit.*, p. 428.
9. Tate, *op. cit.*, pp. 113, 116–7; Opie & Tatum, *op. cit.*, p. 26.
10. O'Grady (1892), *op. cit.*, p. 59; O'Meara, *op. cit.*, p. 78.
11. Loyd, *op. cit.*, p. 17.
12. Stokes (1868), *op. cit.*, p. 11; Gregory (1994), *op. cit.*, pp. 493–4; Gantz (1981), *op. cit.*, p. 71.
13. Gregory (1994), *op. cit.*, pp. 190, 285; O'Grady (1999), *op. cit.*, pp. 152–3.
14. Gantz (1976), *op. cit.*, pp. 185–91.
15. Gregory (1994), *op. cit.*, pp. 466, 468, 522; O'Rahilly, *op. cit.*, 152; Gantz (1981), *op. cit.*, pp. 170, 202; Gwynn, *op. cit.*, vol. 3, pp. 257–9; Stokes, W. (1895): 'The Rennes Dinnshenchus', *Revue Celtique XV*, p. 450.
16. Green (1992a), *op. cit.*, p. 135, Meyer (1907), *op. cit.*, p. 31; MacSweeney, *op. cit.*, p. 185; Ó hÓgáin, *op. cit.*, p. 131.
17. Green (1992a), *op. cit.*, p. 174; Green (1992), *op. cit.*, p. 212; Gantz (1976), *op. cit.*, p. 81.
18. Green (1996), *op. cit.*, pp. 101–2; Green (1992), *op. cit.*, pp. 160–1; Cocker & Mabey, *op. cit.*, p. 427; Green (1992a), *op. cit.*, pp. 157–8.
19. Green (1992), *op. cit.*, p. 126.
20. Gantz (1981), *op. cit.*, p. 260; Gantz (1976), *op. cit.*, p. 233; MacNeill, E., *op. cit.*, p. 168; Frazer, *op. cit.*, p. 32; O'Sullivan, D. C., *op. cit.*, p. 111.
21. Best, *op. cit.*, pp. 120–25.
22. Crossley Holland, *op. cit.*, pp. 61, 67; Tate, *op. cit.*, p. 114.
23. Ingersoll, *op. cit.*, p. 161; Armstrong (1958), *op. cit.*, p. 79; MacAlister, *op. cit.*, Pt 1 pp. 121–3; Gantz (1981), op cit., p. 57.

24. Opie & Tatum, *op. cit.*, p. 111, 324; Tate, *op. cit.*, pp. 113–4; Green (1992), *op. cit.*, p. 89; Watters, *op. cit.*, p. 64; Forbes, *op. cit.*, p. 324.

25. Cabot, *op. cit.*, p. 102.

26. Cocker & Mabey, *op. cit.*, p. 424; www.birdwatchireland.ie

27. Cabot, *op. cit.*, p. 102.

28. Cocker & Mabey, *op. cit.*, pp. 425, 427.

POSTSCRIPT

1. Eberhard, W. (1986): *A Dictionary of Chinese Symbols*, London, p. 229; Tate, *op. cit.*, p. 102.

2. Frazer, *op. cit.*, pp. 499, 676–7.

3. Eberhard, *op. cit.*, pp. 174–5, 248; Tate, *op. cit.*, pp. 136–7.

4. Armstrong, *op. cit.*, pp. 190–1.

Bibliography

An Roinn Oideachais (Dept. of Educ.) (1978): *Ainmneacha Plandaí agus Ainmhithe,* Oifig an tSoláthair, Baile Átha Cliath

Anderson, G. (2008): *Birds of Ireland: Facts, Folklore and History,* The Collins Press, Cork

Armstrong, E. (1955): *The Wren,* Collins, London

— (1958): *The Folklore of Birds* (1970), Dover Publications, New York

Atwood Lawrence, E. (1997): *Hunting the Wren: Transformation of Bird to Symbol,* University of Tennessee Press, Knoxville, TE

Ball, F. E. (1920): *A History of the County Dublin,* vol. 6, RSAI, Dublin

Best, R. I. (1916): 'Prognostications from the Raven and the Wren', *Ériu* vol. 8, 120–146, Dublin

Breathnach, P. (1986): *Maigh Cuilin: A Táisc agus a Tuairisc,* Indreabhán Cló, Connemara

Brennan, J. (2013): *Donegal Folk Tales,* The History Press, Dublin

Bulfinch, T. (1993): *The Golden Age of Myth and Legend,* Wordsworth Editions Ltd, Hertfordshire

Cabot, D. (1995): *Irish Birds,* (2004), HarperCollins, London

Carmichael, A. (1900, 1928, 1941), *Carmina Gadelica,* vols 1, 2, 4, Oliver & Boyd, Edinburgh

Chambers, E. K. (1903): *The Medieval Stage,* vol. I, Oxford University Press

Cocker, M; Mabey, R. (2005): *Birds Britannica,* Chatto & Windus, London

Cooper, J. J. (1993): *Brewer's Book of Myth and Legend,* Helicon Publishing, Oxford

Crofton Croker, T. (1824): *Researches in the South of Ireland* (1969), Irish University Press, Shannon

Crossley Holland, K. (1980): *The Penguin Book of Norse Myths,* Penguin Books, London

Curtin, J. (1890): *Myths and Folktales of Ireland,* Dover Publications (1975), New York

— (1894) *Hero Tales of Ireland,* Macmillan Press London

Danaher, K. (1966): *Irish Country People,* Mercier Press, Cork

— (1967): *Folk Tales from the Irish Countryside,* Mercier Press, Cork

— (1972): *The Year in Ireland – Irish Calendar Customs,* Mercier Press, Cork

D'Arcy, G. (1999): *Ireland's Lost Birds,* Four Courts Press, Dublin

De Bhaldraithe, P. (2012): 'True or False? The Crane Revisited', *Archaeology Ireland,* 22–24

Dillon, M. (1946): *The Cycle of the Kings*, Oxford University Press, Oxford
— (1962): *Lebor na Cert*, Irish Texts Society, Dublin

Dinneen, P. S. (1927): *Foclóir Gaedhilge agus Béarla*, Irish Texts Society, Dublin

Eberhard, W. (1986): *A Dictionary of Chinese Symbols*, Routledge & Kegan Paul, London

Ellis, E. (1899): *1,000 Mythical Characters Briefly Described*, Hinds & Noble, New York

Forbes, A. R. (1905): *Gaelic Names of Beasts*, Oliver & Boyd, Edinburgh

Frazer, J. G. (1922): *The Golden Bough*, The Macmillan Press Ltd, London (1987)

Gallagher, M. (2009): *Tuar na h-Aimsire: Traditional Weather Signs*, Browne Printers, Letterkenny

Gantz, J. (1976): *The Mabinogion*, Penguin Books
— (1981): *Early Irish Myths and Sagas*, Penguin Books

Green, M. (1992): *Animals in Celtic Life and Myth*, Routledge, London
— (1992a): *Dictionary of Celtic Myth and Legend*, Thames and Hudson London
— (1996): *Celtic Art*, Orion Publishing, London

Gregorson Campbell, J. (1900): *Superstitions of the Highlands and Islands of Scotland*, James MacLehose & Sons, Glasgow
— (1902): *Witchcraft and Second Sight in the Highlands and Islands of Scotland*, James MacLehose & Sons, Glasgow

Gregory, Lady A. (1902,1904): *Complete Irish Mythology*, The Slaney Press (1994), London
— (1920): *Visions & Beliefs in the West of Ireland*, Colin Smythe (1970), Toronto

Grigson, G. (1958): *The Englishman's Flora* (1996), Helicon Publishing, Oxford
— (1959): *The Cherry Tree*, Phoenix House, London

Gwynn, E. (1913,1924,1935): *The Metrical Dindshenchus*, vols 3, 4, 5, Dublin Institute for Advanced Studies, Dublin

Gwynn Jones, T. (1930): *Welsh Folklore and Folk Custom*, Metheun & Co. Ltd, London

Hastings, C. (2009): *Ag Bun na Cruaiche: Folklore & Folklife from the Foot of Croagh Patrick*, Nonsuch Publishing, Dublin

Hobson, J. C. (2009): *Backyard Ducks and Geese*, The Crowood Press, Wiltshire

Hyde, D. (1890): *Beside the Fire: a Collection of Irish Gaelic Folk Stories*, David Nutt, London

Hynes, S. B. E. (1928): *Legends of St Kevin*, CTSI Pamphlet No. 959, Minnesota

Ingersoll, E. (1923): *Birds in Legend, Fable and Folklore*, Longman's Green London

Jackson, K. (1971): *A Celtic Miscellany*, Penguin Books Ltd, London

Keating, G. (1902, 1908–14): *The History of Ireland*, (Trans. Comyn, D., Dinneen, P.), Irish Texts Society, London

Kelly, F. (1997): *Early Irish Farming*, Dublin Institute for Advanced Studies

Kendrick, T. D. (1927): *The Druids*, Methuen & Co. Ltd, London

Loyd, L. (1882): *Bird Facts and Fallacies*, Hutchinson, London

Lucas, A. T. (1960): 'Furze: A Survey of its History and Uses in Ireland' *Béaloideas* Iml. 26, Galway

Macalister, R. A. S. (1938–9, 1956): *Lebor Gabála Érenn Parts 1, 2, 5*, Irish Texts Society, Dublin

McCullough, J. A. (1930): *The Mythology of All Races*, vol. 2, Marshall Jones Co., Boston

Mac Giolla Léith, C. (1993): *Oidheadh Chloinne hUisneach*, Irish Texts Society, Dublin

Mac Gréine, P. (1932): 'Further Notes on Tinkers' Cant', *Béaloideas*, Iml. 3, Uimh. 3, 302, Galway

McKinnon, D. (1904–8): 'The Glenmasan Manuscript', *Celtic Review*, Vol. 3, Norman McLeod, Edinburgh

Mac Neill, E. (1908) & Murphy, G. (1933): *Duanaire Finn*, Irish Texts Society, Dublin

MacNeill, M. (1962): *The Festival of Lughnasa*, Oxford University Press, Oxford

Macsweeney, P. (1904): *Martial Career of Conghal Cláiringhneach*, Irish Texts Society, London

Meyer, K. (1890): 'The Hiding of the Hill of Howth', *Revue Celtique*, vol. 11, Paris
— (1901): *King and Hermit*, David Nutt, London
— (1902): *Comrac Liadaine ocus Cuirithir, or Liadain and Cuirithir*, David Nutt, London
— (1904): 'Finn and the Man in the Tree' *Revue Celtique*, vol. 25, Paris
— (1906): 'The Triads of Ireland', *Todd Lecture Series*, No. 13, London
— (1907): 'The Colloquy between Fintan and the Hawk of Achill' *Anecdota I*, Halle/Saale.
— (1910): 'Reicne Fothaid Canainne', *Fianaigecht*, Dublin

Minihane, P. (2003): *Beara Woman Talking: The Lore of Peig Minihane*, Mercier Press, Cork

Muller, S. (1996 / 1997): 'The Irish Wren Tales and Ritual. To Pay or Not to Pay the Debt of Nature', *Béaloideas* Iml. 64 / 65, 131–169, Galway

Murphy, G. (1933): *Duanaire Finn Part II*, Irish Texts Society, London
— (1956): *Early Irish Lyrics*, Four Courts Press, Dublin

Ní Shéaghdha, N. (1967): *Toruigheacht Diarmaid agus Gráinne*, Irish Texts Society, Dublin

Northall, G. F. (1892): *English Folk-Rhymes*, Kegan Paul, Trench, Trübner & Co., London

Ó Baoill, D. (1992): *Amach as Ucht na Sliabh*, Cumann Staire agus Seanchais Ghaoth Dobhair, Ballyshannon

Ó Cléirigh, T. (1928): 'Gleanings in Wicklow', *Béaloideas*, Iml. Uimh. 3, 250, Galway

Ó Coigligh, C. : *Seanchas Inis Meáin*, Coisceim Press, Dublin

Ó Cróinín, S. (1980): *Seanachas Amhlaoibh Í Luínse*, Irish Folklore Commission, UCD, Dublin

— (1985): *Seanachas ó Chairbre*, Irish Folklore Commission, UCD, Dublin

Ó Cuinn, C. (1990): *Scian a Caitheadh le Toinn – Scéalta Inis Eoghain*, Coiscéim Press, Dublin

Ó Cuiv, B. (1980): 'Some Gaelic Traditions about the Wren', *Éigse* vol. 18 / 1, 43–66, Dublin

Ó Danachair, C. (1957): 'Some Distribution Patterns in Irish Folk Life', *Béaloideas*, Iml. 25, pp. 108–123, Galway

Ó Dochartaigh, L. (1977/79): 'An Spideog i Seanchas na hÉireann' *Béaloideas*, Iml. 45 / 47, 164–98, Galway

— (1982): 'An Spideog i Scéalaíocht na hÉireann' *Béaloideas*, Iml. 50, 90–125, Galway

O'Donoghue, D. (1893): *Brendaniana: St Brendan the Voyager in Story and Legend*, Browne & Nolan, Dublin

Ó Duilearga, S. (1948): *Leabhar Sheáin Uí Chonaill*, Irish Folkore Commission, UCD, Dublin

— (1981): *Leabhair Stiofán Uí Ealaoire*, Irish Folklore Commission, UCD, Dublin

O'Farrell, P. (2004): *Irish Folk Cures*, Gill & Macmillan, Dublin

O'Grady, S. (1892): *Silva Gadelica*, Williams and Norgate, London

— (1892): 'Agallamh na Senorach', *Silva Gadelica* (1999) Cambridge, Ontario

O'Hegarty, P. S. (1943): 'The Wren Boys', *Béaloideas*, Iml. 13, 275–76, Galway

Ó hEochaidh, S. (1969/70): 'Seanchas Éanlaith Iar-Uladh', *Béaloideas*, Iml. 37 / 38, 210–337, Galway

Ó hÓgáin, D. (1991): *Myth, Legend and Romance – An Encyclopaedia of the Irish Folk Tradition*, Prentice Hall Press, New York

O'Keeffe, J. G. (1913): *Buile Suibhne*, Irish Texts Society, Dublin

O'Meara, J. (1978): *The Voyage of St Brendan*, Dublin

— (1982): *Gerald Of Wales: The History and Topography of Ireland*, Penguin Books, Middlesex

Ó Murchadha, G. (1932): 'Eachtraí, Véursaí, agus Paidreacha ó Iarthar Chorcaighe', *Béaloideas*, Iml. 3 Uimh. 4, 456–66, Galway

Ó Murchú, P. (1996): *Gort Broc: Scéalta agus Seanchas ó Bhéarra*, Coisceim Press, Dublin

O'Rahilly, C. (1924): *The Pursuit of Gruaidhe Griansholus*, Irish Texts Society, London

— (1967): *Táin Bó Cuailnge*, Irish Texts Society, Dublin

Ó Ruadháin, M. (1955): 'Birds in Irish Folklore' *Proceedings of XI International Ornithological Congress*, Basel

Ó Súilleabháin, S. (1967): *Irish Folk Custom and Belief*, Comhar Cultúra Éireann, Dublin

O'Sullivan, D. C. (2009): *The Natural History of Ireland by Philip O'Sullivan Beare*, Cork University Press

O'Sullivan, P. V. (1991): *Irish Superstitions and Legends of Animals and Birds*, Mercier Press, Cork

— (2008): *The Magic of Irish Nature*, Nonsuch Publishing, Dublin

O'Sullivan, S. (1966): *Folktales of Ireland*, Routledge & Kegan Paul Ltd, London

— (1977): *Legends from Ireland*, B. T. Batsford Ltd, London

O'Toole L. & O'Flaherty, R. (2011): 'Out of Sight, Out of Mind? On the Trail of a Forgotten Irish Bird', *Archaeology Ireland*, 13–16, Dublin

Opie, I. & Tatum, M. (eds) (1989): *A Dictionary of Superstitions*, Oxford University Press, Oxford

Owen, T. (1959): *Welsh Folk Customs*, National Museum of Wales, Cardiff

Pauli, R. (1889): *The Life of Alfred the Great*, Trans. by B. Thorpe, Bell & Daldy, London

Plummer, C. (1922): *Lives of the Saints*, Clarendon Press, Oxford

Power, P. (1914): *Lives of Ss. Declan and Mochuda*, Irish Texts Society, London

Raynor, L. J. (1988): *Legends of the Kings of Ireland*, Mercier Press, Cork

Reeves, W. (1874): *Adamnán's Life of St Columba*, Edmonston & Douglas, Edinburgh

Roe, H. (1939): 'Tales, Customs and Beliefs from Laoighis', *Béaloideas*, Iml. 9 Uimh. 1, 32, Galway

Scrivener, D. (2008): *Poultry: Breeds and Management*, The Crowood Press, Wiltshire

Sébillot, P. (1906): *Le Folklore de France*, vol. 3, E. Guilmoto, Paris

Sikes, W. (1880): *British Goblins: Welsh Folkore, Fairy Mythology, Legends & Traditions*, Sampson Low, Marston, Searle, Rivington, London,

Smith, C. E. & Kelman, J. H.: *Trees Shown to the Children*, T. C. & E. C. Jack, London

Smyth, D. (1988): *A Guide to Irish Mythology*, Irish Academic Press, Dublin

Stokes, W. (1868): *Cormac's Glossary*, Irish Archaeological & Celtic Society, Calcutta

— (1888): 'The Voyage of Snedgus and Mac Riagla', *Revue Celtique*, vol. 9, 14–25, Paris

— (1890): *Lives of the Saints from the Book of Lismore*, Clarendon Press, Oxford

— (1892): 'The Bodleian Dinnshenchus', *The Folklore Journal*, 467-516, London

— (1893): 'The Edinburgh Dinnshenchus' *The Folklore Journal*, 471-516, London

— (1893): 'The Voyage of the Hui Corra', *Revue Celtique*, vol. 14, 22-69, Paris

— (1894): 'The Rennes Dinnshenchus', *Revue Celtique* vol. 15, 418-84, Paris

— (1907): *The Birth and Life of St Moling*, Harrison, London

Swainson, C. (1885): *Provincial Names and Folk Lore of British Birds*, English Dialect Society, London

Tate, P. (2007): *Flights of Fancy: Birds in Myth, Legend and Superstition*, Random House, London

Thompson, W. (1849, 1850, 1851): *Natural History of Ireland*, vols 1–3, Reeve, Benham & Reeve, London

Thorpe, L. (1966): *Geoffrey of Monmouth: The History of the Kings of Britain*, Penguin Books Ltd, London

Watters, J. (1853), *The Natural History of the Birds of Ireland*, James McGlashin, Dublin

Westropp, P. J. (2000): *Folklore of Clare*, Clasp Press, Ennis

White, G. (1788–9): *The Natural History of Selborne* (1977), Penguin Books, Middlesex

Wilde, W. (1853): *Irish Popular Superstitions*, Irish Academic Press (1979), Dublin

Wood Martin, W. G. (1902): *Traces of the Elder Faiths of Ireland*, Longmans, Green & Co., London

Yarrell, W. (1885): *A History of British Birds*, vols 1–4, John Van Voorst, London

Yeats, W. B. (1888,1892): *The Book of Fairy and Folktales of Ireland* (1994), Octopus Publishing Ltd, London

Index

Note: illustrations are indicated by page
numbers in bold.

Aberdeen 49
Achill, Co. Mayo 117, 118–19, 128, 131–5, 161,
  201–2, 205, 216
Adam 113
Adamnán 160
Adonis 174
Aeneas 99
Aeneid (Virgil) 99
Aeolus 46–7
Aeschylus 175
Aesop's Fables 180–81
Africa 84, 85, 88, 93, 157, 232
Agnar 168
agricultural-ogham 223, 229
Ahenny, Co. Tipperary 153
Ailell 215
Ailne 205
Alfred the Great 117
Amairgen 130–31
America 44, 63, 74, 102, 191, 231, 232
Andersen, Hans Christian 157, 170
Anderson, William 117
angelic spirits 7–8, 94
Annals of the Four Masters 156, 163
Aobh 170
Aodh 160
Aoife, daughter of Dealbhoth 150
Aoife, wife of Lir 170–71
Aongus Óg 5
Aphrodite 99, 174, 184; *see also* Venus
Apollo 46, 73, 99, 135, 174, 175, 220–21
Aran Islands 31–2, 33
Ardfert, Co. Kerry 207
Ares 73
Aristophanes 92
Aristotle 35, 46, 92, 105, 135, 144, 154, 175
Armagh, County 87, 171, 173, 205
Armstrong, Edward 36
art-ogham 223, 224, 225, 226
Artemis 221
Arthur, King 35, 121, 208, 214–15
Assaroe, Co. Donegal 119, 132
Athairne 13, 150, 163
Athene 198, 228–9
Auguries of the Eagle 120
Auraicept na n-Éces 222
Austria 20, 82, 135
autumnal equinox 184
Aztecs 231

Babes in the Wood 18
Bacchus 192
Bachelleries 42–3
Badhbh 153, 162, 200, 204–5
banshee 194–5, 200, 205, 210

Bantry, Co. Cork 114
barn owl 194–5, 199; *see also* owl
barnacle goose 16, 178, 182–3, 185, 227; *see also*
  goose
Battle of Gabhra 214
Bealtaine *see* May Eve/Day
Beara, Co. Cork 70
Beatrix of Bouillon 174
beauty 4, 91–2, 174, 211, 231
Bedfordshire 79, 153, 183
bee 16, 32, 121
Beeton, Isabella 145
Belfast Lough 13, 110–11
Benedict, St 213
Bewick's swan 165, 175, 177; *see also* swan
Bible 98, 100
bird-ogham 222–30
Birds, The (Aristophanes) 92
black-headed gull 48, 52; *see also* seagull
blackbird 13, 14, 15, 20, 91, 104–12, **106**, 119, 135,
  137, 227
blacksmiths 104, 107–8
Blaiman 61, 130
Blaiman, Son of Apple 130
Blodeuedd 120, 197–8
boar 120, 131, 153
Bodhbh Dearg 170–71
Bohemia 20
Boniface of Mayence 156
Book of Invasions of Ireland 62, 100, 204, 220
Borrowed Days 104–5
Boy Bishop 41
Bran 8, 217
Branwen 226
Branwen Daughter of Llyr 217, 226
Brehon laws 9–10, 72, 135, 156, 184, 206, 207, 219
Brendan, St 7, 207
brent goose 16, 178, 182, 185; *see also* goose
Bresal, Prince of Leinster 127
Brian Boru 58, 220
Briefe Description of Ireland (Payne) 175, 192
Brigid, St 53, 76, 128
Britain 20, 21, 24, 38, 39, 51–2, 58, 71, 72, 74, 76,
  79, 81, 86, 88, 89–90, 95, 96, 101, 102, 103, 109,
  111, 112, 116, 120–21, 129, 135, 137, 139, 141,
  145, 154, 155–6, 157, 159, 164, 179, 183, 184–5,
  186–9, 193, 194, 195–6, 202–3, 206, 207, 211,
  216, 217, 219, 221; *see also* England; Scotland;
  Wales
Brittany 17–18, 33, 45, 82, 121, 183, 189
Browne, Sir Thomas 155
Brú na Bóinne, Co. Meath 6, 172
Bruinnech 149
Brynhildr 168
Buide 8–9
Buile Shuibhne see Mad Sweeney
bull *see* cattle
Burgundy 99, 121, 174–5, 216–17

Burns, Robert 140
buzzard 10, 125, 127, 232; see also hawk

Caér Ibormeith 172
Caesar, Julius 72, 183, 198
caged birds 79; see also pets
Cailleach 202, 212
Caireall 218
Cairpre, King 8
Caithness 206
calls 1, 4, 8–9, 13, 18–19, 25, 34, 37, 43–4, 45,
    48–9, 50, 53–5, 56–8, 62, 65, 66–9, 71–2, 75–6,
    85, 86, 89, 98–9, 104, 110–11, 138, 139–41, 142,
    143, 148–9, 154, 163, 175, 177, 188, 194–5, 198,
    201, 209, 218–19, 220–21, 225, 226, 227–8, 229,
    231, 232–3
Cambridgeshire 121, 155, 216
Campbell clan 188
Cana, wedding feast at 42, 43
Canada 102, 185
Canada goose 178; see also goose
Candlemas 104
Cano, son of Gartnán 62, 173
Caoilte 6, 214
Carcassonne 30–31, 42
Carmarthenshire 107
Carnelly, Co. Clare 70
carrier pigeons 101–2
carrion crow 192, 202–3, 206, 217; see also crow
Cascorach 214
cat 121, 156, 193
Catalogus Gloriae Mundi (Chassenaeus) 183
Cath Finnthragha 148–9
Catherine the Great 136
cattle 65, 81, 119, 122, 129, 141, 152, 153, 189–91
Cattle Raid of Cooley 78, 82–3, 109, 119, 128, 130,
    162, 173, 182, 204–5, 213–14, 215
Caxton, William 183
Cellach of Killala, St 34, 204, 213
Celtic art 4–5, 37, 63, 72–3, 121–2, 153, 174–5,
    198, 217
Celtic civilization 9, 36–8, 63, 72, 99, 135, 216–18
Celtic mythology 6, 37, 147, 153, 158, 178, 183,
    200, 209, 212, 229
Ceryx 45, 46–7
Césa MacRí 107
Chance, Edgar 92
Charlemagne 123
Chassanaeus, Bartholomaeus 183
cherry tree 89–90
'Cherry Tree Carol' 90
chicken 9–10, 11–12, 60, 65–74, 67, 156, 222, 226
children, abduction of 116–18
Children of Lir 2, 170–71, 175
China 135, 231, 232
chough 207–8
Christ 17–18, 25, 42, 53, 57, 60, 65, 66, 67–8, 82,
    90, 95, 100, 138–9, 189, 197, 210, 223
Christmas 2, 17, 21–2, 25, 28–30, 33, 40–42, 67,
    96, 104, 223
Cicero 175, 220
Circe 135
Clare, County 48–9, 68, 70, 80, 87, 124, 151, 161,
    167, 186, 195, 200, 210
Clare Island, Co. Mayo 117

Claudius Aelianus 81
Cliodhna 8
Clontarf, battle of 220
Clovis 100
coats of arms see heraldry
cock see chicken
cockatrice 71
cockfighting 74, 226
coins 122, 152, 153, 162, 198, 216, 217
collared dove 94, 96, 102–3, 226; see also dove
Colloquy of the Ancients 108–9, 214
Colman, St 62
Colmcille, St 23, 71–2, 97–8, 160–61, 203–4, 211
colour-ogham 223, 225, 226–7, 228, 229
Columba, St see Colmcille, St
Columella 196
common gull 48; see also seagull
Conaire, King of Tara 6–7
Conall 160
Conchubar 5, 6
Cong, Co. Mayo 97
Congal, King of Ulster 182
Conghal 51, 205–6, 216
Conlaoch 215
Connacht 6, 53, 97, 161
Connemara 29
Constantine the Great 123
Cork, County 20, 27–8, 33, 50, 53, 70, 86–7, 88–9,
    114, 124, 140, 143, 158, 178, 186, 192, 194, 201,
    209
Cork city 27–8
Cormac's Glossary 5, 34, 62, 110, 140, 178, 182,
    205, 213
cormorant 50, 216
corncrake 3, 143–6, 144
Cornwall 35, 38, 48, 51–2, 87, 203, 207
corrguineacht 153, 162
courtship 55, 142, 154, 221, 225
cow see cattle
crane 2, 91, 134, 147–57, 151, 158, 160, 161–4,
    227
Crane-bag of Manannán 150, 161
Crédhe, daughter of Cairpre 5, 92, 111, 148–9
Croagh Patrick 7, 98, 204
Cromwell, Oliver 25
crops 36, 81, 88, 102, 155
crow 9, 11, 34, 51, 55, 107, 118–19, 126–7, 131,
    153, 189, 192, 195, 200–208, 203, 209, 210, 212,
    213, 216, 218, 220, 228
Cruachan 6
Crucifixion 17, 21, 57, 67, 82, 95, 189, 223
Cúchulainn 5, 6, 78, 82–3, 109, 128, 130, 131, 134,
    150, 162, 173, 182, 204–5, 215–16
cuckoo 1, 9, 13, 16, 21, 78, 86–93, 89, 94, 143–4
Cuirithir 99
Culhwch 108, 121, 198
Cumhall, son of Trénmhór 150
cures 6, 8, 20–21, 78, 80, 82, 83, 96, 99, 123, 154,
    156, 158–9, 179, 189, 196, 211, 212–13, 217–18
curlew 2, 12–13, 138–42, 141
curses 19–20, 34, 72, 76, 100, 127, 168, 171, 182,
    189, 213, 220
Cycle of Kings 181
Cynddylan, King 121
Czechoslovakia 183

Dallán, St 62
De Bello Gallico (Caesar) 183
De Bhaldraithe, Padraic 147–8
De Re Rustica (Varro) 101
death 2, 17, 18–19, 20, 33, 34, 56, 66–7, 71, 81, 86,
  90, 95, 96, 105, 116, 139, 180, 186, 194, 195, 198,
  200, 202–3, 205, 207, 209, 210, 211, 213–15, 219,
  220, 232; *see also* souls of the dead
Dechtire 6
deer 14, 82, 83, 109–10, 120, 131, 135, 153, 167, 173
Deirdre 13, 91, 128, 129, 174, 218
Deirdre and the Sons of Uisneach 128, 129
Denmark 87, 122, 198
Derbforgaill 173
Derbyshire 29, 39
Derg Corra 109–10
Derrick, John 192
Derry 71–2
Desmond, Earl of 125
Destruction of Da Derga's Hostel 6–7, 205, 214
devil 69, 70, 188, 207, 209–10, 212
Devon 29, 51–2, 203
Diarmuid 13–14, 57, 110, 129, 130
Dickens, Charles 221
Díma 149
Dingle Peninsula, Co. Kerry 28
Diodorus Siculus 9
Dionysus 192
Dioscorides 78, 83
Dodona, Greece 99
dog 34, 61, 68, 109, 129, 136, 156
domestic chicken *see* chicken
domestic duck *see* duck
domestic goose 12, 178, 181, 183, 184–5, 227; *see
  also* goose
domesticated dove 94, 96; *see also* dove
Domhnall, son of Aed 181–2
Donall 128
Donegal, County 19, 20, 21, 33, 48, 50, 53–4,
  59–60, 65–7, 70, 71, 72, 75, 76–7, 78, 80, 81, 86,
  89, 90, 94–5, 97–8, 104, 105, 107, 118, 119, 124,
  132, 138, 145, 146, 158, 161, 165, 178, 185, 186,
  188, 191, 194, 201, 203–4, 209
Donncha Mór of Ossory 6
Dorset 176, 177, 217
dove 7, 11, 13, 15, 16, 21, 78, 90, 92, 94–103, **95**,
  188, 220, 226
dovecotes 96, 101, 136
Drayton, Michael 18
Dream of Óengus 172, 175
Dream of Rhonabwy 214–15
dreams 46, 66, 99, 114, 118, 214–15
Dreanacht 34
druids 9, 25, 225
Drum Ceat 160
Dublin 7, 52, 64, 85, 136, 137, 139, 156, 164, 199, 209
Dublin, County 140, 220
duck 10, 12, 14, 50, 59–64, **61**, 116, 128, 130, 164,
  166, 173, 211, 222, 224
Dunraven, Earl of 212
Dunstable, Bedfordshire 79

eagle 2, 12, 13, 26, 32, 35, 39, 41–2, 77, 108,
  113–24, **115**, 127, 131, 135, 136, 197, 198,
  201–2, 212, 222, 229–30, 231

Eagle's Nest, Co. Kerry 113, 114, 124
Easter 60, 70–71, 82, 166, 212
Edward I 39
Edward the Confessor 226
eggs 4, 9–10, 18, 45, 46, 52, 55, 58, 61, 63, 65,
  70–71, 72–3, 74, 86, 88, 92–3, 99, 101, 107, 108,
  130, 175, 176, 178, 180–82, 185, 196, 202, 213,
  218, 231
Egil 168
egret 152
Egypt 101, 135, 154
Eibhir 5
eider-duck 224; *see also* duck
Elsa of Brabant 174
Emain Macha 173, 205
enchantment 57, 60–61, 80, 135, 161, 165, 166,
  167–73, 182, 203–4, 205
England 18, 20, 29–30, 38, 41, 42, 48, 51–2, 70, 72,
  76, 79, 81, 85, 86, 87, 89–90, 95, 96, 118, 121,
  122, 139, 140, 145, 148, 153, 155, 157, 166–7,
  176–7, 180, 183, 187, 188, 195, 196, 202–3, 206,
  208, 212, 216, 217, 221, 229; *see also* Britain
Eochaid 172
Epona 217
Ériu 205
Erris, Co. Mayo 171, 178
Essex 29
Estiu 8
Esus 152
Étaín 5, 172
Ethelbert II 156
Euripides 175
Eve 113
evil spirits 65, 68–9
Exile of the Sons of Uisliu 218
Expugnatio Hibernica (Gerald of Wales) 156, 163
extinction 2, 113, 124, 147, 155

fairies 21, 61, 65, 68–9, 70, 78, 90, 97, 196, 205,
  214
falcon *see* hawk; peregrine falcon
falconry 125, 128, 129–30, 135–7, 156, 163, 193,
  224
Fannell 82–3
Fate of the Children of Uisneach 174
Ferdia 82, 130, 215
Fergus 130, 182, 215
Fermaise 214
fertility 36, 37, 63, 73, 152, 153
Fiachaireacht 218–19
Fiachna, son of Baeton 129
Fianna 6, 13, 25, 57, 82, 91, 107, 109, 110, 119–20,
  128, 130, 141, 145, 205, 214, 218
Finn and the Man in the Tree 109–10
Fionn Mac Cumhaill 13, 25, 62, 78, 82, 91, 107,
  109–10, 128, 145, 161–2
Fir Bolg 133
Feast of Dún na nGéd 181–2
Feast of Fools 40–41
Feast of the Ass 40
Feast of the Innocents 41
feathers 4, 5, 45, 47, 65, 71, 96, 101, 116, 142, 173,
  178, 185, 197, 198, 203, 231; *see also* plumage
feral pigeon 96; *see also* dove; pigeon
Finian of Clonard, St 127

Fionntan Mac Bóchna 120, 131–5, 205
Fitzgerald, Gearóid Iarla, Earl of Desmond 125
Fitzstephen, Robert 62
Fjalar 73
flesh *see* meat
flight 2, 4, 9, 26, 75–6, 80, 84, 125, 130, 138, 141, 142, 154, 158, 179, 201, 221, 224–5
Fomhar na nGéan 184
Fomorians 134, 216
fox 31–2, 34, 59, 114–16, 127, 148, 180, 195, 202, 211, 212, 221
France 9, 17–18, 25, 29–31, 33, 37, 38, 40–41, 42–3, 45, 63, 72–3, 76, 82, 87, 88, 99, 100, 101, 105, 121, 135, 144, 152, 153, 156, 174–5, 183, 184, 188, 189, 212, 216–17
Franco-Prussian War 101
Frazer, James 36
Freya 122, 135, 184
furze 27, 28, 29

Gabriel's Hounds 139, 180
Galen 78
Galloway 38
Galway, County 29, 31–2, 33, 65, 88, 105, 113, 124, 155, 178, 179, 180
gannet 140
Gaul 9, 63, 72–3, 99, 152, 184, 216, 217
Gazza Ladra, La (Rossini) 191
Genii Cucullati 73
Geoffrey of Monmouth 120, 206
Gerald of Wales 46, 62, 72, 128, 145, 154, 155, 156, 163, 183, 192, 213
Gereint and Enid 129–30
Germany 18, 37, 73, 81–2, 86, 87, 88, 96, 107, 121, 123, 141, 152, 168, 174, 189, 198, 212, 230
ghosts 68, 139, 180
giants 23, 60–61, 73, 83, 96–7, 122, 135
Glamorgan 195
Glas, son of Derga 215
Glasgow 24
Glendalough, Co. Wicklow 78, 108, 128, 181, 213
Glenveagh National Park, Co. Donegal 124
goat 139, 225
goldcrest 35
golden eagle 2, 113, 124, 157; *see also* eagle
golden plover 56, 58; *see also* plover
goldfinch 125
goose 9–10, 12, 16, 148, 153, 156, 178–85, **180**, 222, 227
Goronwy 120–21
goshawk 136, 137, 224; *see also* hawk
Gráinne 13–14, 110, 129
greater black-backed gull 48; *see also* seagull
greater celandine 83–4
Greece, ancient 45, 78, 83–4, 85, 92, 99–100, 105, 122–3, 184, 194, 196, 198, 218
Greece, modern 18, 37, 81
Green, Miranda 152
green plover *see* lapwing; plover
Greenland 185
Greenland white-fronted goose 178, 185; *see also* goose
grey crow *see* hooded crow
grey plover 56; *see also* plover
greylag goose 178, 184; *see also* goose

Grimms' Fairy Tales 170, 197
grouse 11, 14, 15, 16, 143
Guaire, King 34, 204, 213
gull *see* seagull
Gullinkampi 73
Gundestrup cauldron 121–2
Gwydyon 120
Gwynn ap Nudd 196
gyrfalcon 156; *see also* hawk

Hag of the Temple 162
hags 68, 162, 169, 170, 202, 205, 212
halberd 154
halcyon *see* kingfisher
Halcyon Days 45, 47
Halcyone 45, 46–7
Halloween 2, 6, 16, 116, 127, 172, 212
Hamlet (Shakespeare) 142
Hampshire 217
hare 82, 179
harrier *see* hen harrier
hawk 2, 10, 12, 61, 78, 83, 88, 92, 107, 116, 122, 125–37, **126**, 156, 161, 163, 201, 205, 212, 222, 224
Hawk of Achill 128, 131–5, 161, 205, 216
healing springs 59, 63, 99, 217
Hebrides 50–51
Hecate 198
Helreid Brynhildar 168
Helyas 174
hen *see* chicken
hen harrier 10, 116, 125, 127, 212; *see also* hawk
Henry II 156, 164
Henry IV 136–7, 167
Henwen 121
Heracles 123
heraldry 21, 24, 39, 117–18, 167, 176, 220, 223–30
Herefordshire 87
Hermes 73, 135; *see also* Mercury
heron 10, 13, 16, 136, 147–53, 156, 158–64, **159**, 193, 227
herring gull 48, 52; *see also* seagull
Hertfordshire 206
Hesse, Germany 81–2
Highlands 38, 53, 55, 86, 87, 91, 116, 127, 159, 166, 202, 206, 211
Histories of the Counties of Waterford and of Cork (Smith) 155
History and Topography of Ireland (Gerald of Wales) 46, 128, 183, 192, 213
History of Animals (Aristotle) 35
History of Ireland (Keating) 6, 9, 97–8, 160
History of the Kings of Britain (Geoffrey of Monmouth) 120
Hobbit, The (Tolkien) 112
Holy Spirit 94, 100, 226
holly 27–8, 61
Homer 154
hooded crow 11, 34, 51, 126–7, 153, 195, 200–208, **203**, 209, 210, 212, 213, 216; *see also* crow
Horace 198
horse 81, 129, 136, 153, 217
Horus 135
hound *see* dog
house martin 84, 85; *see also* martin
How Culhwch won Olwen 108, 121, 129, 198

Hraesvelg 122
Hungary 103
hunting (of birds) 10, 25–31, 35–43, 60, 62, 63, 141–2, 156, 163, 179, 207
Hydin, Ranulph 192
Hyginus, Gaius Julius 154

Idun 122, 135
Ilbhreac 150
Iliad (Homer) 154
Image of Ireland (Derrick) 192
Imbolc *see* St Brigid's Day
India 73, 135
Inisbofin, Co. Galway 113
Inishglory, Co. Mayo 171
Inishkea, Co. Mayo 151, 161
Intoxication of the Ulaid 182, 215
Isle of Man 29, 30, 36, 38, 39, 139
Italy 37, 106, 154
Iuchra 150

jackdaw 200, 207
Japan 135
Jesus *see* Christ
John the Baptist, St 88
John the Evangelist, St 41–3
Joseph, St 90
Julius Caesar (Shakespeare) 198
Juno 184
Jupiter 121, 122–3, 152; *see also* Zeus

Kalends 40; *see also* New Year
Kartaga 232
Keating, Geoffrey 6, 9, 97–8, 160
Kenneth, St 51
Kent 153, 206
Kentigern, St 23–4
Kerry, County 20, 28, 29, 45, 59, 70, 75, 113, 114–16, 124, 165–6, 207
kestrel 125, 129–30, 136; *see also* hawk
Keteler, Alice 70
Kevin, St 78, 108, 181, 213
Kieran of Clonmacnoise, St 149
Kieran of Saighir, St 149
Kildare, County 128
Kilkenny, County 70
Killarney, Co. Kerry 113, 114–16, 124
Killorglin, Co. Kerry 165–6
King Lear (Shakespeare) 45
kingfisher 45–7, **47**
kingship 25, 26–7, 35, 37–8, 41, 116, 123, 173, 197, 225, 229–30
kite 2, 10, 34, 204, 213, 224; *see also* hawk
Knight of the Swan 171, 174
Koronis 221
Kronos 78

Labhraidh Loingseach 191–2
Labhrán 119
Lake Derravarragh, Co. Westmeath 170–71
lamb *see* sheep
Lammas Day 116, 127, 212
Lancashire 122, 187
landrail *see* corncrake
Languedoc 212

Laois, County 70
lapwing 2, 52, 55, 56, 58, 202, 222, 228; *see also* plover
lark *see* skylark
Laoi 130
Latin America 63, 74
Laurence, Elizabeth Atwood 36
laws 9–10, 72, 135, 136–7, 156, 184, 206, 207, 219
Lebor Gabála Érenn 62, 100, 204, 220
Lebor na Cert 51
Lent 71, 108, 183, 185
lesser black-backed gull 48; *see also* seagull
L'Estrange *Household Book* 58
leucism 105
Liadain (mother of St Kieran of Saighir) 149
Liadain (poet) 99
Life of Columba (Adamnán) 160
Life of Saint Abbán 147
Life of Saint Ailbe 155
Life of Saint Cellach of Killala 34, 213
Life of Saint Colmán 136, 175
Life of Saint Máedoc of Ferns 62
Life of Saint Moling 34–5, 98
Limerick, County 20
Lincolnshire 122, 155
Lir 170–71
little owl 198; *see also* owl
Liverpool 48, 58
livestock 36, 65, 116, 127, 212, 221; *see also* cattle; pig; sheep
Lleu Skilful Hand 35, 37, 120–21, 197–8
Llyr 226
Log na nDeamhan, Croagh Patrick 204
Lohengrin 174
Loki 122, 135
London 79, 212, 221
long-eared owl 194, 199; *see also* owl
Lord of Misrule 40, 41
love 5, 86, 90, 94, 99–100, 171–2, 232
Luan 8–9
luck 2, 9, 18, 19–20, 28, 33, 48, 60, 66–7, 70, 71, 80–81, 82, 85, 86–7, 90, 140–41, 143–4, 157, 159, 165, 166, 181, 186–8, 195, 198, 200, 203, 207, 209, 220, 232
Lugh 6, 134, 150, 205, 216
Lughaidh 51, 98, 205–6, 216
Lun Dubh Mac Smola 107
Lúnasa *see* Lammas Day

Macbeth (Shakespeare) 211
Mac Coise, Urard 168
Macha 204, 205
Mac Lochlainn, Proinsias 191
Mad Sweeney 14–15, 35, 58, 91, 98–9, 110, 142, 162, 182–3
Máedoc, St 62
Maeve 5
magpie 9, 105, 107, 136, 186–93, **190**
Maigh Tuireadh, battle of 131, 133–4, 205, 216
Malahide, Co. Dublin 140
mallard 59, 60, 62, 63–4, 211, 224; *see also* duck
Manannán Mac Lir 5, 150, 161
Manlius, Marcus 184
Maolughra 21
Marbán 16, 99, 110, 175, 182

March Cock 68–9
marriage 43, 86, 89, 90, 99–100, 105, 186, 187, 232
Mars 153, 183
Marseille 30–31
marten 116, 127, 212
Martial 100, 135, 218
Martial Career of Conghal Cláiringhneach 8, 51, 205–6, 216
martin 81, 84, 85, 225
Martinmas *see* St Martin's Eve/Day
Mary, Queen of Scots 136
Mary, Virgin 17, 21, 56–7, 60, 76, 90, 100
Mary II 18
Mason, Sir Thomas 137
Math Son of Mathonwy 35, 120–21, 197–8
May Eve/Day 87, 88, 107, 116, 127, 212
Mayo, County 17, 33, 48, 60, 65, 66, 97, 104, 117, 118–19, 124, 128, 131–5, 138, 146, 151, 161, 165, 171, 178–9, 185, 187, 188, 201–2, 205, 216
meadow pipit 92–3
Meargach 205
meat 4, 9–10, 52, 58, 63, 65, 74, 79, 96, 100, 101, 102, 108–9, 139, 141–2, 145, 156, 163–4, 176, 178, 184–5, 231
Meath, County 104, 155
Medinat temple, Egypt 101
Medyr, son of Medyredydd 35
Mercury 73, 152, 154; *see also* Hermes
merlin 125, 136; *see also* hawk
messages, carrying of 94, 100, 101–2, 209
Metrical Dindshenchus 8–9
Michael, St 98
Michaelmas 74, 98, 184–5
Midhir 150, 172
Midsummer Night's Dream (Shakespeare) 195
migration 1, 46, 84, 85, 88, 93, 144, 150, 154, 155, 185
Milesians 62, 134
Mionn 22
Mirrour of the World (Caxton) 183
mistle thrush 111, 112, 228; *see also* thrush
Mo Chua, St 72
Mochaomhóg 171
Moling, St 34–5, 98
Mongán 172–3
Monmouthshire 183, 195
moon 84, 105, 114, 122, 159
moorhen 143
Morrigan 6, 204–5, 215
Moryson, Fynes 192
Mossad, son of Maen 129
mouse 32, 76–7, 164, 199
Moycullen, Co. Galway 105
Muffet, Thomas 145
Muller, Sylvie 36
mummers 28–9
Munster 6, 21, 28, 97
Muscovy duck 63; *see also* duck
Muses 192
mute swan 165, 175, 177; *see also* swan

Nanosuelta 217
Naoise 13, 91
Nar 8–9
Native Americans 63, 231, 232
Natural History of Dublin (Rutty) 193

Natural History of Ireland (O'Sullivan Beare) 25–6, 105, 112, 138, 141–2, 155, 164, 175, 192
Navan Fort *see* Emain Macha
Neotus, St 203
nests 19–20, 24, 33, 46, 55, 56, 60, 64, 75, 76, 80, 81, 82, 84, 92–3, 95, 96, 114, 117–18, 123, 138–9, 145, 152, 157, 175, 188–9, 199, 211
Netherlands 137
nettle 145
Neville, George 156, 163
New Year 25, 30, 40, 60, 127
Nguni people 232
Niamh of the Golden Hair 174
Nigeria 232
nightingale 192, 232
Nisus 78
Noah 100, 189, 220
Norfolk 18, 52, 81, 155, 157, 216, 217
Normandy 82
Normans 38–9, 129, 135–6, 156, 163
Norse mythology 73, 122, 135, 184, 219–20
Norsemen *see* Vikings
Norwich 155
Nuadu 131, 133

oak 120, 121, 122
O'Brien, Teigue 167
O'Brien clan 167
Ó Dálaigh, Donnchadh Mór 35
Odette 171–2
Odile 172
Odin 122, 184, 216, 217, 218, 219–20
O'Drive, Darby 202
Óengus 172
Offaly, County 149, 155
O'Flaherty, Ronan 147, 153, 154
ogham alphabet 222–30
Oisín 91, 109, 110, 111–12, 119, 128
Old Crow of Achill 118–19, 201–2
Olwen 129
O'Nery, Donald 189–91
Only Son of Aoife 215
O'Quinn clan 167
Orkney Islands 206
Ornithologia (Willughby) 155
ornithology 1, 92, 103
ornithomancy 9
O'Rourke, Daniel 114
Orpheus 175
Oscar 214
osprey 2, 128
O'Sullivan Beare, Philip 25–6, 105, 112, 138, 141–2, 155, 164, 175, 192
O'Sullivan clan 21, 223
O'Toole, Lorcán 147, 153, 154
O'Toole clan 181, 200
Ovid 78, 198
Owein 214–15
owl 9, 27, 120, 194–9, **196**, 228–9
oystercatcher 50, 53–5, **54**

Pallas Athene 198, 228–9
Paris 101, 152
partridge 136, 145
Patrick, St 7, 91–2, 98, 109, 139, 204
Payne, Robert 175, 192

peace 45, 94, 95, 99, 100, 166, 226
peacock 156, 189, 231
peewit *see* lapwing
Pembrokeshire 30, 39
Peredur Son of Evrawg 218
peregrine falcon 2, 116, 125, 130–31, 136, 163, 193, 212, 224; *see also* falcon; hawk
Perigord, France 87
Persia 135, 232
Peter, St 76
pets 149, 150, 156, 206, 207, 212, 219, 221
pheasant 222
Picts 38
pig 121, 135, 217
pigeon 11, 94–6, 97, 100, 101–2, 136; *see also* dove
pigeon fancying 102
pigeon racing 102
pink-footed goose 178; *see also* goose
pintail 59; *see also* duck
place names 10–13, 21, 33, 55, 91, 96, 97, 127, 145, 147–8
Plato 175
Pliny 35, 70, 84, 92, 123, 135, 154, 175, 198, 213, 220
plover 13, 56–8, **57**; *see also* lapwing
plumage 1, 4, 17–18, 21–2, 45, 47, 53, 60, 85, 100, 104, 105–6, 165, 186, 209, 211, 218, 226–7, 228, 231; *see also* feathers
poetry, early Irish 2, 13–16, 35, 51, 78, 91, 98–9, 110–11, 119–20, 130–31, 163, 175, 182, 216
Poland 103
Polycronicum (Hydin) 192
Prometheus 123
prophecy 4, 25, 34–5, 37, 99, 113, 116, 120, 186, 209, 218–19, 220, 232
Pursuit of Gruaidhe Ghriansholus 130, 173

quail 144
Quetzacoatl 231
quetzal 231

Ra 135
Ragnarok 73
ram *see* sheep
rat 164, 199, 221
raven 1, 2, 4, 9, 12, 34, 51, 60, 100, 116, 127, 131, 168, 188, 195, 200, 202, 204, 205–6, 209–21, **210**, 228, 232
Red Book of Ormond 136
red kite *see* kite
Reims, France 73, 100
Resurrection 65, 67, 71, 82, 226
Rhiannon 8
Rhodes 81
rhynchokinesis 140
Richards, Solomon 193
ringed plover 56; *see also* plover
ritual offerings 152, 162; *see also* sacrifices
robin 1–2, 7, 17–24, **19**, 33, 78, 90, 94, 223
Robin Hood 42
rock dove 94, 95, 96; *see also* dove
Romania 217
Romans 9, 26, 35, 40, 73, 83–4, 85, 99–100, 101, 121, 123, 152, 184, 196, 198, 217–18, 220–21, 23
Ronan, St 14
rook 136, 200, 207, 211, 222, 228

rooster *see* chicken
Roscommon, County 6
Ross Lewin family 210
Royston crow *see* hooded crow
Russia 37, 44, 123, 230
Rutty, John 193

sacrifices 36, 63, 70, 217, 232
St Brigid's Day 75, 116, 127, 212
St James's Day 88
St John's Eve/Day 88
St Kevin and the Blackbird 2
St Martin's Eve/Day 45, 65, 185
St Patrick's Day 87, 175
St Stephen's Day 25–30, 41–2, 74
St Vitus' Day 212
salmon 108, 119, 120, 131, 132, 173, 182
Samhain *see* Halloween
sand martin 85; *see also* martin
Saturnalia 40
sayings 20, 31, 50, 56, 66, 74, 78, 85, 90–91, 180–81, 200, 202, 210
scaldcrow *see* hooded crow
Scattery Island, Co. Clare 151, 161
Scotland 23–4, 31, 38, 39, 48, 49, 50–51, 53, 55, 56, 60, 62, 70, 75, 76, 79, 82, 86, 87, 88, 90–91, 95, 104, 105, 106, 108, 116, 117, 120, 127, 139, 140–41, 143, 144, 159, 166, 173, 183, 186, 188, 189, 195, 202, 206, 211–12; *see also* Britain
screech owl *see* barn owl
Scylla 78
sea eagle *see* white-tailed eagle
Sea of Moyle 171
seagull 12, 16, 48–52, **49**, 53–4, 59–60, 205–6, 222, 224
seal 124, 173
Second World War 101
Seneca 175
seers 120, 130–31, 205
Sequana 63
Serf, St 24
Seven Whistlers 139, 180
Shakespeare, William 45, 142, 195, 198, 211, 233
Shannon Callows 146
sheep 61, 65, 113, 124, 206, 217, 221
sheldrake 224; *see also* duck
Shetland Islands 117, 139
short-eared owl 194, 199; *see also* owl
shoveler 59; *see also* duck
Shropshire 202–3
Siegfried 171–2
Sigurd 220
Sirona 73
Six Swans, The 170
skua 50
sky gods 121–2, 135, 216
skylark 15, 21, 75–9, **77**, 90, 94, 143, 222, 229, 232–3
Slagfid 168
sleep 6, 8, 57, 62, 172
Slieve League, Co. Donegal 118
Sligo, County 185
Smith, Charles 155
snake 122, 153, 227
snipe 140–42, 222, 224–5
Somerset 157
song *see* calls

song thrush 14, 111, 112; *see also* thrush
Sons of Tuireann 128, 172
souls of the dead 4, 7, 48, 60, 94, 95, 105, 123, 165,
  179, 211, 212, 224, 226, 231–2
sparrowhawk 2, 10, 88, 125, 130, 136, 137; *see also*
  hawk
spring 20, 48, 55, 75, 81, 87, 152, 157, 212
stag *see* deer
Stanley family 39, 117–18
starling 130, 192, 222, 226
Stephen, St 25
stoat 82, 164, 221
stock dove 94, 96; *see also* dove
stonechat 105, 143
stork 57, 157, 227
Storks, The (Andersen) 157
Suffolk 20, 29, 139
Suibhne Geilt see Mad Sweeney
summer 1, 20, 33, 75, 80, 87–8, 91, 143, 145, 225
sun 63, 73, 121–2, 135, 226
Sussex 202
Suttung 122
swallow 1, 57, 80–85, **83**, 225, 232
swan 7, 60, 62, 128, 156, 165–77, **169**, 222, 229
Swan, John 196
Swan Lake (Tchaikovsky) 171–2
swan marks 166, 176
swansong 175
Sweden 56–7, 167–8, 189, 195
Sweeney *see* Mad Sweeney
swift 84, 85
Swift, Jonathan 193
Syria 135

Tadhg Mac Céin 5–6, 8
Tadhg son of Cian 5–6, 8
Táin Bó Cuailnge 78, 82–3, 109, 119, 128, 130, 162,
  173, 182, 204–5, 213–14, 215
Tale of Volund 167–8
Tara 51, 205–6, 216
tawny owl 194, 197; *see also* owl
teal 59, 62, 224; *see also* duck
Thor 135
Three Powerful Swineherds of Britain 121
Three Wonders of Connacht 161
thrush 14, 16, 20, 104, 108, 111–12, 222, 227–8
Tipperary, County 20, 153
Tír na nÓg 109
tit 222, 226–7
Tolkien, J. R. R. 112
tomtit *see* tit
Topsell, Edward 156
Tory Island, Co. Donegal 203–4
Tower of London 212
trade-ogham 227
Tralee, Co. Kerry 28
Travellers 159, 189, 200
Tréfuilngidh 134
Trier, Germany 152
Tuan Mac Cairill 120
Tuatha Dé Danann 107, 131, 133–4, 150, 170, 214, 220
turkey 176
turtle dove 13, 15, 16, 94, 96, 98–9, 226; *see also* dove
'Twelve Days of Christmas' 96
Twelve Swans, The 168–70, 182
Twelve Wild Geese, The 182

Tyrol 20, 82
Tyrone, County 104

Ulster 5, 6, 21, 27, 38–9, 48, 51, 53, 104–5

Valerius 220
Valkyries 168
Varro 101
Venus 99; *see also* Aphrodite
Vidofnir 73
Vikings 66, 220; *see also* Norse mythology
Villiers, France 43
Virgil 99
Volund 167–8
Von Rothbart 171–2
Voyage of the Hui Corra 7
Voyage of St Brendan 7
vulture 9

Wales 8, 20, 29, 30, 35, 38, 39, 51, 56, 87, 107, 108,
  116, 120–21, 129–30, 180, 183, 195, 196, 197–8,
  202, 203, 206, 214–15, 217, 218, 226; *see also*
  Britain
war 6, 73, 101, 125, 147, 153, 158, 160, 162, 200,
  204–5, 209
Wasting Sickness of Cúchulainn 215
weather lore 2, 20, 33, 45, 48, 56, 59, 65, 75, 80,
  88–9, 95, 104–5, 138, 141, 144, 158, 178–9, 188,
  195–6, 201
Wedding of Maine Morgor 128
Wellesley, Arthur, Duke of Wellington 101
Westmeath, County 170–71
Westphalia, Germany 81
Westropp family 195
Wexford, County 193
White, Gilbert 84
white-tailed eagle 2, 113, 117, 121, 124; *see also*
  eagle
whooper swan 165, 175, 177; *see also* swan
Wicklow, County 78, 108, 128, 181, 187, 200, 213
wigeon 59; *see also* duck
Wild Swans, The (Andersen) 170
'Wild Swans at Coole' (Yeats) 177
willow 152, 191
Willughby, Francis 155
wine 42–3, 192
winter 2, 21, 36, 45, 46–7, 48, 65, 152, 155
winter solstice 36, 45, 46, 47
wisdom 113, 194, 198, 209, 228–9
witches 23, 50–51, 60–61, 70, 180, 189, 198
wolf 18, 116, 121, 122, 127, 173, 212
woodcock 15, 140, 141–2
woodpecker 16
woodpigeon 94, 95, 96, 100, 102; *see also* dove;
  pigeon
Wooing of Emer 5
Wooing of Étaín 172, 220
Worcestershire 87
wren 4, 9, 16, 17, 20, 25–44, **26**, 123, 197, 222, 225
wrenboys 25, 27–31, 33, 35–43

Yeats, W. B. 177
Yggdrasil 73, 122, 135
Yorkshire 70, 90, 187, 196

Zeus 78, 122–3; *see also* Jupiter